MY YEARS
IN THE 1980s
NEW YORK ART SCENE

collezionemaramotti

Realizzato in occasione della mostra /
Published on the occasion of the exhibition
Scene
4 May – 31 July 2014

Jeannette Montgomery Barron

MY YEARS
IN THE 1980s
NEW YORK ART SCENE

SilvanaEditoriale

1980

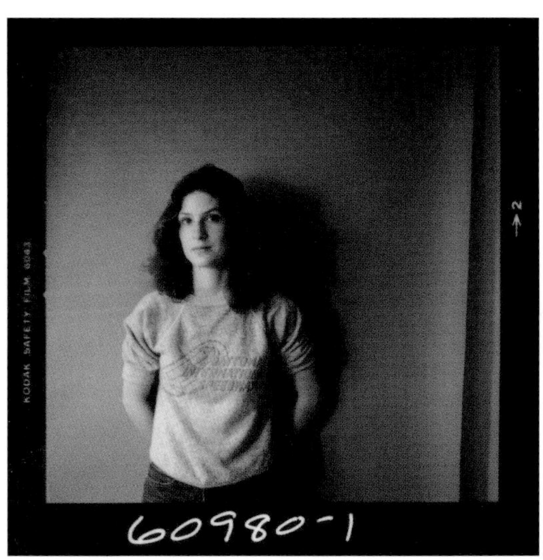

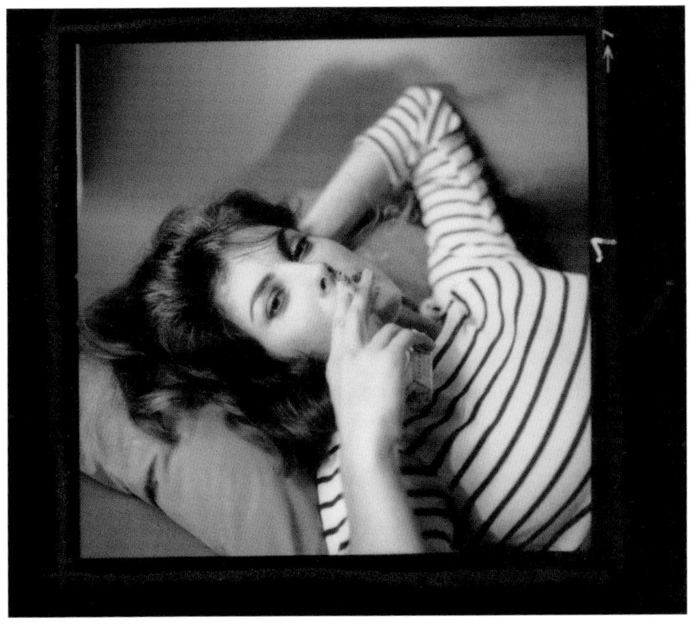

Kathryn Bigelow came to my apartment one day to be photographed. She took a picture of me, too. I love it.

My brother Monty and I photographed each other in Lugano, Switzerland. He arranged for me to photograph the famous film director Douglas Sirk and his wife, Hilde, the next day.

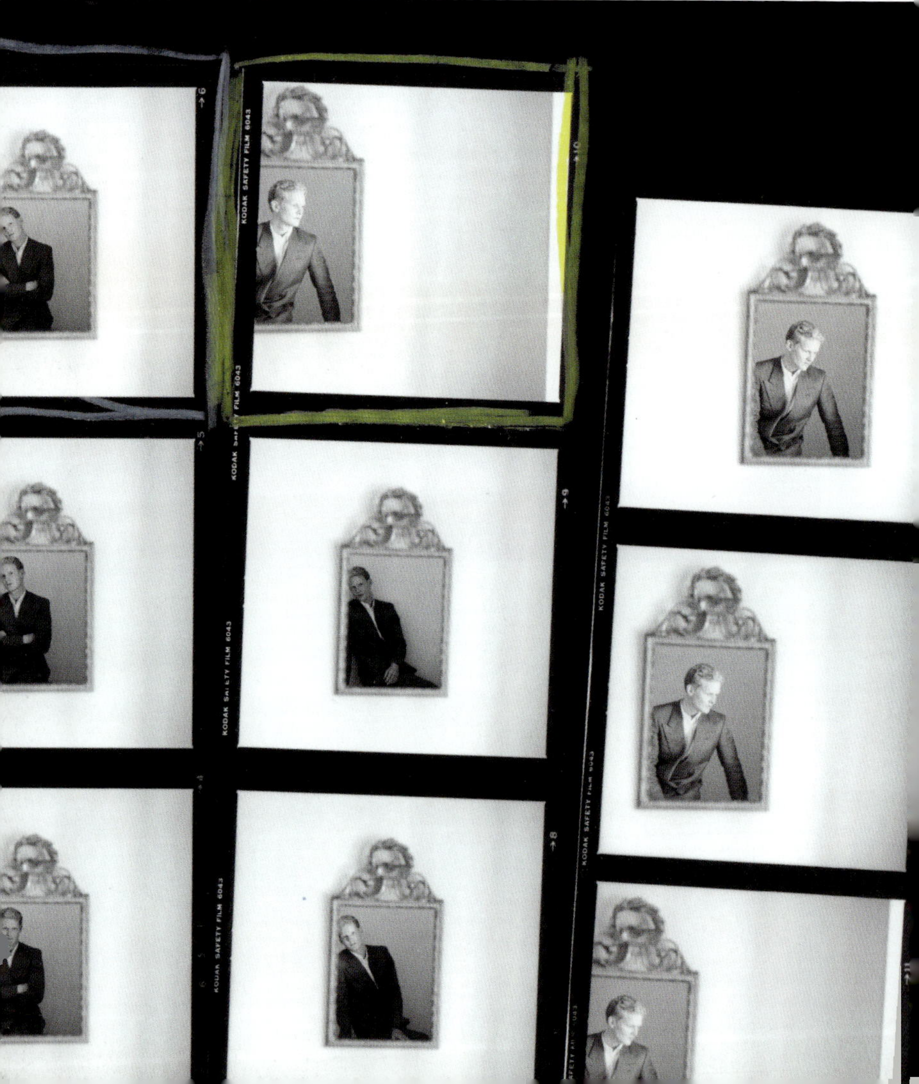

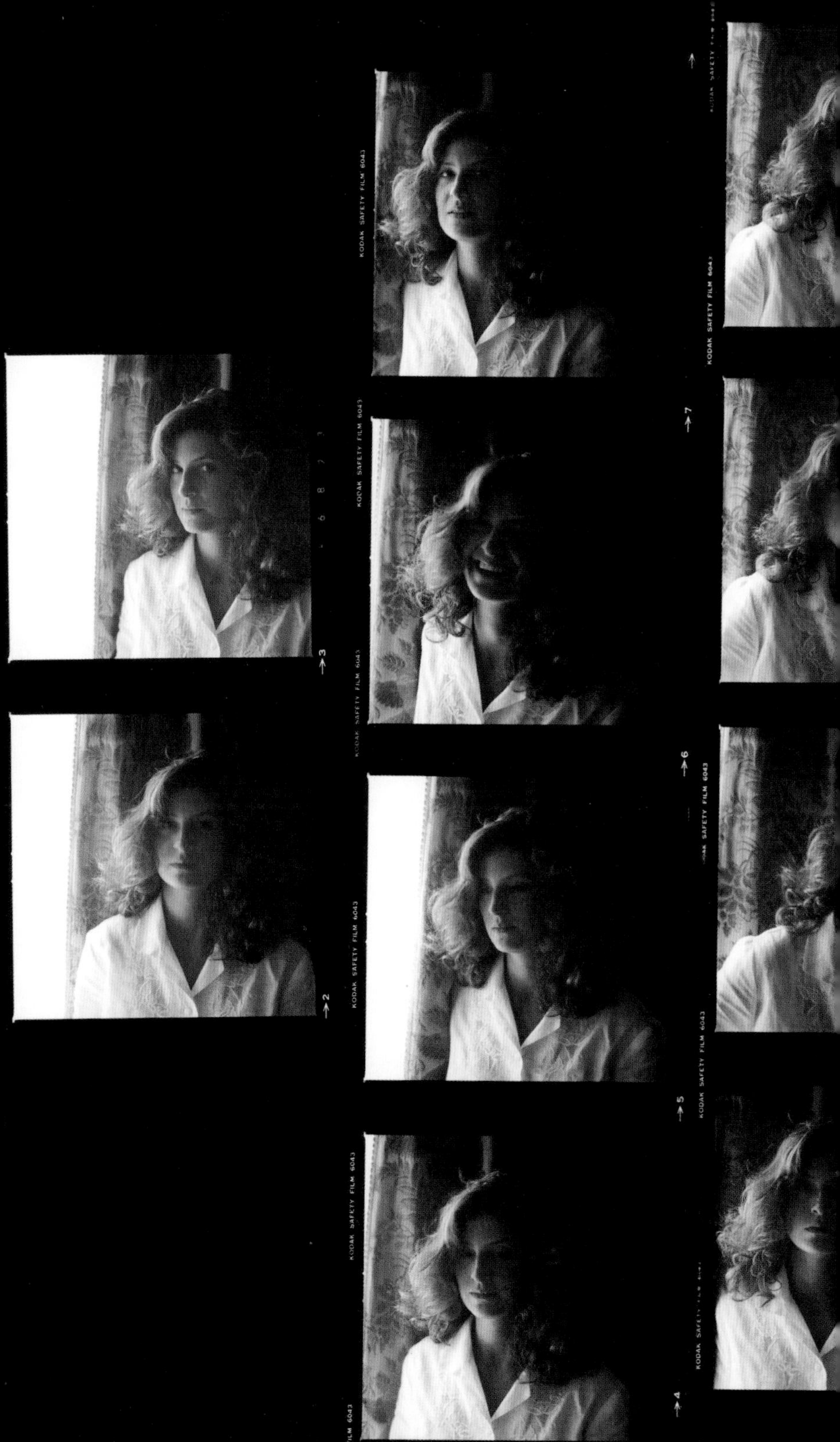

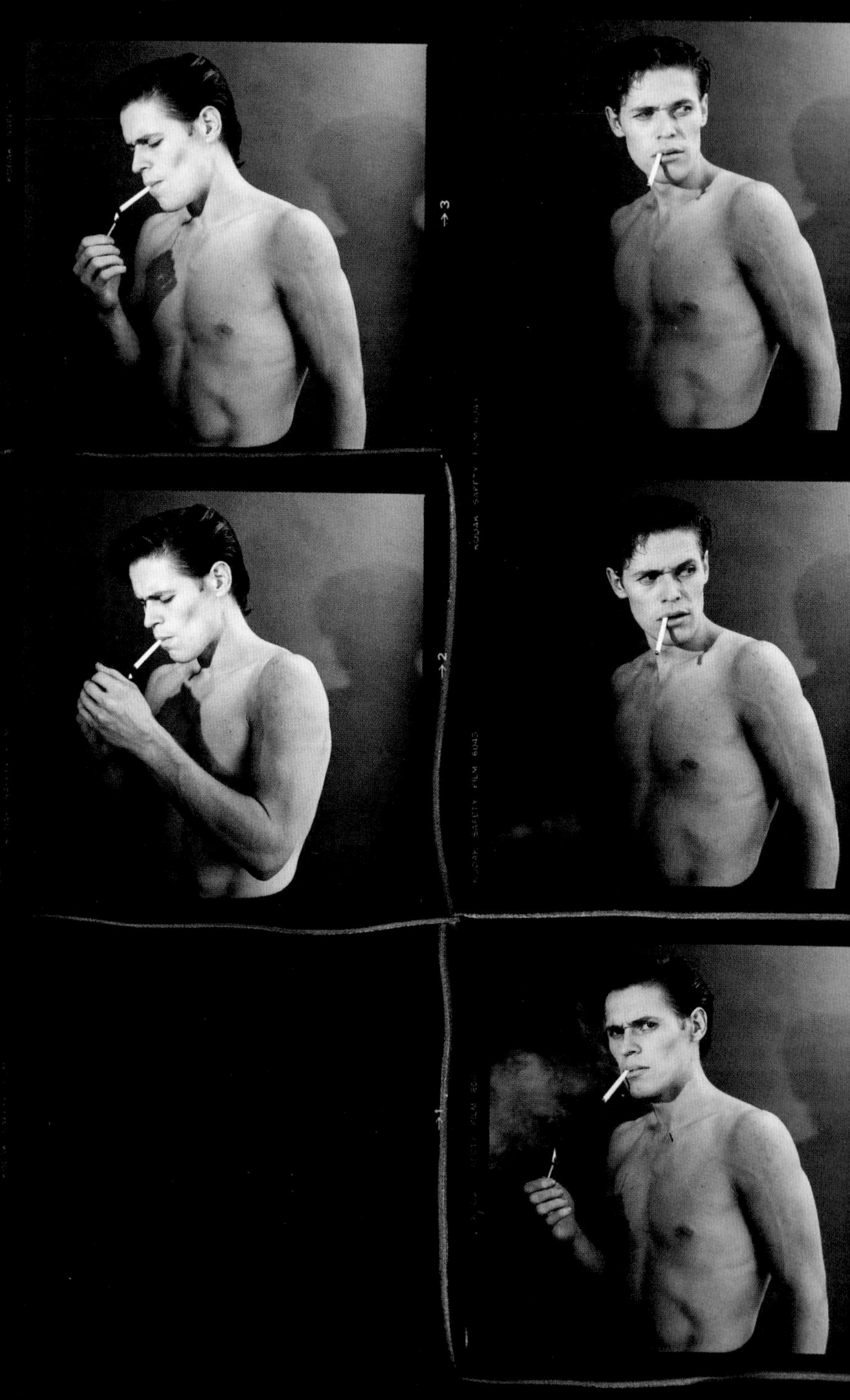

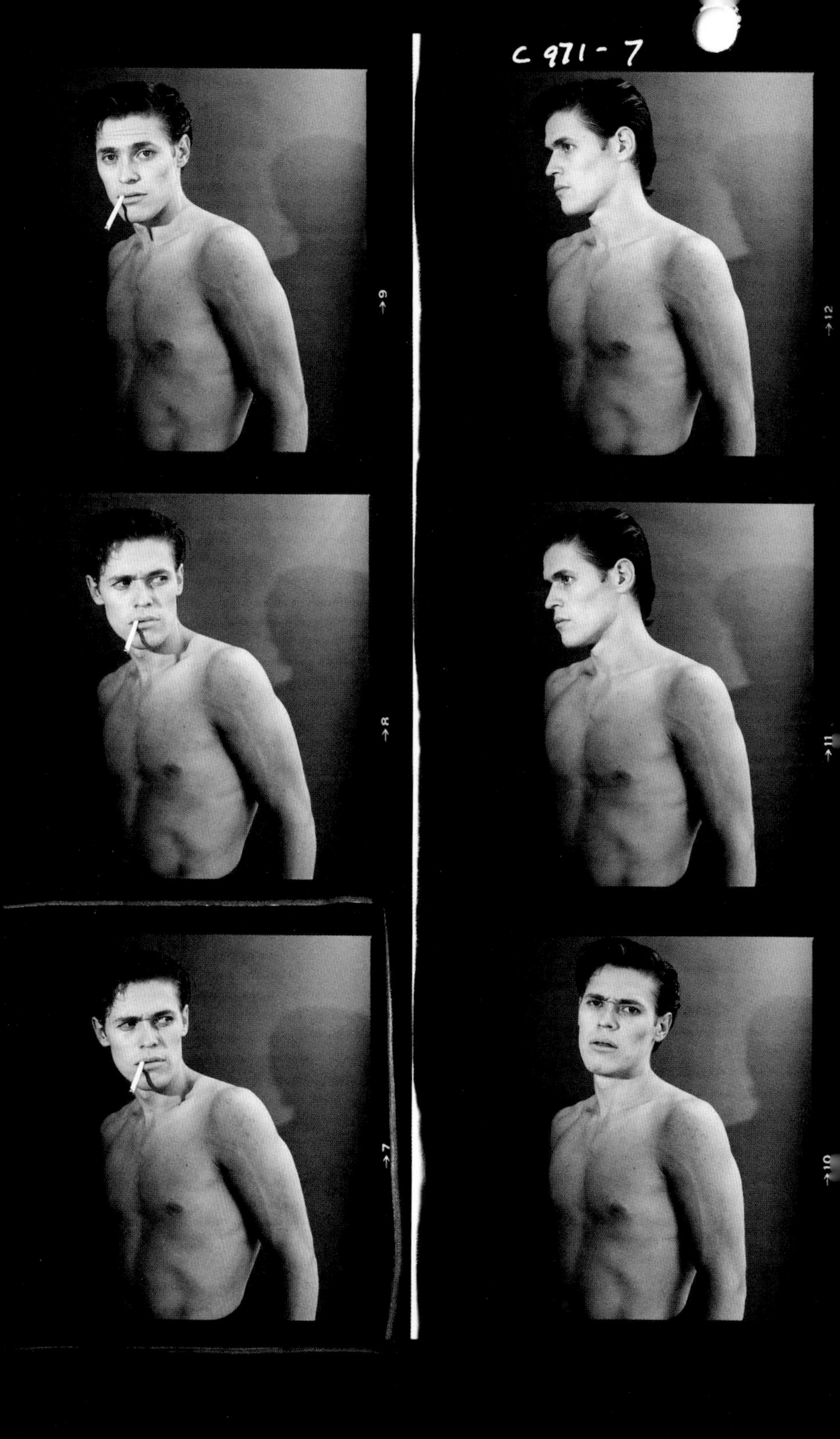

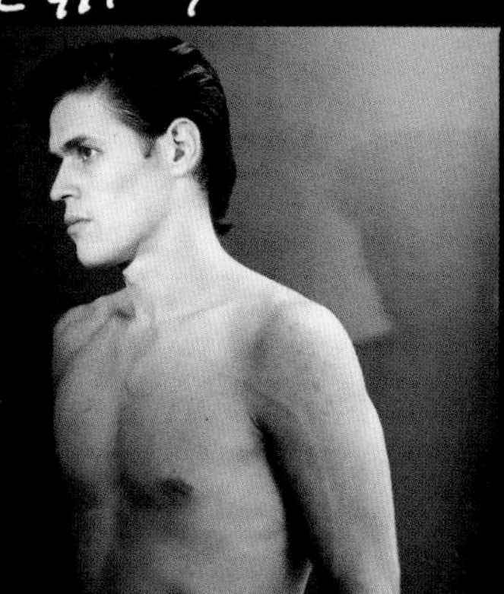
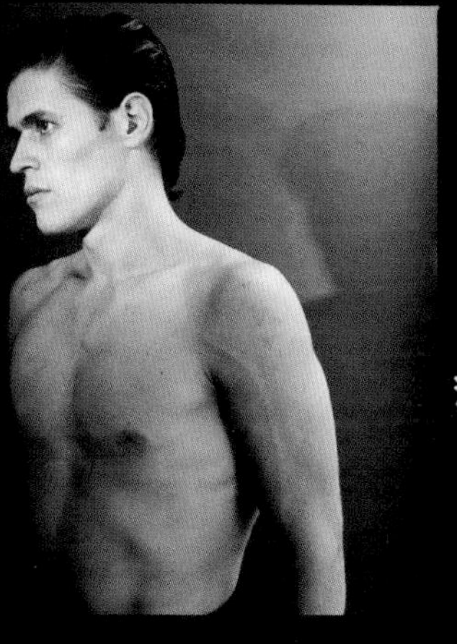
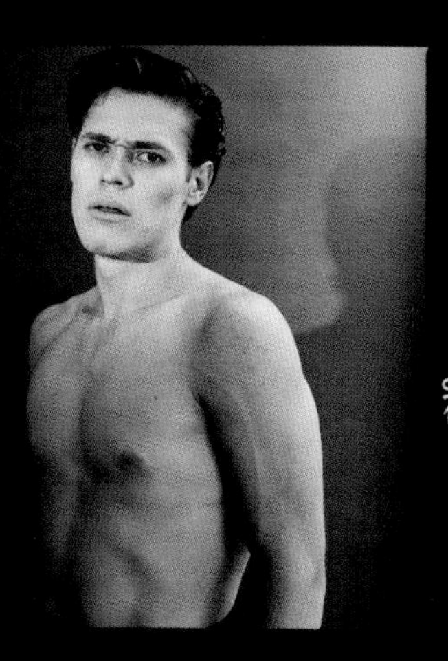
C 971 - 7

KODAK SAFETY FILM 5063
KODAK SAFETY FILM 5063
KODAK SAFE
→6A
→7
→7A
→8
→8A
→9
5063
KODAK SAFETY FILM 5063
KODAK SAFETY FILM 5063
→11
→11A
→12
→12A
→13
→13A
→14

1981

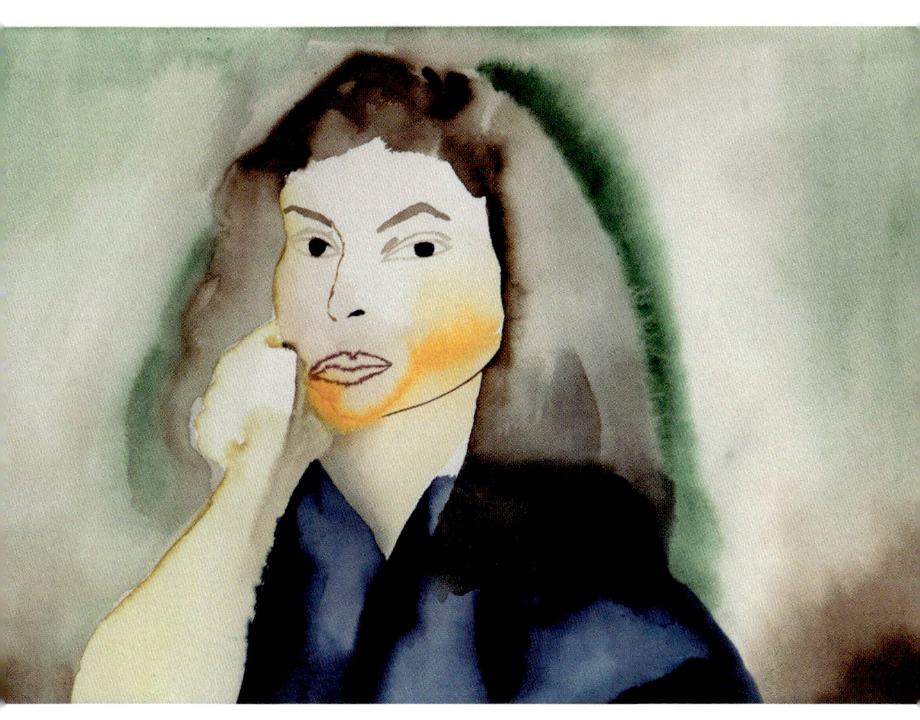

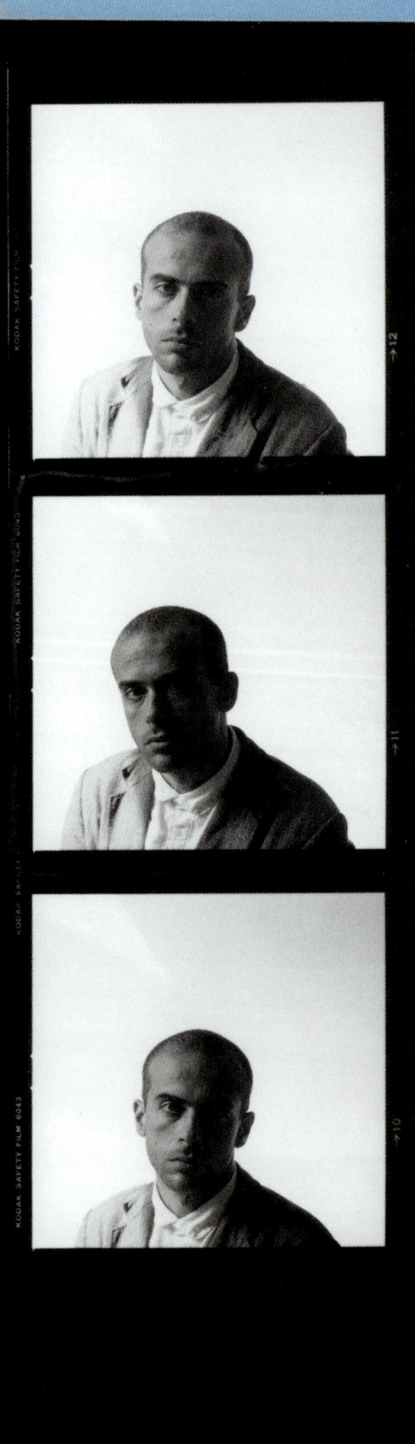

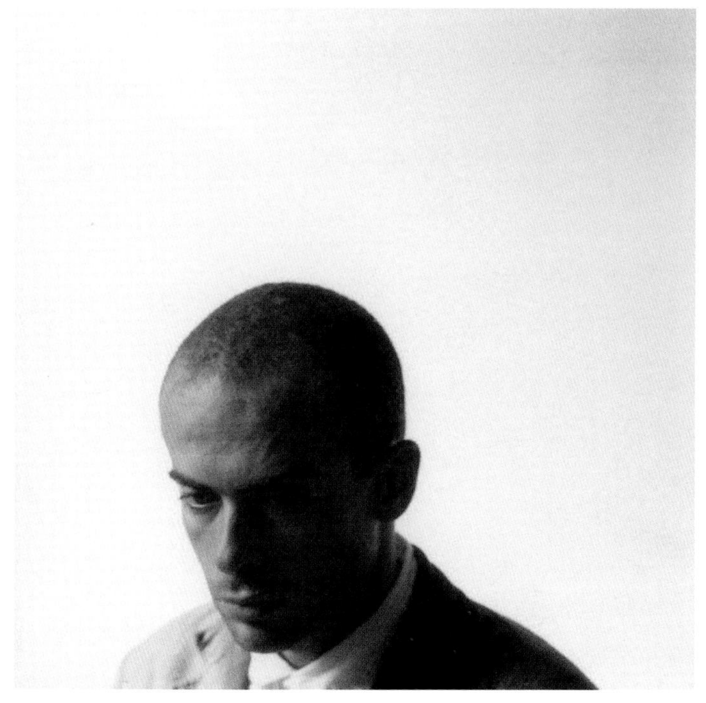

Matthias Brunner, me and Thomas Ammann.
We were joking that Thomas was doing
so well that he even had a Picasso on
his terrace.
My brother took the photo.

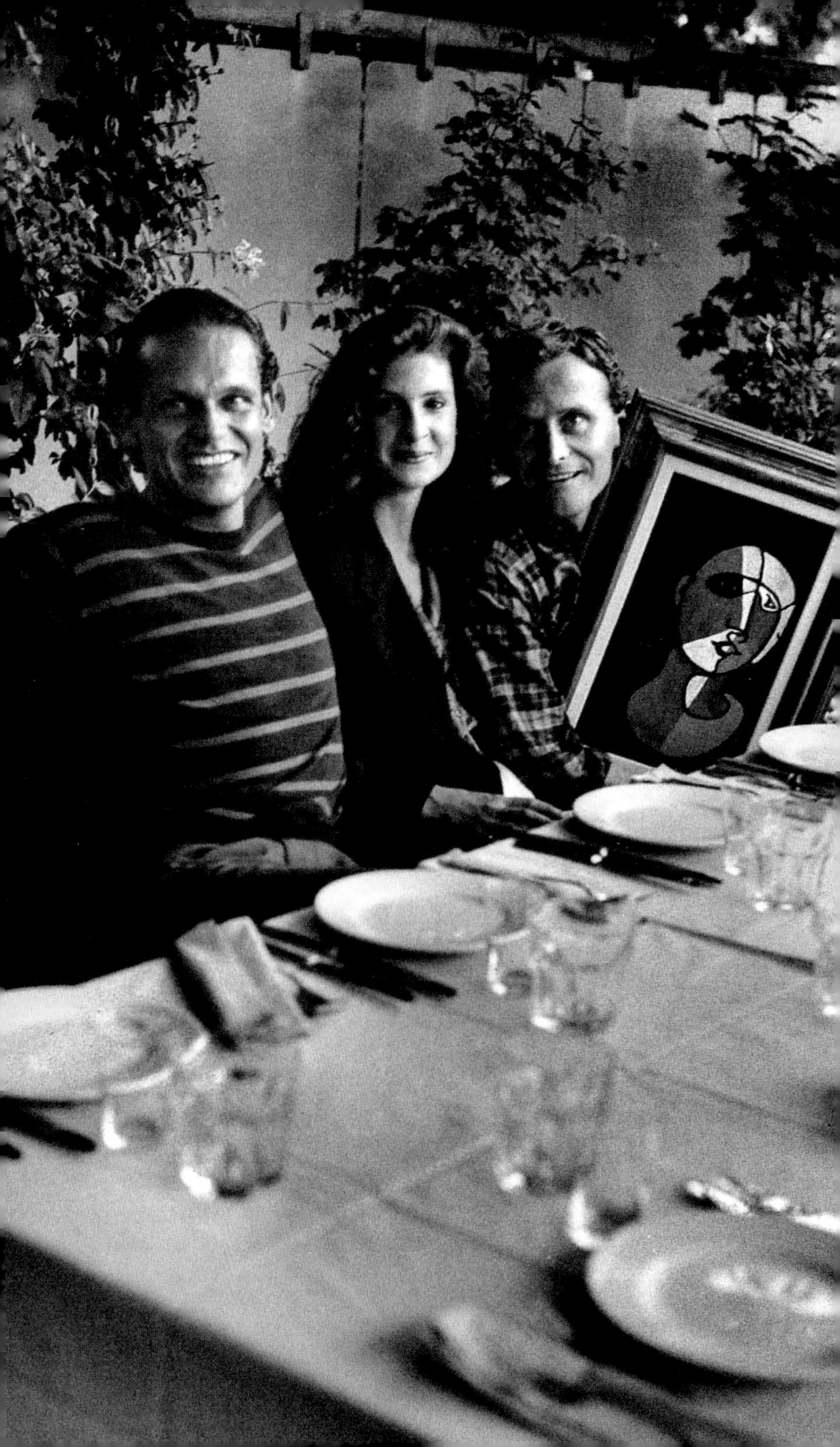

1982

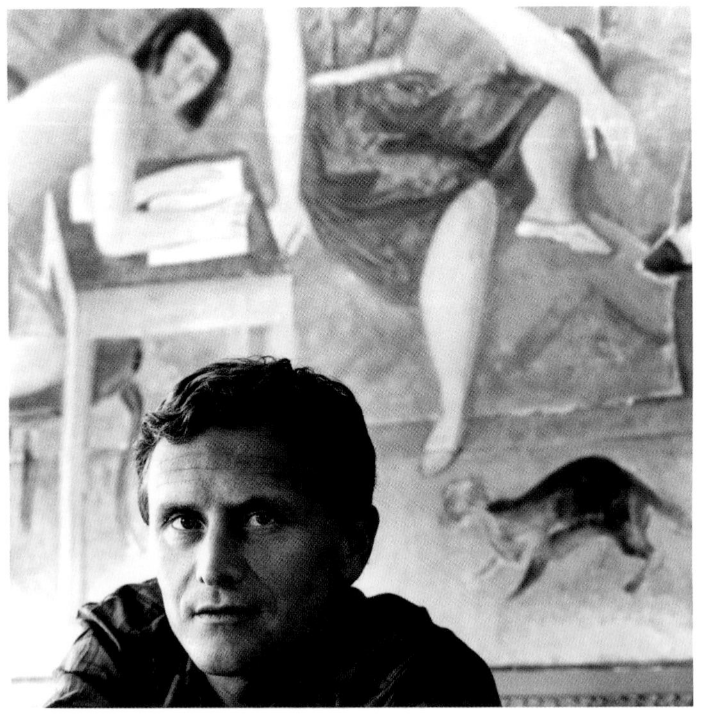

for Jeanette
Love Thomas

THOMAS AMMANN   Zürich, October 8, 1982

Dear Janet,

Thank you ever so much for the lovely
photos you sent me, especially the ones
with BALTHUS.

They are so fantastic that I absolutely
need two more copies of each. I would
very much appreciate if you could send
them to me soonest, together with your
bill for expenses.

Thank you very much in advance.
With best regards,

                              Yours,

                              Thomas Ammann

BOMB

No.4   Painters & Writers 1982 $3.00

Kiely Jenkins, *plastic, metal, light bulbs spray enamel, marker,*
April 1981.   Fun Gallery

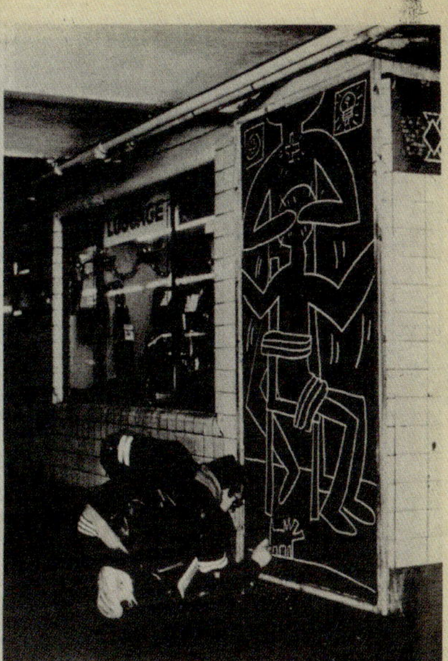

Photograph, Tseng Kwong Chi Courtesy Tony Shafrazi **Keith Haring**

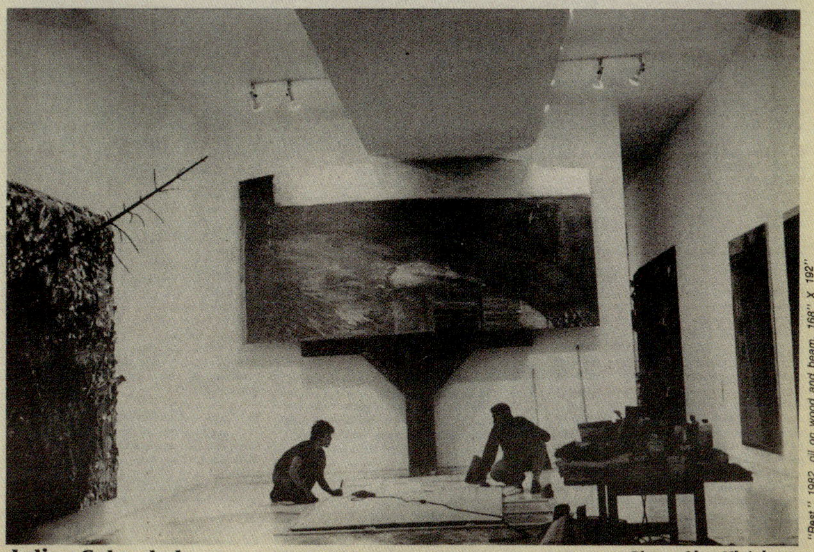

Julian Schnabel, *Installation at Mary Boone Gallery, 1982*   **Photo: Alan Kleinberg**

"Rest," 1982, oil on wood and beam, 168" X 192"

SIDNEY JANIS GA

WEST 57th STREET NEW YORK 10019 TELEPHONE 5

Page 2

15.	Gandy BRODIE	<u>Birth of a Fawn</u> 1975
16.	Jon BOROFSKY	<u>Disintegrating Clay H</u> unfired clay, steel h 13¾ x 13¾" Collection
17.	Robert LONGO	<u>The Swing</u> 1979 cast a <u>Collection</u>: Jeanne Si
18.	Jedd GARET	<u>Precarious Notoriety</u>
19.	David SALLE	<u>Middlebrow Literature</u> canvas 85-3/4 x 104¾
20.	Jean Michel BASQUIAT	<u>Diagram of the Ankle</u> canvas 60 x 120"
21.	Jon BOROFSKY	<u>As I was awakening I</u> <u>by the spirits at 2,</u> canvas 108 x 72"
22.	Eric FISCHL	<u>Untitled</u> 1982 oil on
23.	Keith HARING	<u>Untitled</u> 1982 ink or <u>Untitled</u> 1982 vinyl (in o:
24.	Roberto JUAREZ	<u>Blanca</u> 1982 oil on
25.	Malcolm MORLEY	<u>Macaws, Bengals, wit</u> canvas 120 x 80"
26.	Susan ROTHENBERG	<u>Asian Sex</u> 1982 oil o
27.	Julian SCHNABEL	<u>Winter (Rose Garden</u> <u>She was a Little Gir</u> bondo on wood 108 x
28.	Robert ZAKANITCH	<u>Yellow Pants</u> 1982 ac

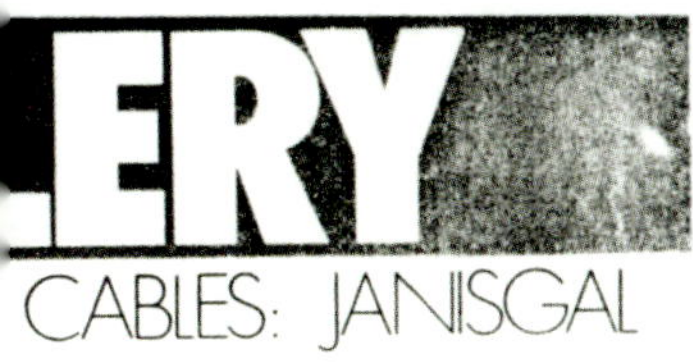

LERY

CABLES: JANISGAL

canva

2,607
wood
renob

21 x

l on

il an

xed n

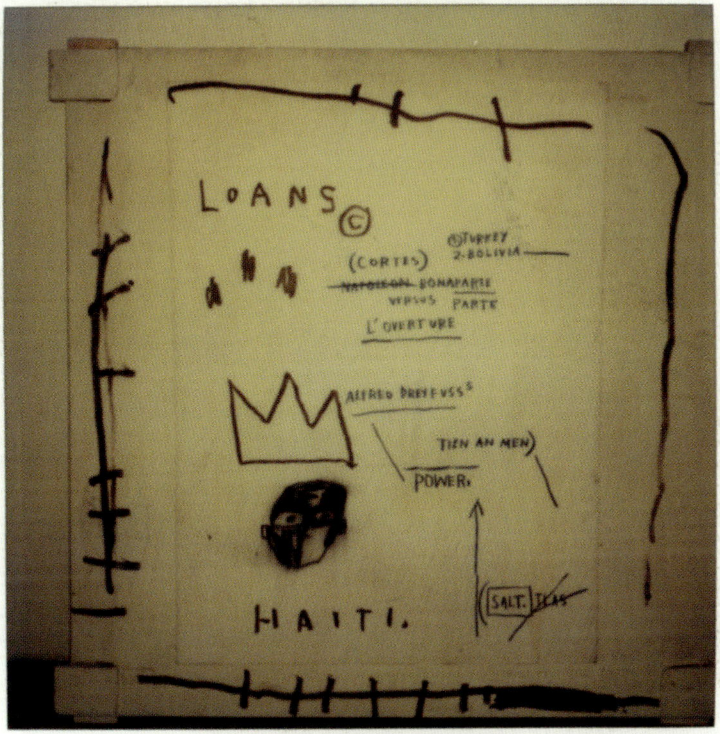

I we
1982

84 x

38 x

l tai

96 x

1982 oil on

62 x 62"

cqueline Built When
oil, plates and

n canvas 88 x 78"

me. I've never had a call

e're going to come and rip

d with some intensity. She
books about art dealers—
mentor." And she hunted
were sitting on our rears,
iend at the time. "She was
were actually up to."
976, Boone began dealing
assembled a syndicate of
igure sum (they now own
she moved into 420 West

Gary Stephan, a well-re-
hnabel, a beginner. Now
y a minuscule couple of
was hardly the point. The
oused Leo Castelli and
patriarchs of modern-art
world. "Getting a gallery
at 420 was fantasy." The
oung woman were hardly

OVENT SEEMED OF MINOR
"We shared the building
d packers," he observed.
ced they were going to
e to a new gallery." They
Mary Boone?' First of all

ng together with a female
with a Caribbean tan, at
restaurant for the art
added, indicating our
able." The restaurant is
bles, and linen napkins,
le were painters Jasper
with a young man from
er puppy eyes. "Jasper!,"
g a glass of Frescobaldi.
ordfish, decorously, but
to focus on one thing at
about his beginnings in
is first show, Alfred Barr
d over," he said. Alfred
eum of Modern Art, and
sts who have charisma.

'62 maybe. I showed a
beach ball. Jasper came
that?' he asked.
oung artist. 'Well, I really
he said. I said, 'Think

l, I thought about it,' he
ortant.' "
s seemed as palpable as
ting. "Leo sees with his
t Hughes. "He's a cross

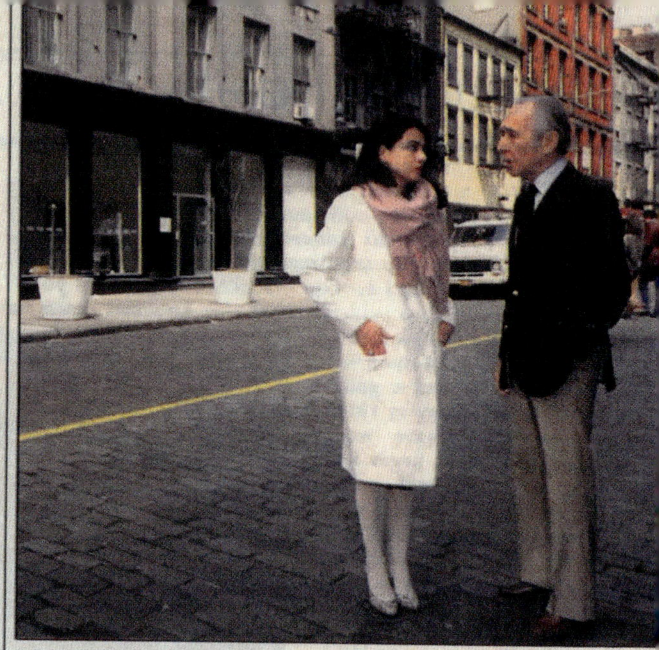

His and hers: *Mary Boone and Leo Castelli chat*

between a Mafia don and Dumbo the Elephant." But for years
his ears picked up nothing new. "It seemed that nothing new
was coming up," he said. "My stable is made up of charis-
matic artists. Of course, there are incidental artists who just
came into the gallery."

Mary agreed. Everybody has incidental artists.

"But I had to wait till something occurred I was really
interested in."

That something was Julian Schnabel.

"Here was something I was confronted with," Castelli said.
"I went in, and it was like when I went to see Jasper in '57,
or Stella in '59. It was a *coup de foudre.*" Which is to say, a
thunderclap. Castelli began helping himself to his compan-
ion's carpaccio.

SUCH EXTRAVAGANCE DOESN'T SURPRISE JULIAN
Schnabel in the remotest. Schnabel was born in
Brooklyn in 1951—the same year as Boone—and
studied at the University of Houston. In the mid-
seventies he came back to New York; if he was
oppressed by self-doubts, they were not too visible. "I'm going
to be a great painter," he told a young woman.

"What do you do now?" she asked. "Right now, I'm a cook.
But I'm going to be the most famous painter in New York."

Right now, though, he was indeed a cook, working at such
joints as the Ocean Club, part of the army of arts graduates
who work as carpenters or plumbing contractors, carouse at
Puffy's, McGovern's, or Barnabas Rex, grouse about the
gallery system, and dream of the one-man, sellout show.

He was not to be part of this army for long. Spotting Boone
in a restaurant in which he was working, he asked her to visit
his studio. "I was struck by the incredible physicality of the
paint," Boone says. The canvases were huge, unfashionably
imagistic. "It was lush. Holes were dug out of it. I was a bit

Bongard, the German critic, who wrote a fierce attack
nabel in *Stern* magazine. "It is a phenomenon," he told
t is a very fashionable thing. But I do not trust its staying

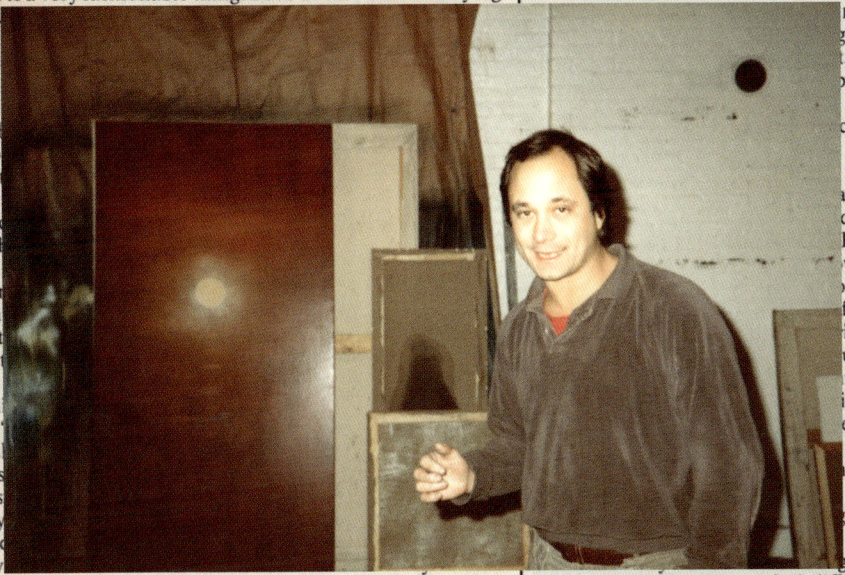

collect the hot items, the hot commoditi
doesn't cut much ice anymore."

tried out. And they have a very short life."
ew weeks ago, David Salle had a Boone-Castelli three-
y show. Peter Schjeldahl, in the *Voice*, described the
ng but wrote that "this show would be an Event if
ed with a box of Chiclets and held
ubway toilet." John Russell, in the
, however, described it as "dis-

okumenta," one of Europe's most
ntial contemporary-art extrav-
zas, is held in Düsseldorf every
ears. It is to be held this summer,
he organizers let it be known that
er Julian Schnabel nor David
would be included. In the case of
abel, it seems to be an aversion to
aintings; in the case of Salle, to
ype. The decision on Salle was
sed at the last minute a couple of
s ago.

oseudonymous critic in *Art/World*
ared Schnabel to the artist who
ted those pictures of large-eyed
ren in sombreros that hang on the
of the Texas Chili Parlor back
," but this writer's seriousness is
asy to gauge since he (she?) also
s John Russell and Robert
es.

tually, the interesting news seems
that criticism itself isn't quite
it used to be when Clement
nberg and Harold Rosenberg is-
their *Diktats*. "I just don't think
s are as influential as they were,"
es says. Things have probably be-
too big, too disparate. "It's what
ctors are told by dealers, it's what
collectors are doing," Grace
ck, of the *Times*, told me. "You

eyeing it angrily. "I may feel differently
He eyed it further. "The drawing's go
"It's the same crazy mind," Boone sa
Doesn't the act of painting clear thin

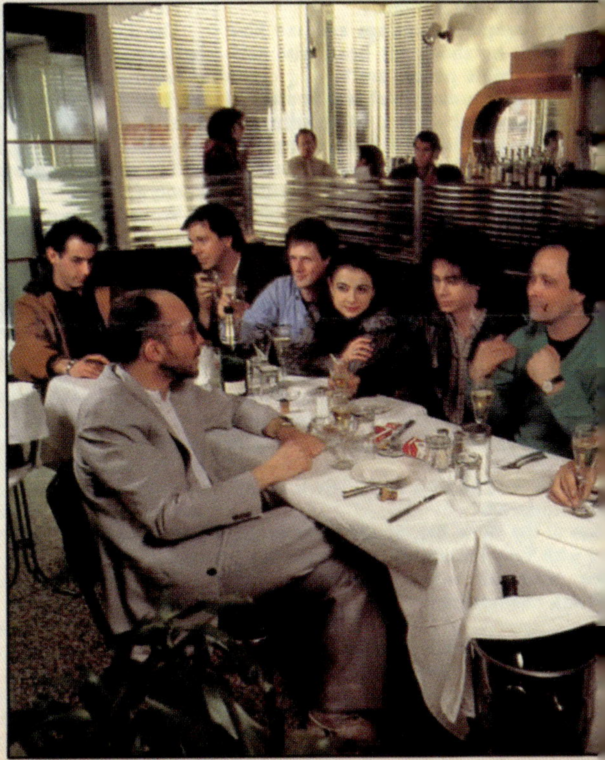

The Odeon group: *Boone with artists Gary Stephan (foreground)*
Salle, Matt Mullican, Michael McClard, Troy Brauntuch, Ross Bleckne

Painting with a Past

A new generation of Italian painters is defyin[g] the avant-garde's historical trend toward Minimalism, inventing images and styles fro[m] personal, art historical, and cultural sources.

by Attanasio di Felice

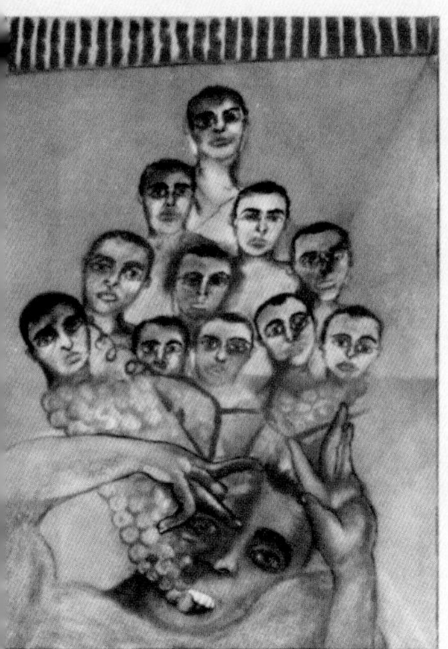

*Above: Francesco Clemente and his Trans-avantgarde colleagues draw upon many sources; Tantric iconography informs his 1980 pastel self-portrait Star. 37x30 ¾". Bobby Heller collection. **Below:** This eclecticism is consistent with such earlier Italian works as Giorgio de Chirico's 1926 oil The Roman Comedy. Private collection.*

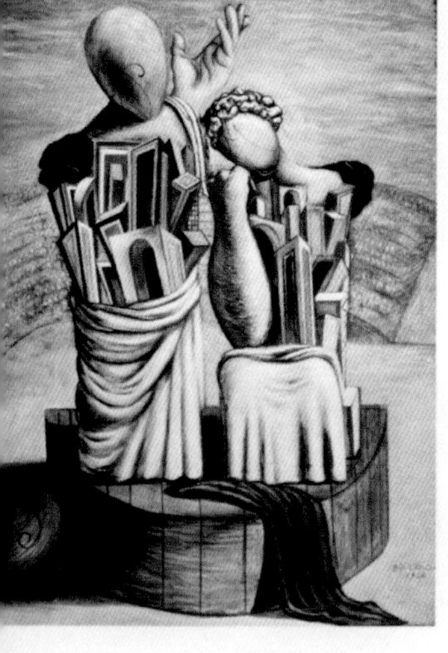

Two years ago in February 1980, Gillo Dorfles, a dean of Italian art criticism involved with the Italian cultural scene since the 1920s, gave—with firm, dismayed conviction—some advice to a colleague. One might as well abandon any efforts to encourage an interest in contemporary Italian art in New York, he said, since the nearly total ignorance of twentieth-century Italian art had created an insuperable gap in American art-historical consciousness.

A year and a half later, Andy Warhol and *Interview* editor Bob Colacello were talking with Mick Jagger. The conversation, recorded in the August 1981 *Interview*, turned to buying art:

Mick: . . . Of the people you've seen around, including yourself, what do you think I should buy? Not too crazy. I'm talking about someone new, that's not too expensive.

BC: Sandro Chia does really beautiful paintings. Do you like his work, Andy?

Andy: Yes, but his prices are high.

What had happened in the year and a half between Dorfles's pessimism and the more than casual interest of Warhol, the most astute artist/businessman since Marcel Duchamp? Five days before Dorfles made his pronouncement, Sandro Chia's first New York one-man show had closed and in s[uc]ceeding months several of his c[ol]leagues, among them Enzo Cuc[co] Francesco Clemente, Nicola De Ma[ria] Luigi Ontani, Ernesto Tatafiore, a[nd] Filippo Di Sambuy, showed in N[ew] York, many for the first time. This n[ew] wave countermanded Dorfles's sta[te]ment and challenged New York's he[ge]mony over the international art sce[ne].

The international recognition w[on] by these young painters, notably [the] five known as "The Italian Tra[ns]avantgarde," bespeaks a changing a[es]thetic perception as well as a chang[ing] and often political art market. At [the] end of the 1970s, Minimalism, Conc[ep]tualism, performance art, and e[ven] video seemed to support the claim t[hat] painting was on its deathbed. By 19[80] however, certain American dealers [in] contemporary art were already aw[are] of the reappearance of narrati[ve,] figurative, and decorative content [in] the work of a few New York artists, a[nd] of burgeoning painterly energies [in] Italy and Germany. At the Ven[ice] Biennale this new painting received f[ur]ther validation in *Open 80*, an inter[na]tional group show curated by Ital[ian] critic and art historian Achille Bon[ito] Oliva and Harald Szeemann t[hat] included paintings by Chia, Cuc[chi,] and Clemente, along with a selection

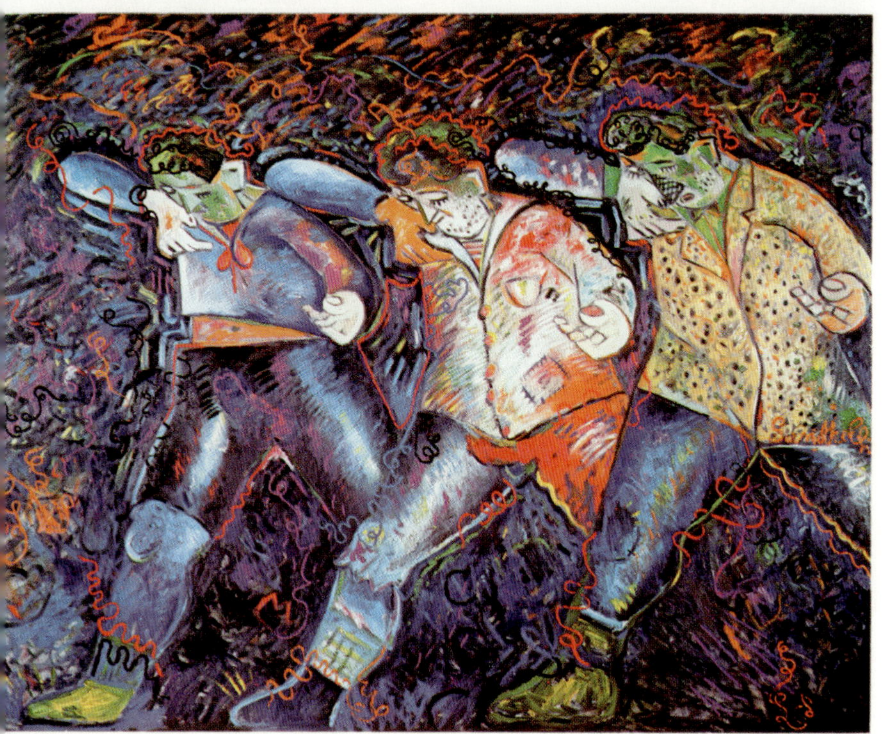

orks by young American artists. ther European exhibitions spurred terest in this new work. Now, after a ate of gallery shows in New York, the lian scene receives further exposure th the April opening of *Aspects of lian Art Now* at the Guggenheim.

Nevertheless, in one sense Dorfles as correct. Many Italian artists of the unger generation are deeply indebt- to the post-World War I works of iorgio de Chirico and his contempo- ries, and Americans' unfamiliarity th modern Italian painting makes it fficult to understand what the latest velopments mean in the context of lian art history and culture.

The larger context, the development innovative painting in Italy in this ntury, focuses on Futurism and its termath. An aggressive, dynamic

response to Neo-Impressionism, Cub- ism, and the machine age, Futurism had already begun to fade during World War I. The movement's stellar painter, Umberto Boccioni, had devel- oped an expressionistic style close to his Calabrian roots in the months before his death in 1916; by the war's end Carlo Carrà and Gino Severini (both of whom were born in the 1880s and died in 1966) were gravitating toward more contemplative modes. Subsequently Carrà, De Chirico, and other artists of their generation—Giorgio Morandi, Ottone Rosai, Primo Conti, Felice Casorati, Filippo de Pisis, Mario Sironi, and De Chirico's brother Alberto Savinio—briefly espoused an illusive, irrational style known as Meta- physical Painting. In his 1918 book, *Metaphysical Painting*, Carrà defends the

Above: Sandro Chia combines cartoonlike figures and expressionistic color in Brutes as Protagonists of a Monkey's Erotic Fantasy. *1979–80. Oil on canvas, 67⅜ x84". Private collection.*

validity of applying Renaissance tech- niques to twentieth-century imagery drawn from the irrational and uncon- scious. This position continues to reverberate in the work of Italy's most advanced painters today.

But rigid adherence to any single twentieth-century art movement has been the exception, volubility of style the rule. De Chirico, Savinio, de Pisis, and many of their colleagues shared a deep attachment to literature and myth. They found inspiration in re- gional Italian culture, Mediterranean archaism, the Renaissance, Orien-

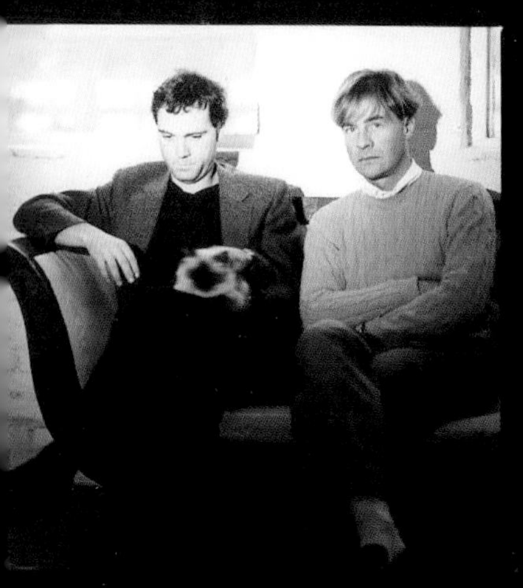

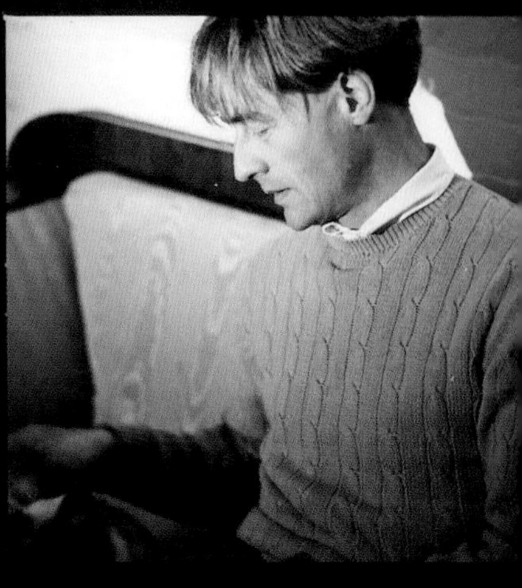

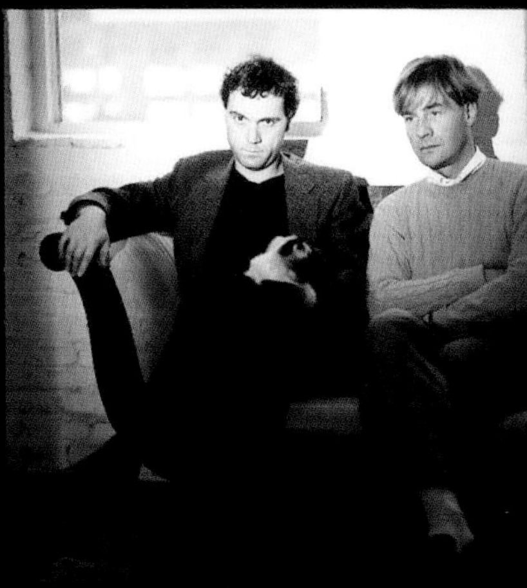

I was amazed by the fact that a person like Heiner liked my work and wanted to be in a picture with me... Heiner was very close to Joseph Beuys a happening and performance artist as well as pedagogue of art. Apparently my art was very different from Joseph Beuys work. Heiner was aware that even very different ways to make art share common roots and in these roots reside the meaning as well as the enigma of art.

Sandro Chia

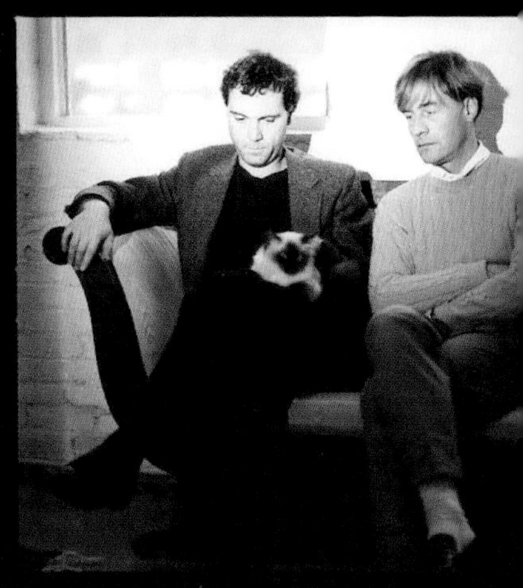

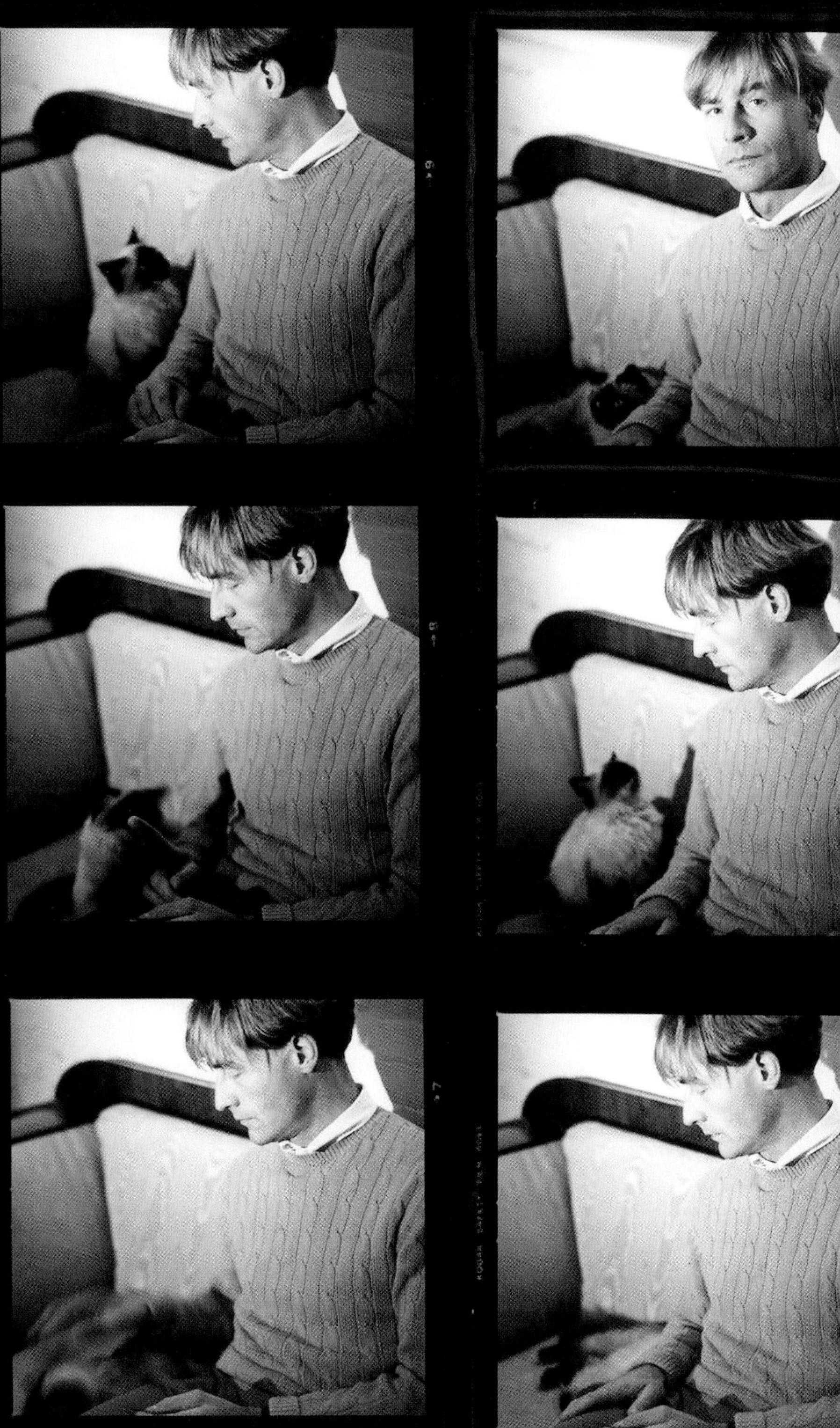

Dear Jeannette

Here I mail you
a first copy of
the catalogue — you
will get more — the
moment I get them.
Thank you very much
again — and I truly
hope you will continue
portraying the artists
so we can do a book
one day.
Very sincerely yours
Heiner

Venice. Matthias Brunner took this photo.

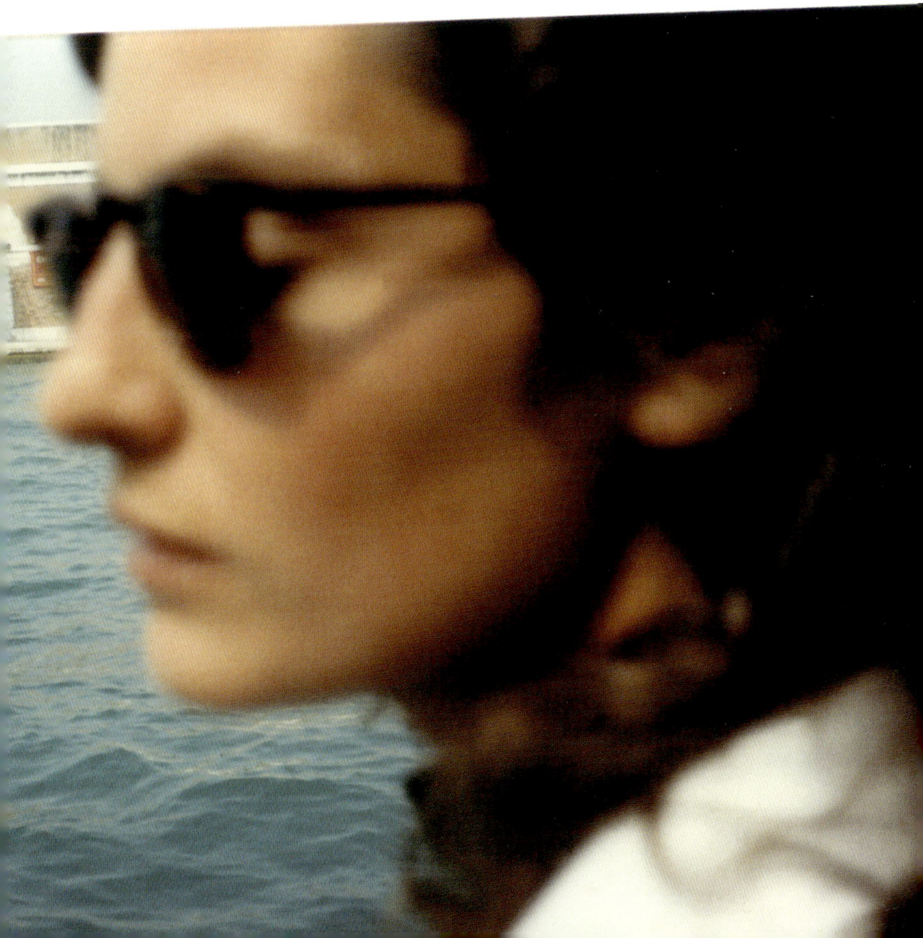

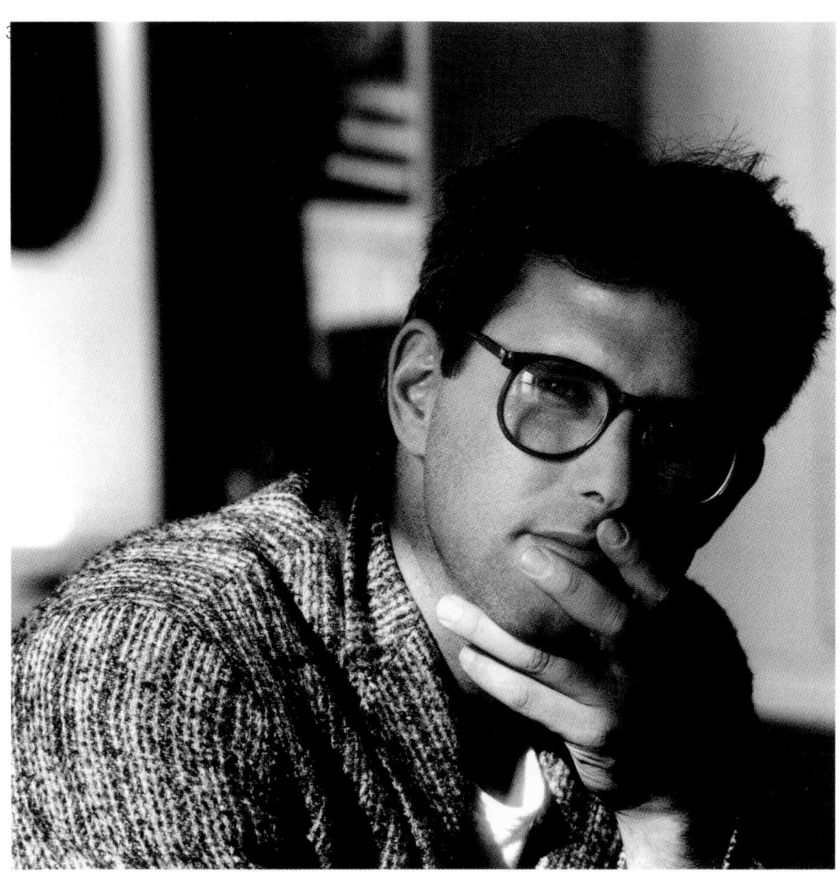

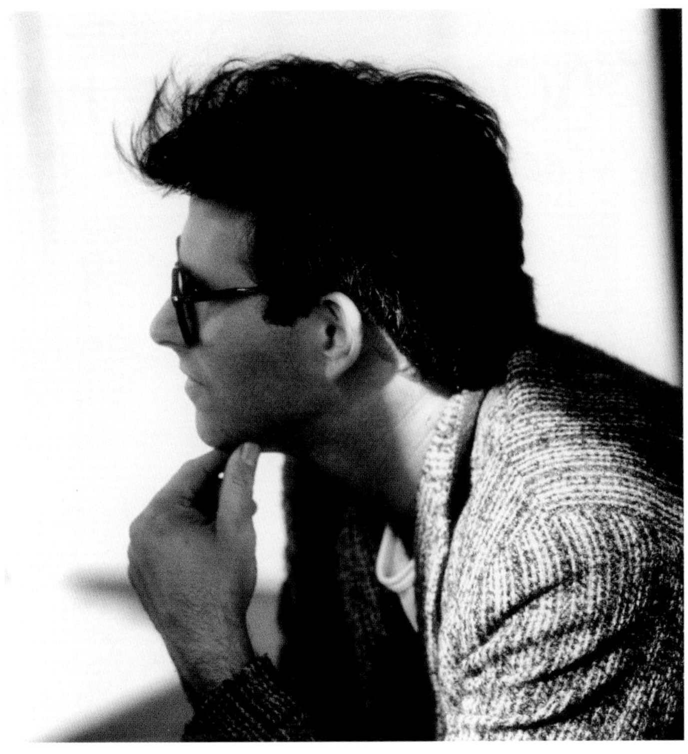

"HOT-DOG-FRESH-FACE

A VIDEOTAPE SHOW AT THE MUD...

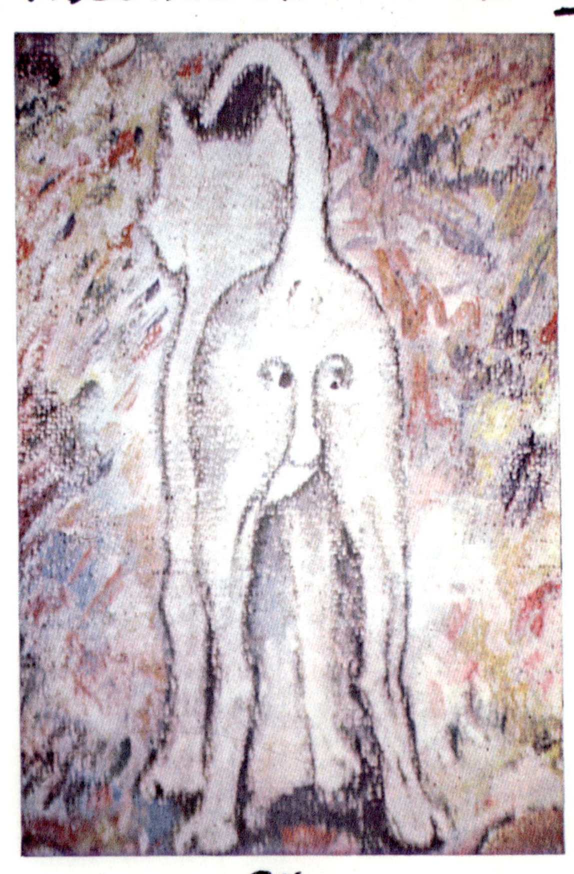

BY

SANDRO CHIA

ALBERTO RIZZO

SUNDAY NIGHT, FEB. 3, 77 WHITE ST. NEW YO
(N.Y.)

JMB: In 1986 I remember coming to your studio for a party after one of your openings—or it may have been an event at your loft to raise money for AMFAR—probably Bianca Jagger invited me because we hung around a lot in those days. I could not help feeling back then that a lot of your painting was about loss and memory—those friends who we saw leaving this world much too soon. And I say "leaving this world" because your work had the feeling that there was another world for them after. There was a brightness, not sadness. At least that's what it seemed to me.

RB: Dear Jeannette, you probably came to my house with Bianca for some fundraiser that I was having. Usually some kind of Christmas dinner, on behalf on ACRIA (AIDS Community Research Initiative of America), an AIDS research, education and prevention organization that has grown to be one of the biggest in the country. We worked with doctors and pharmacies to try to expedite cutting edge medications to people who most needed it. We held workshops in minority communities to create awareness of the health issues the stigma and the prevention/ treatment options. So a typical day in 1986 was me being in my studio working on paintings that i felt had to deal with the urgency of the rapidly shifting paragigm from the industrial optimism and progress of the previous generation to its dislocation by young people's sudden awareness of the possibility of mortality. I tried to reflect both ends of this contradictions in my work.
I've always been a creature of habit so a typical day in 1986 would not be that different from a typical day in 2014. I get up early, meditate, read the paper, exercise, get to work at 10-10.30, stop for a few minutes at 1 to eat the same thing every day (yogurt and granola), work again until about 4, return any calls or deal with any annoying stuff that comes up in the day in NYC, go home and rest, go out to dinner at 8 since I have never cooked, try to get home by 10-10.30, read and try to be asleep by midnight. I essentially repeat this scenario *ad infinitum.* I've never been a big TV watcher, nor do I need to be entertained so I don't really go to dance or theatre. I always wonder why I live in NYC, but can never figure out any other place to go, except for the summers when I go out to my house in the Hampton and basically repeat the process above, the only difference being that I get to work much earlier and go to the gym, etc in the late afternoon.
I really only have 5-6 hours of creative energy a day so I have to use it as effectively as I know how. All my best,

Ross Bleckner

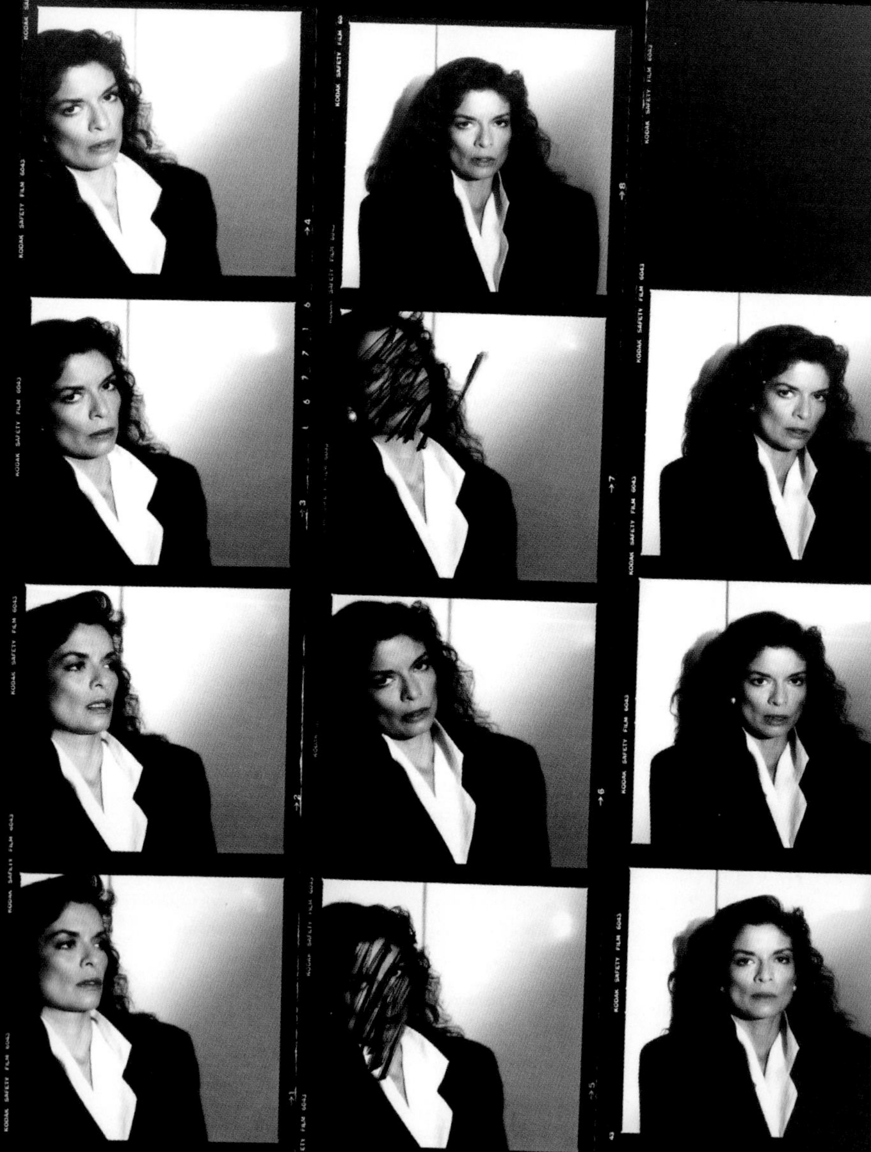

Model Release

Date

PHOTOGRAPHER

Address

For valuable consideration, I hereby irrevocably consent to and authorize the use and reproduction by you, or anyone authorized by you, of ~~any and all photographs~~ which you have this day taken of me, negative or positive, proofs of which are hereto attached, for any ~~purpose whatsoever~~, without further compensation to me. All negatives and positives, together with the prints shall constitute your property, solely and completely.

I am over 18 years of age.   Yes _______   No _______

MODEL ____

Signature of Model

Address:____

Witnessed by:_____________________________________

Signature of Witness

• • • • • • • • •

If the person signing is under 18 consent should be given by parent or guardian, as follows:

I hereby certify that I am the parent or guardian of_____________

The model named above, and for value received I do give my consent without reservations to the foregoing on behalf of him or her or them.

DATED:____

Signature of Parent or Guardian

WITNESSED by:____________________________________

Signature of Witness

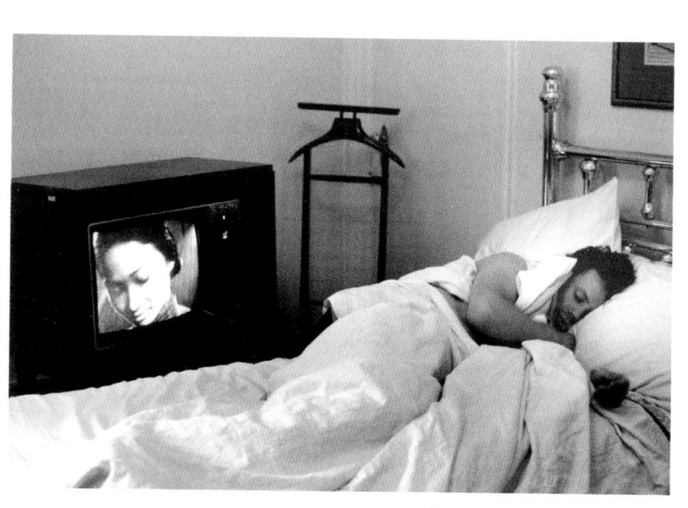

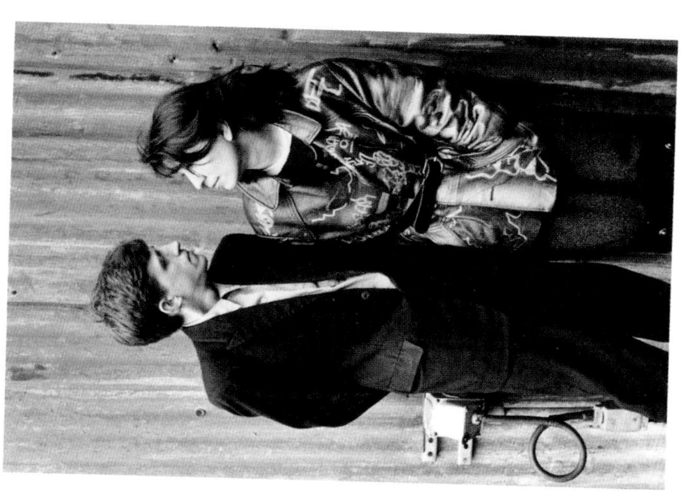

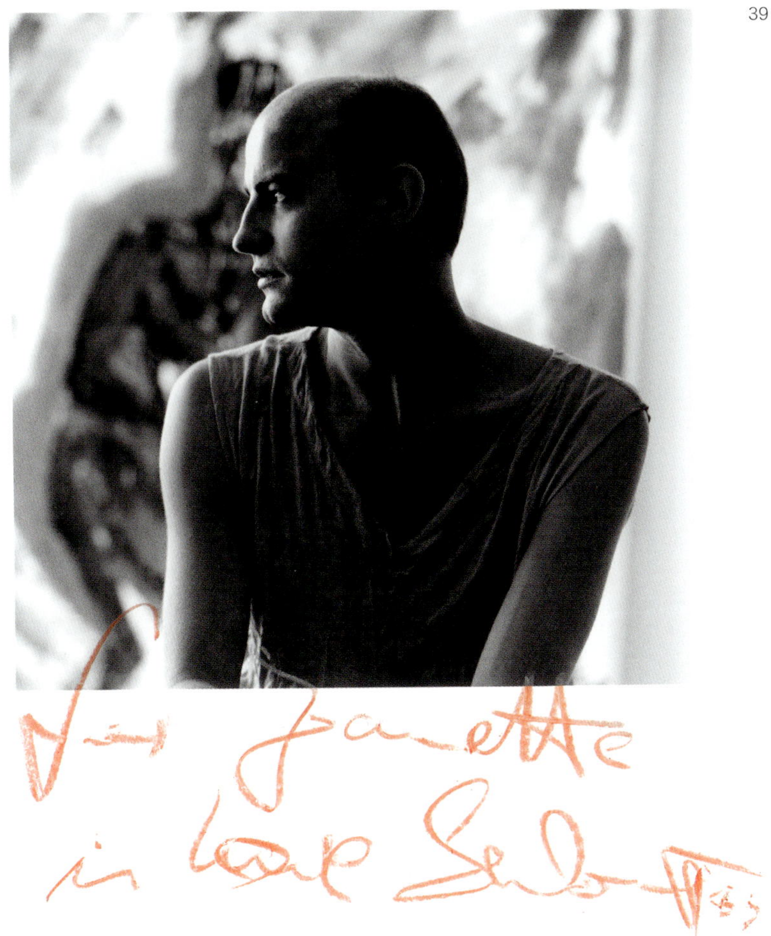

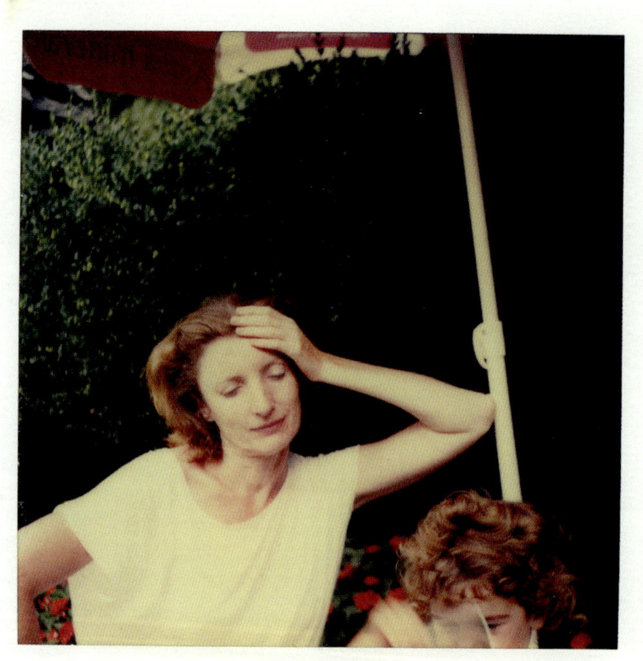

1984

The Locarno Film Festival, Summer 1984.
Viva Auder was invited to be a judge.
She brought along her daughters Gaby
Hoffman and Alexandra Auder. I'm
pretty sure Gaby snapped that polaroid

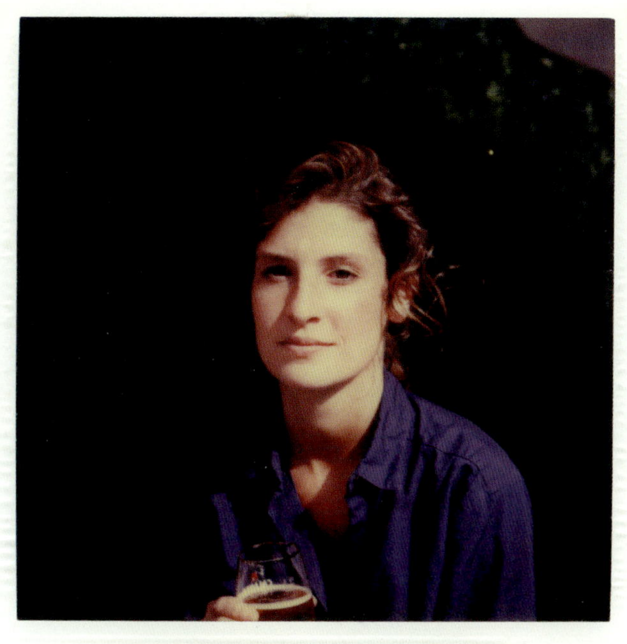

of me. And Viva took the photo
of me with Gaby.
   I was really addicted to Polaroid
that summer! Thomas Ammann and
Matthias Brunner posed for me in
their bathing suits.

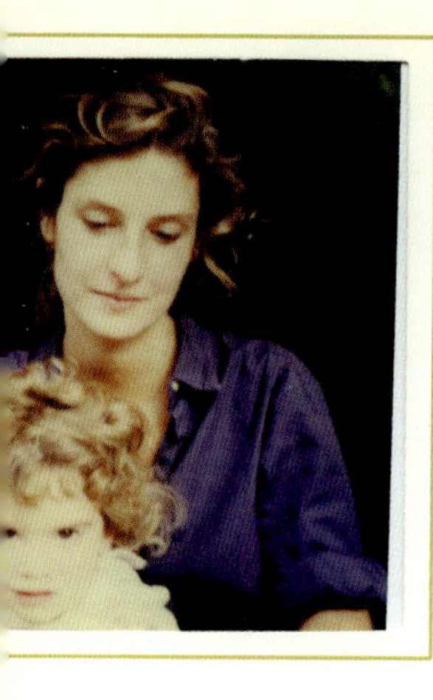

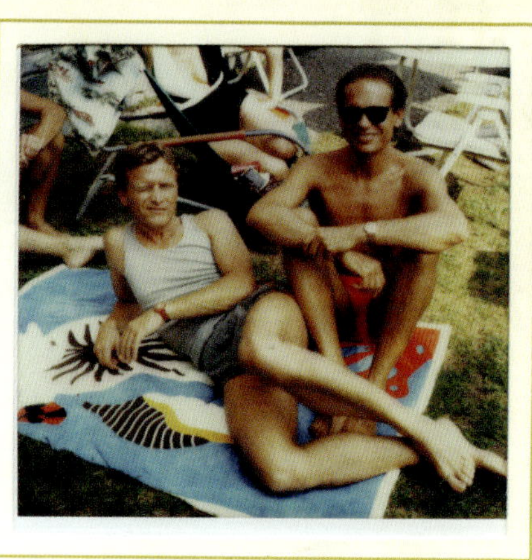

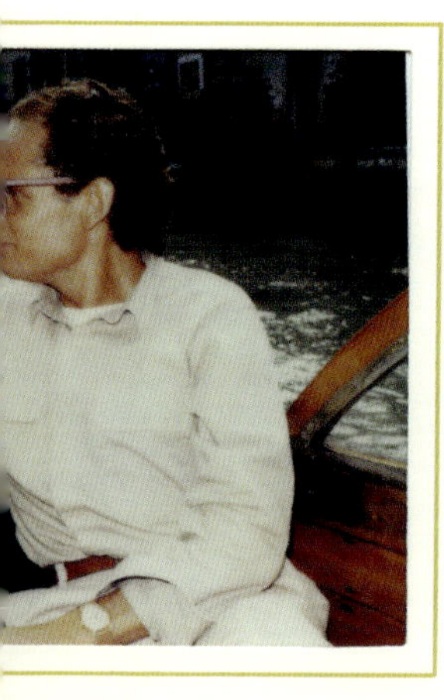

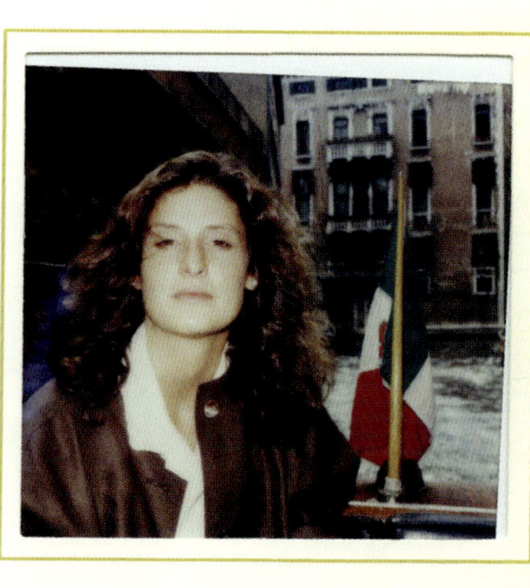

MATTHIAS BRUNNER
SEEFELDSTRASSE 90
8008 ZÜRICH
01·47 47 83

10/9/84

Dear Jeannette,

after all these wonderful days with you and now this sudden lack of you, I feel even more that you live at the wrong place. Call the transporters, and mover over Darling!

I just spent the most fabulous weekend in Paris. Can you imagine us all together: Thomas, Ed, Paul (Morrissey), Samya, Wolf, Juliette and many more... It was so funny and great, often
we all had the best time and you were part of the subject! (Always only in the most positive way of course!) So everybody sends you their love. We cannot wait till you are back in Europe in fall.

I asked Ed for the adress of David Kalstone. It is 471 West 22nd Street, N.Y. 10011. He said that you really should get in touch with him. Ed will help you a lot with all the american and french writers he knows who live in Paris. So you can make photographs of them too. Now, as I know him better, I think even higher of him. He is really a very special person. I can hardly wait to read all his books.

I am still in a terrible rush and hope you forgive me, if this letter is just a short one.

love and

a big kiss,

Thes

MAY 16 PARADISE
1984 AT GARAGE ★
KEITH HARING
LARRY LEVAN
OF LIFE AT 84 KI
MUSIC BY LARRY LE
ART AND VIDEO BY
$5.00 ADMISSION W
K. Haring 84

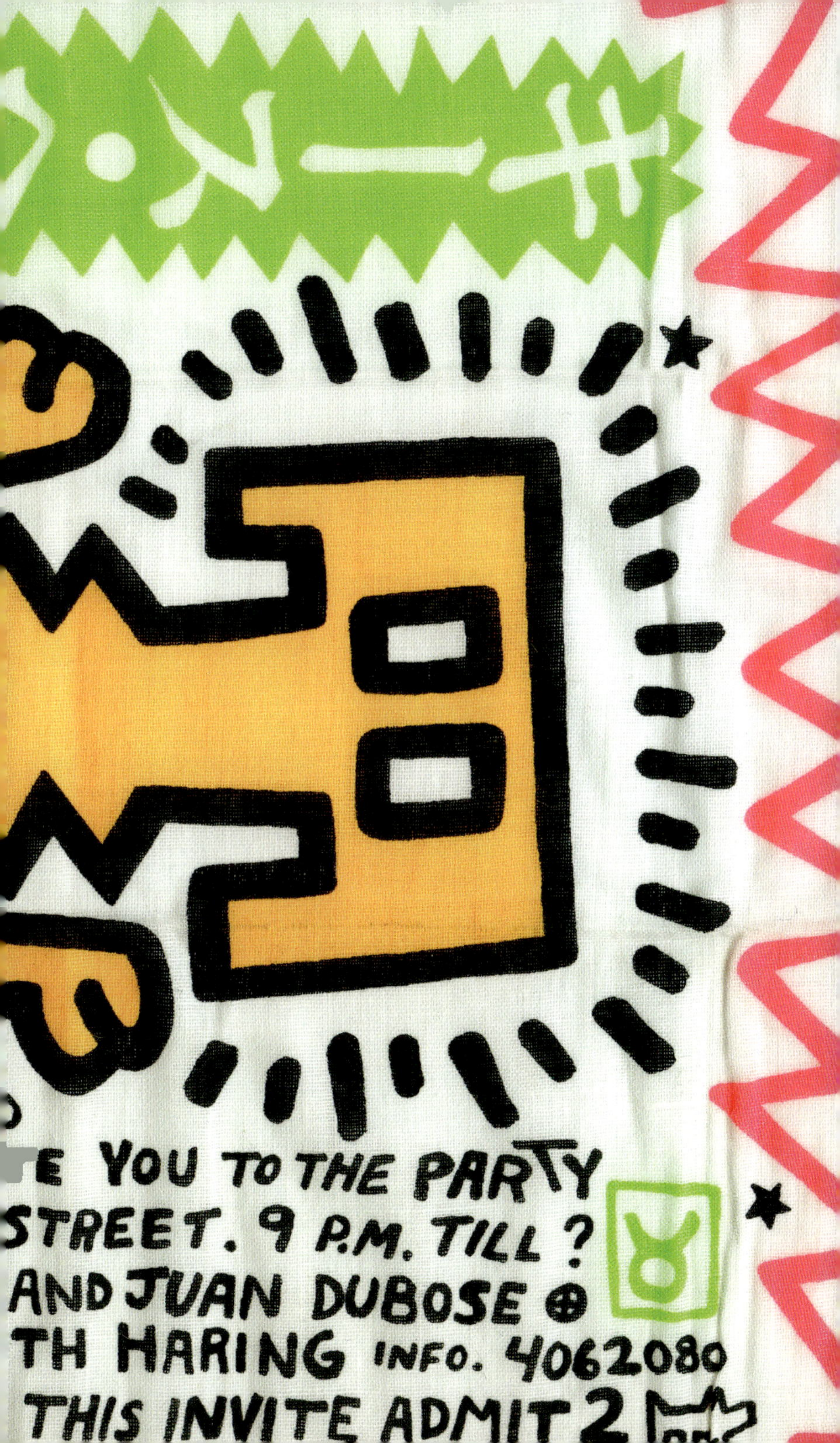
E YOU TO THE PARTY
STREET. 9 P.M. TILL ?
AND JUAN DUBOSE
TH HARING INFO. 4062080
THIS INVITE ADMIT 2

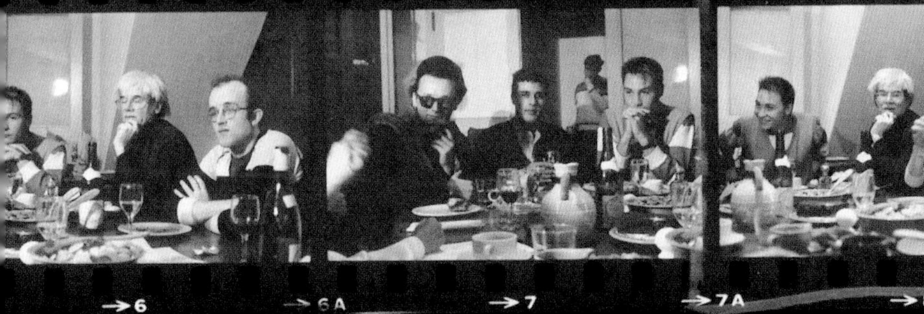

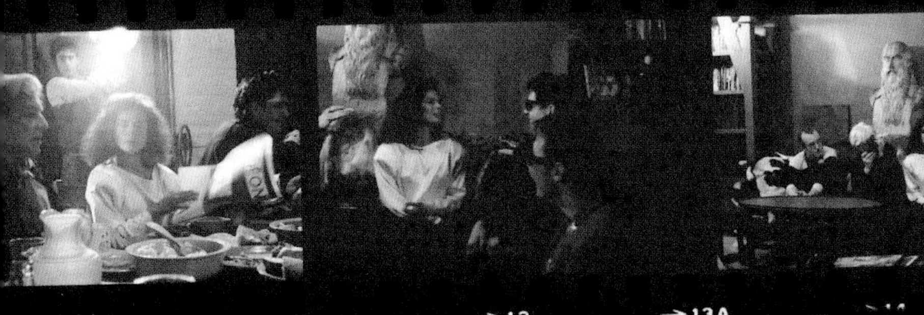

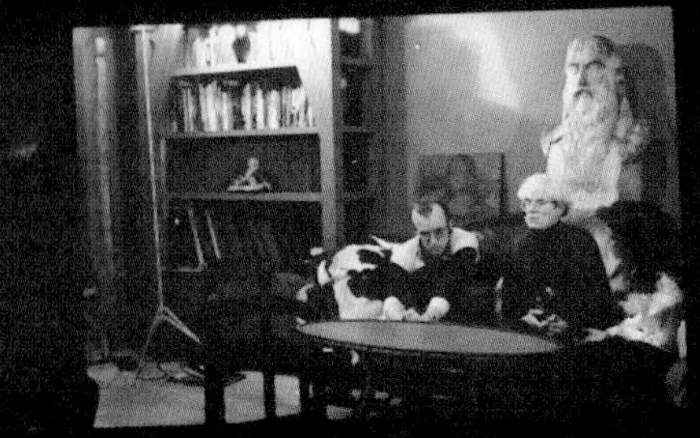

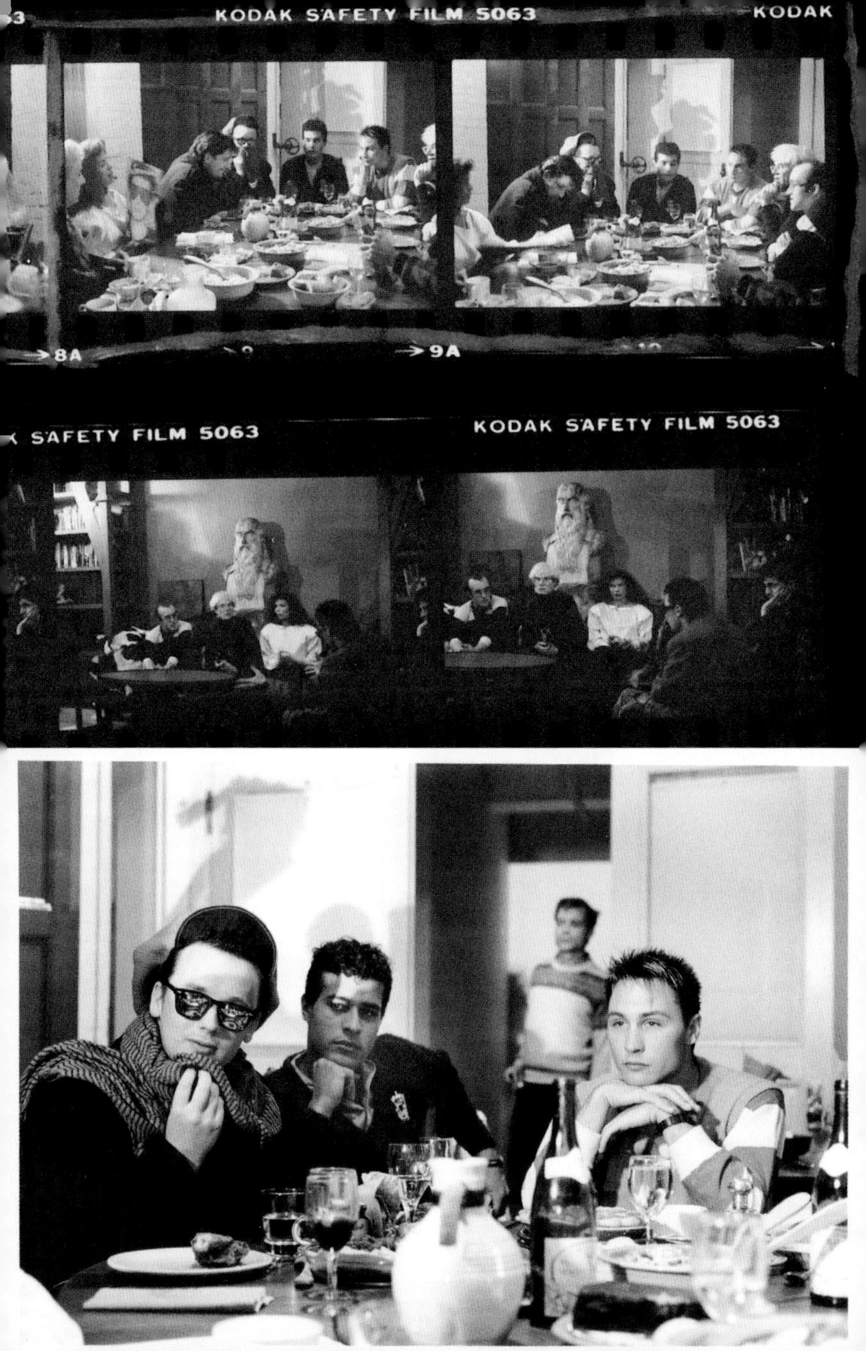

to create an "uptown salon" atmosphere.

Since September, Sharpe has shown figurative artists who make what

> **East Village art can be separated into a number of different esthetic trends that individually are closer kin to art made elsewhere than to each other.**

could be called extended self-portraits—work that embellishes a central figure with props and pictorial attributes for an overall effect of lyrical subjectivity. This group includes ceramic sculptors Arthur Gonzalez

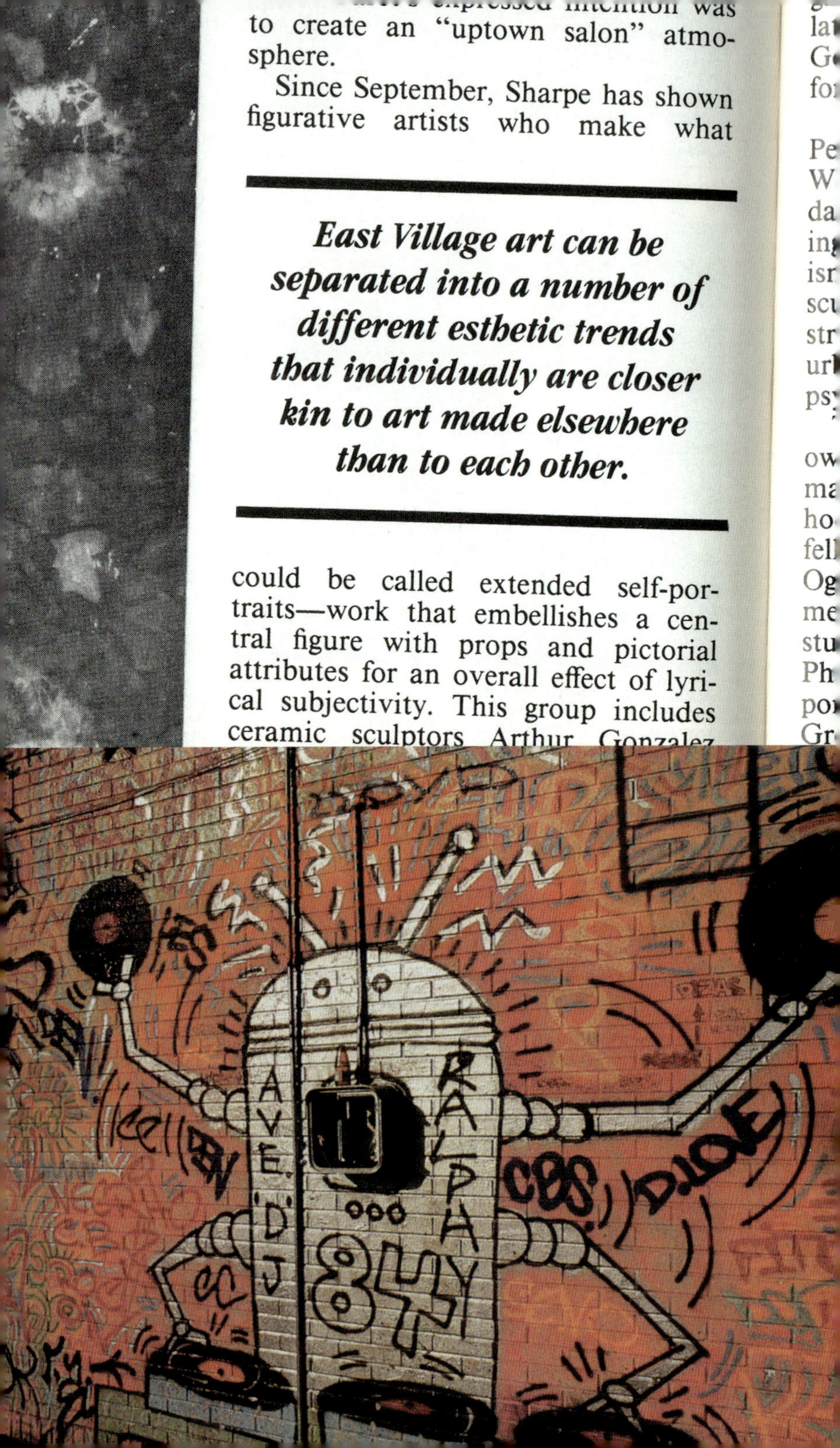

The East Village picture was completed, geographically if not chronologically, with Pat Hearn's opening in December '83 on East Sixth St. and Avenue B after extensive renovations of a completely wrecked corner building. Her relatively large space (1,100 sq. ft.) is at present the easternmost commercial gallery, and is particularly stylish, complete with glass bricks, tortoise-shell tiles and a miniature, cactus-dotted "sculpture garden" in one corner.

No East Village gallery has a clearer esthetic disposition than Pat Hearn, who has found, apparently without much difficulty, an entire group of artists intent on recapitulating the visual motifs of Surrealism. Some, like George Condo, make works in almost direct imitation of Dali and Magritte; others, like Peter Schuyff, take up new positions on Surrealism's stylistic spectrum (his paintings could fit in somewhere between Tanguy and Ba-

One of the scene's most sensationalist figures is Mike Bidlo, who recreates others' works and reenacts events from their lives.

ziotes). Hearn's March show consisted of elaboratively framed cliché-verre by Stephen Pollack, who incorporates undated notions of Surrealist icono-

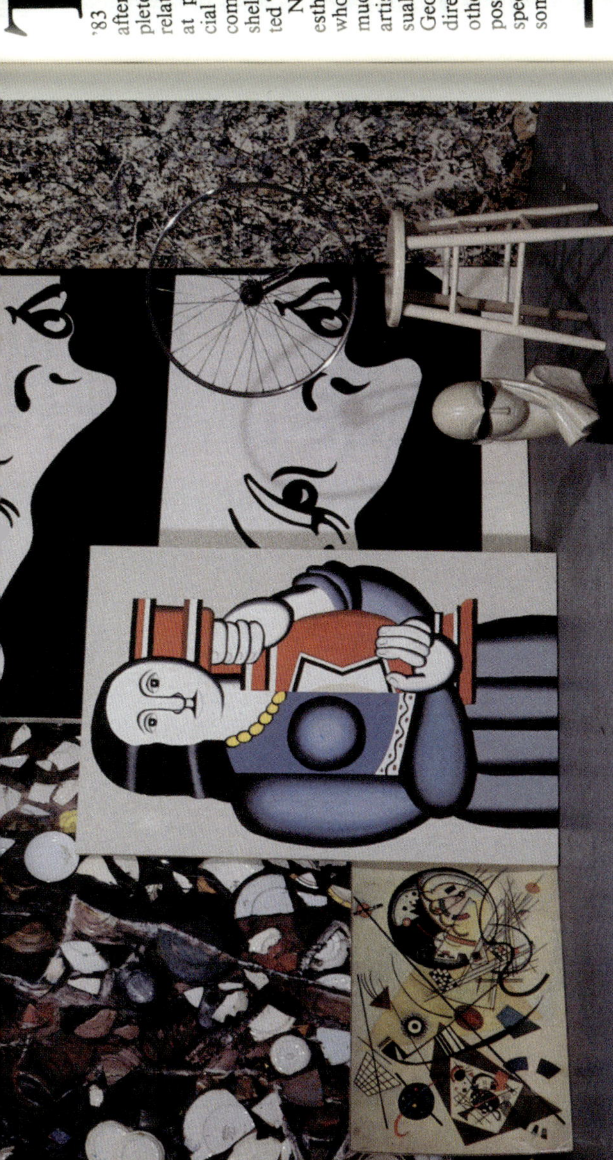

Bidlo's recreations of works by (from left) Schnabel, Kandinsky, [.]r, Warhol, Brancusi, Duchamp and Pollock. Gracie Mansion.

[.]ke Bidlo: A Chicken in Every Pot and a Pollock Over Every Couch, 1983, [.]n "Sofa/Couch" at Gracie Mansion. Photo Philip Pocock.

Richard Hambleton, Romance and Catastrophe, 1984, acrylic on canvas, 40 by 28 inches. Piezo Electric.

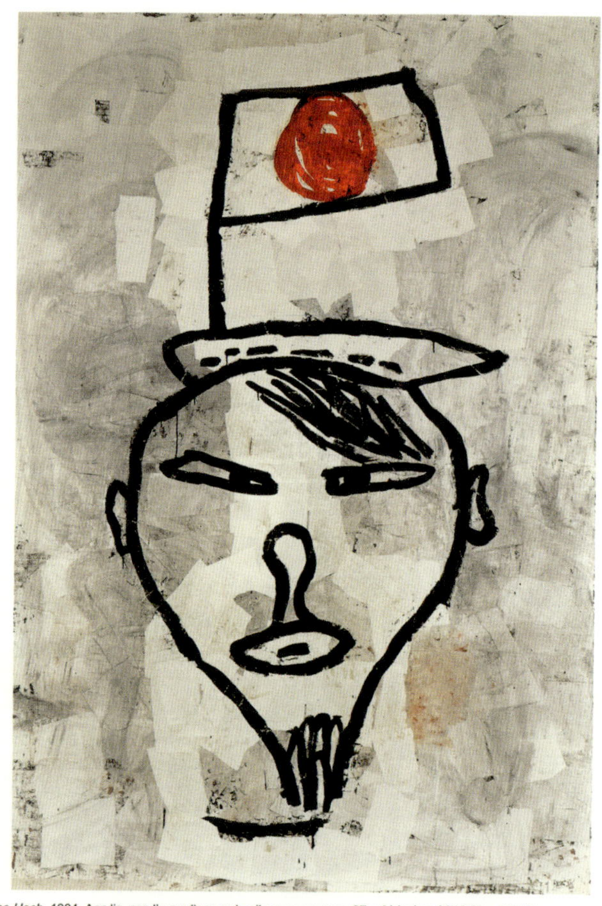

Donald Baechler, *Die Fahne Hoch,* 1984, Acrylic, acrylic medium and collage on canvas, 97 x 64 inches / 246.38 x 162.56 cm
Courtesy Tony Shafrazi Gallery, New York

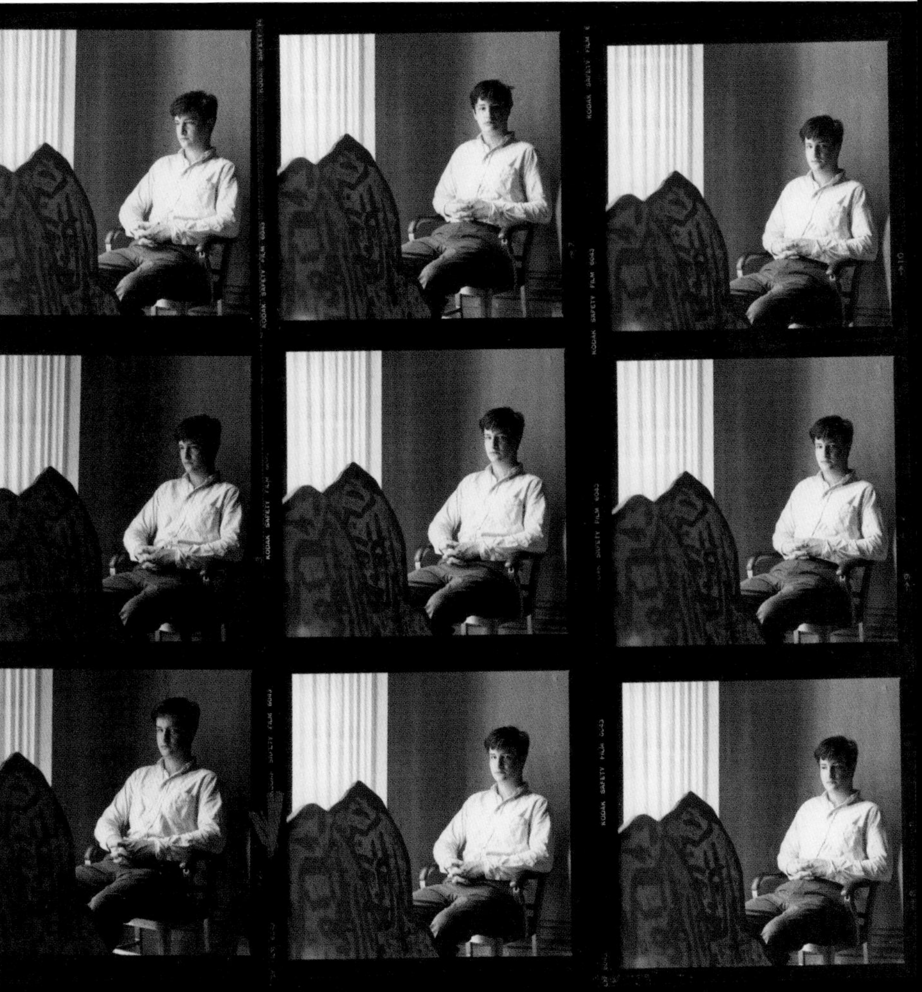

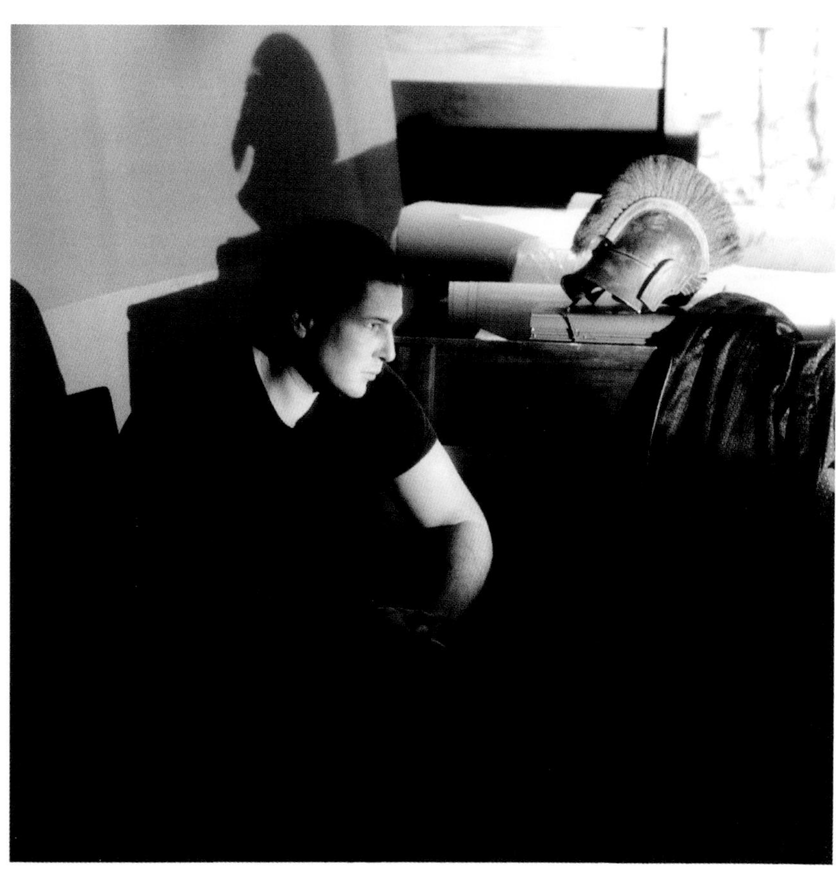

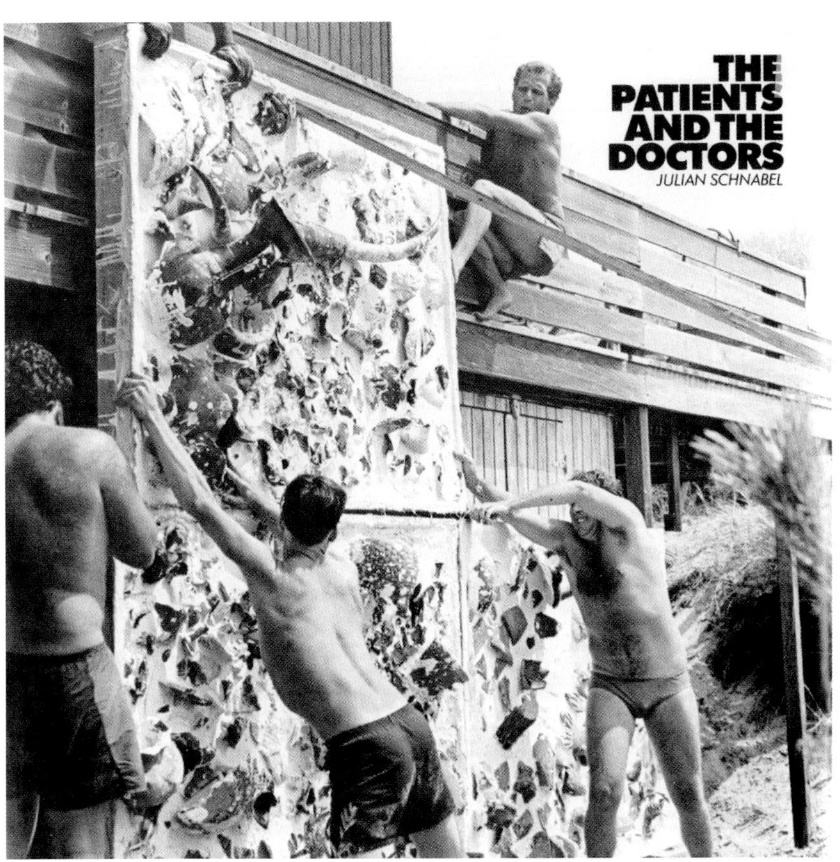THE
PATIENTS
AND THE
DOCTORS
JULIAN SCHNABEL

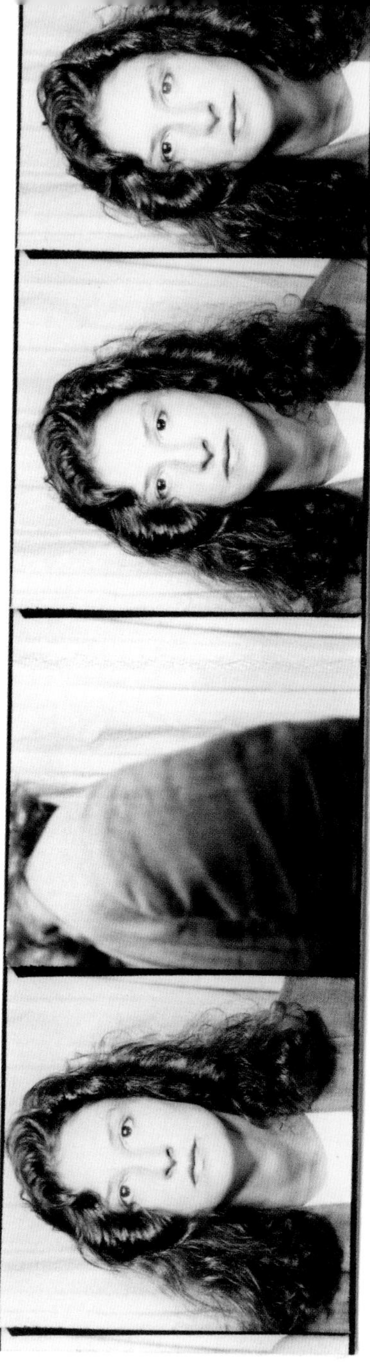

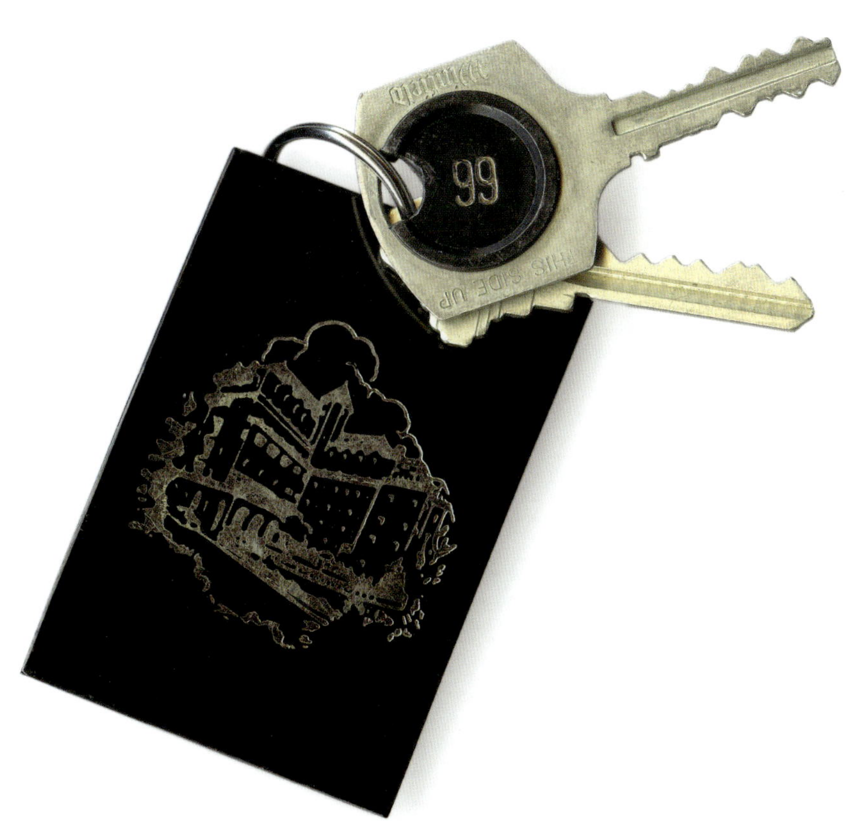
99
THIS SIDE UP

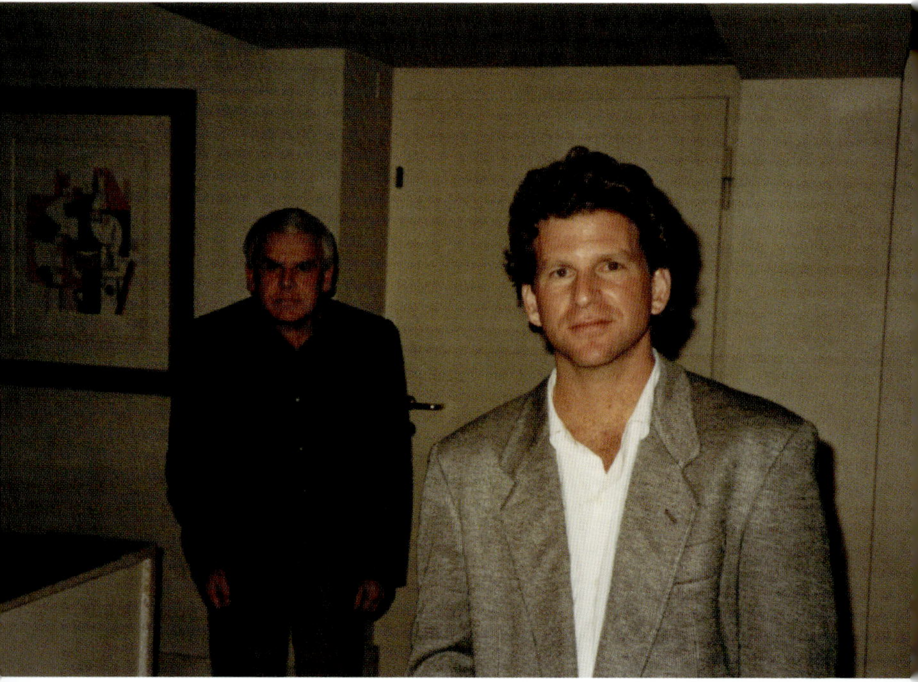

When I first met Jeannette, her idea of making breakfast was picking up the phone, dialing the Greek diner and saying, «Hey, Joey, it's Jeannette. Can you send me coffee, a Coke and a BLT?»

So it came as a surprise that she became -- almost overnight -- an incredible cook. Whenever we had a dinner party, our guests would ask how she made the salad dressing.
«Oil, vinegar, salt, pepper,» she'd say.
«That's it?»
We'd all laugh.
«That's it.»

Her photos are just like that: simple ingredients, the right proportions, and a bit of magic.

James Barron

LEONA M. HELMSLEY
DUNNELLEN HALL
521 ROUND HILL ROAD
GREENWICH, CONNECTICUT 06830

August
2012

Thank You, J. M. B   (as in
For the extra-lovely   Jean
Stamps — not to   Michel
mention the photo   Basquiat)
in itself a lovely
Surprise

We look so
                      young
We were so
                      young

X.X   Rene Ricard

Jeannette Montgomery Barron
P.O Box 97
215 South Kent Road

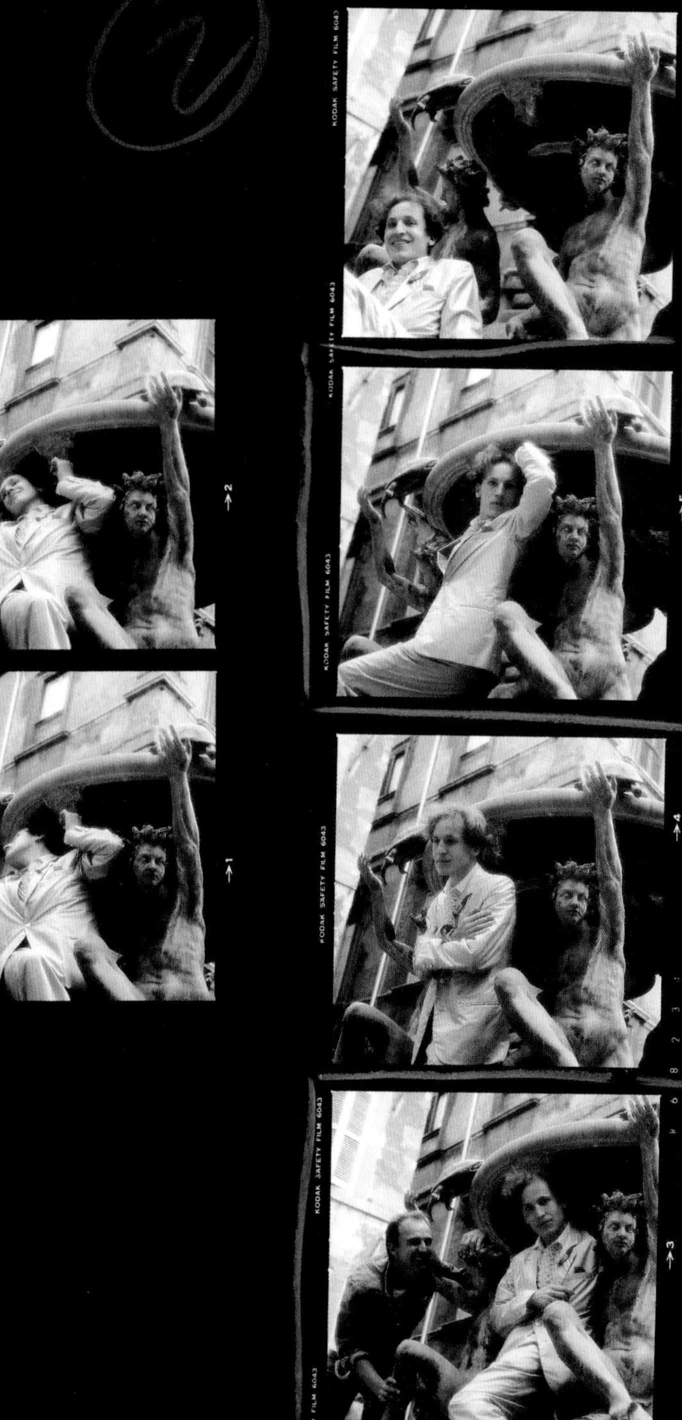

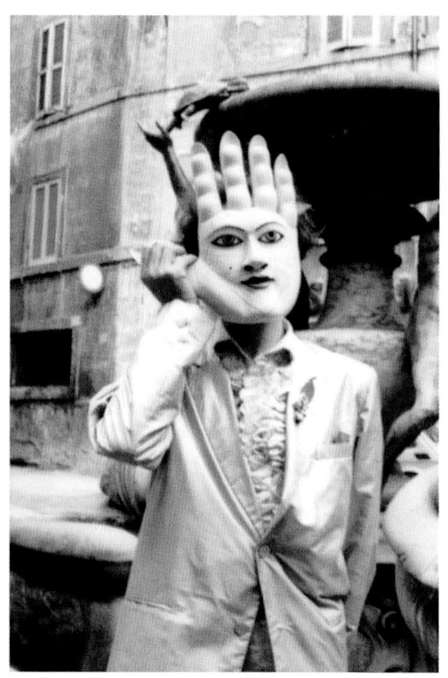

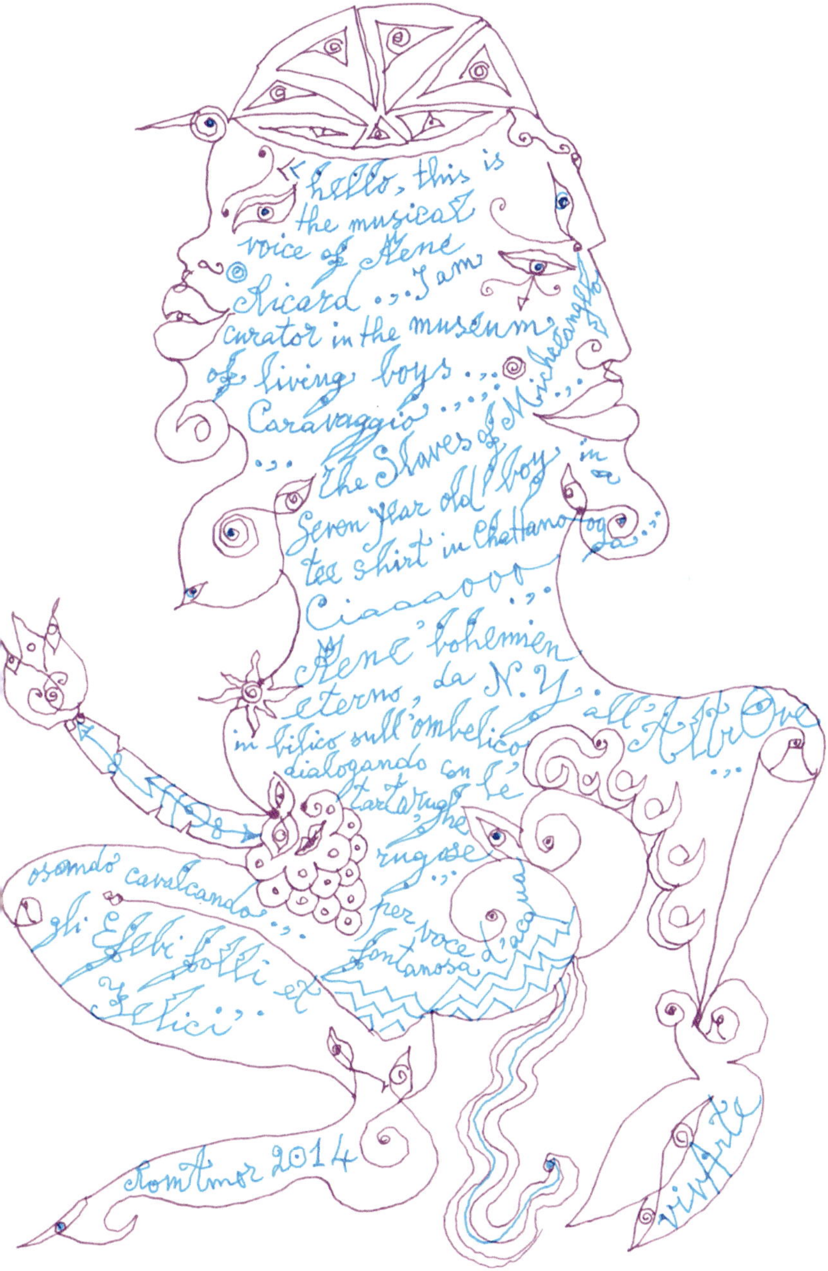

hello, this is
the musical
voice of Gene
Ricard ... I am
curator in the museum
of living boys ...
Caravaggio ...
... the Slaves of Michelangelo ...
Seven year old boy in a
tee shirt in Chattanooga ...
Ciaaooo ...
Gene bohemien
eterno, da N.Y. all'Altrove
in bilico sull'ombelico
dialogando con le
tartarughe
rugose ...
osando cavalcando ... per voce d'acqua
gli Elefoli folli et fontanosa ...
felici ...

RomAmor 2014   vivArte

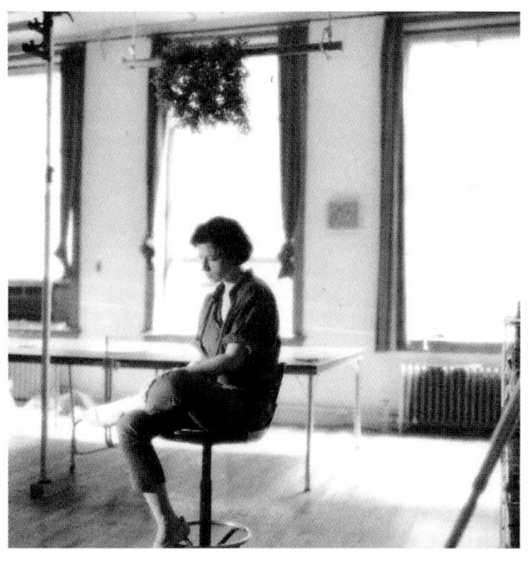

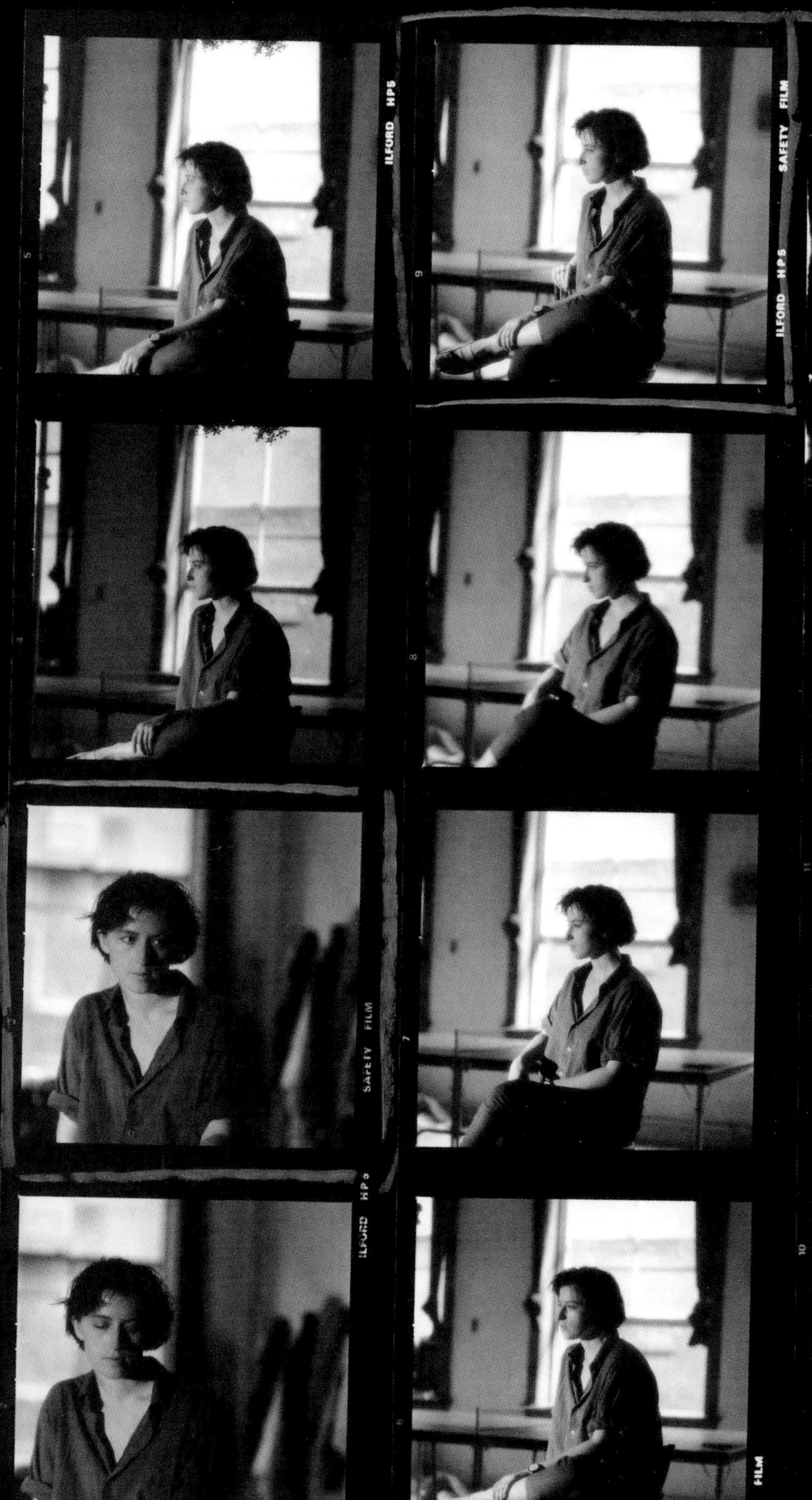

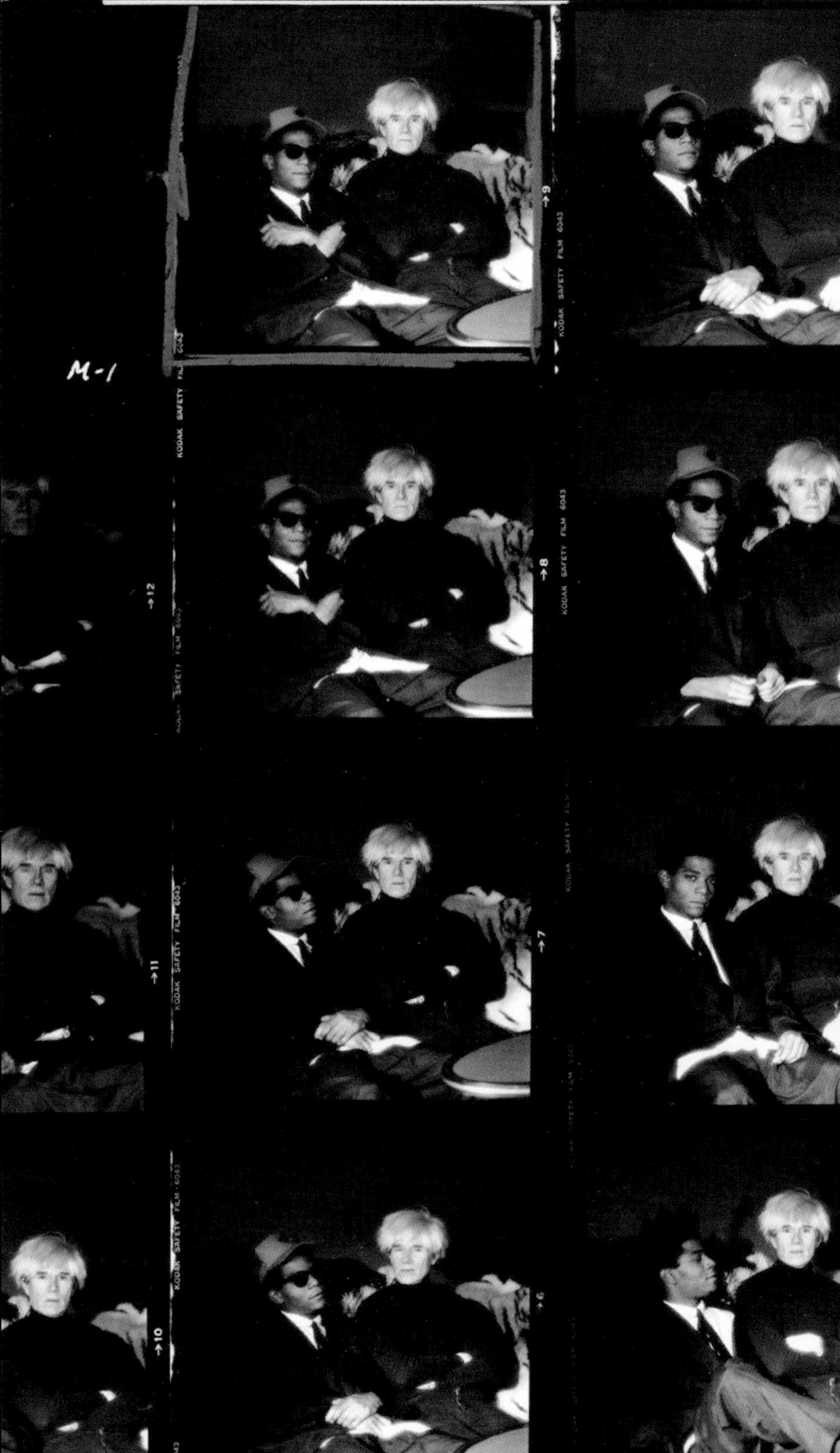

M-1

Model Release

Date_______________________

PHOTOGRAPHER_ *JEANNETTE MONTGOMERY*

Address____

____

For valuable consideration, I hereby irrevocably consent to and authorize the use and reproduction by you, or anyone authorized by you, of any and all photographs which you have this day taken of me, negative or positive, proofs of which are hereto attached, for any purpose whatsoever, without further compensation to me. All negatives and positives, together with the prints shall constitute your property, solely and completely.

I am over 18 years of age.   Yes _________   No _________

MODEL_ *JEAN-MICHEL BASQUIAT*

Signature of Model

SIGNATURE
~~Address~~:

Witnessed by:_______________________

Signature of Witness

• • • • • • • • • •

If the person signing is under 18 consent should be given by parent or guardian, as follows:

I hereby certify that I am the parent or guardian of_______________

____

The model named above, and for value received I do give my consent without reservations to the foregoing on behalf of him or her or them.

DATED:_ *Beth Phillips*______ *12/2/84*

Signature of Parent or Guardian

WITNESSED by:_______________________

Signature of Witness

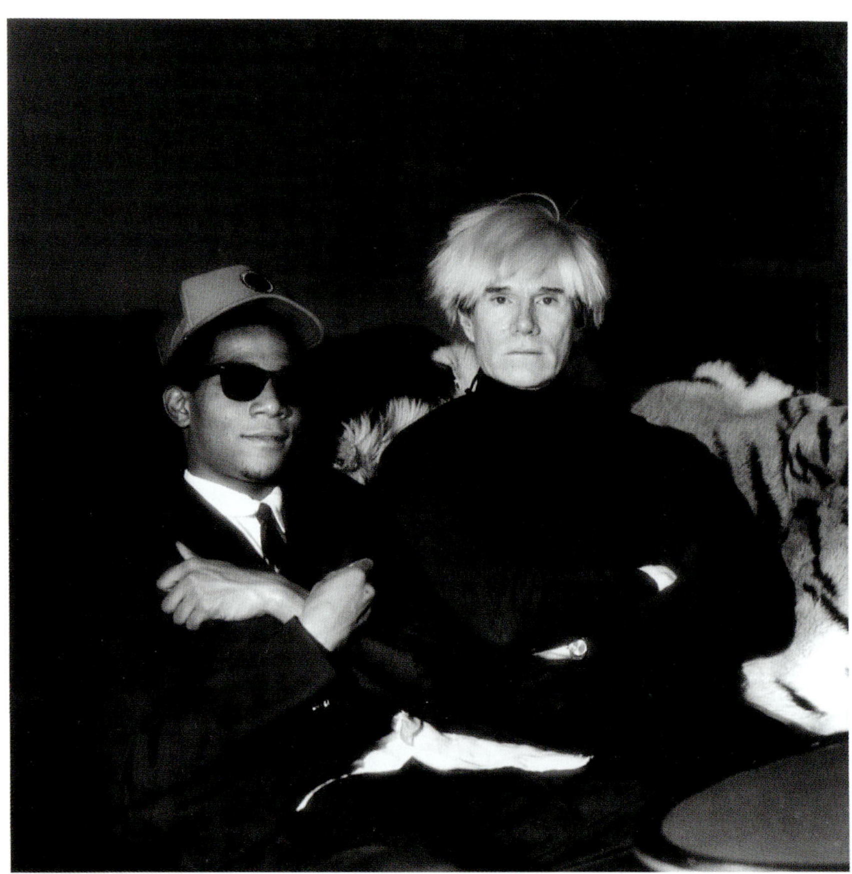

1985

Model Release

Date_ *APRIL 30, 1985*

PHOTOGRAPHER_ *JEANNETTE MONTGOMERY*

Address_

For valuable consideration, I hereby irrevocably consent to and authorize the use and reproduction by you, or anyone authorized by you, of any and all photographs which you have this day taken of me, negative or positive, proofs of which are hereto attached, for any purpose whatsoever, without further compensation to me. All negatives and positives, together with the prints shall constitute your property, solely and completely.

I am over 18 years of age.   Yes __X__   No ______

MODEL_ *ANDY WARHOL*

Signature of Model

Address:_

Witnessed by:_

Signature of Witness

· · · · · · · · · ·

If the person signing is under 18 consent should be given by parent or guardian, as follows:

I hereby certify that I am the parent or guardian of_______

The model named above, and for value received I do give my consent without reservations to the foregoing on behalf of him or her or them.

DATED:_

Signature of Parent or Guardian

WITNESSED by:_

Signature of Witness

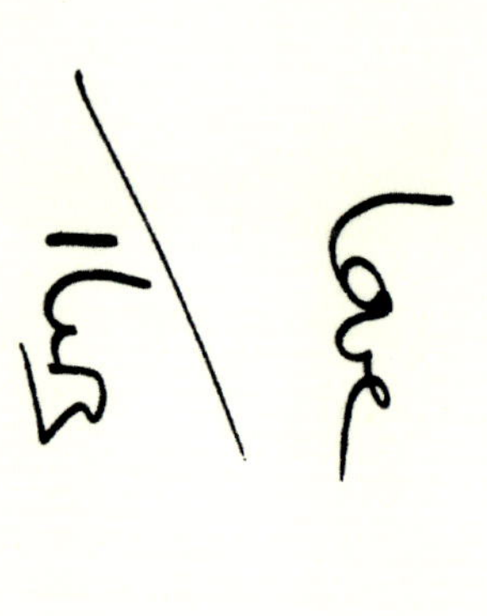

Collection "PORTRAITS DE CINEMA" (1re série)
6. **Léo Mirkine.** Robert Mitchum, Cannes (1954)

Editions ADMIRA, 13100 Aix-en-Provence, tél.: 42.27.26.67

PHN 66   © 1987 Editions ADMIRA & Yves MIRKINE

Reproduction interdite pour tous pays. Imprimé en France.

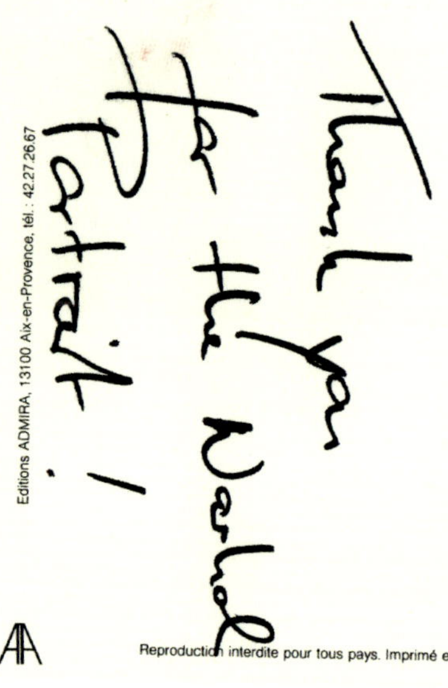

Thomas Ammann

Dear Jeannette,

Thank you so much for the wonderful photograph of Andy. It made me very happy.

I have seen the other photographs as well, they are all wonderful; I was, however, a little bit jealous of This for the fantastic Ross Bleckner. Could I order one, too?

Kind regards

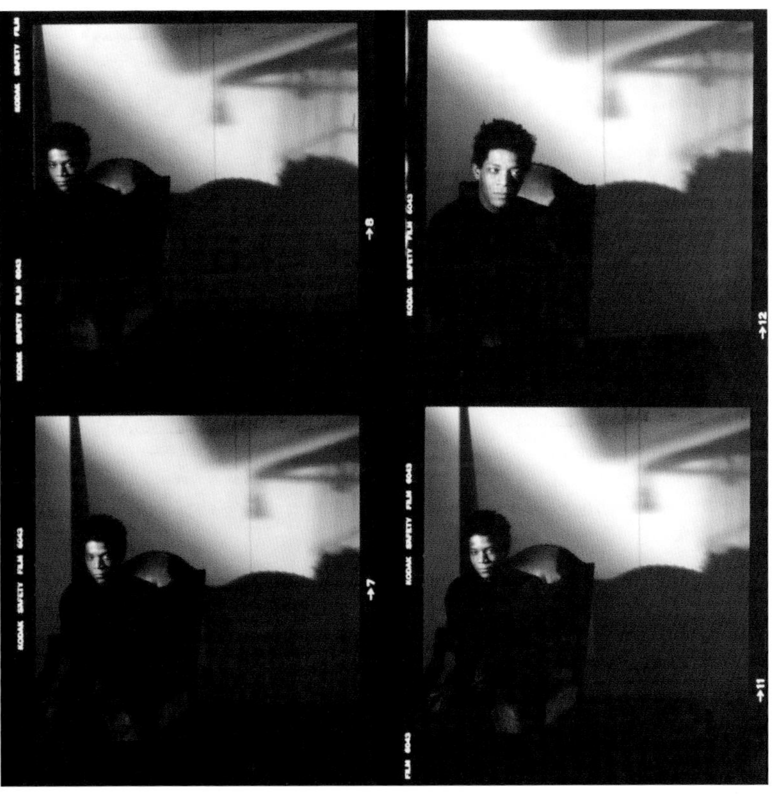

SECOND ANNUAL "PARTY OF LIFE" AT
THE PALLADIUM - 126 E. 14 ST. N.Y.C.
MAY 22 - WEDNESDAY - 11 PM - 1985
KEITH HARING INVITES YOU TO THE

Model Release

Date ____________________

PHOTOGRAPHER ____________________

Address ____________________

____

For valuable consideration, I hereby irrevocably consent to and authorize the use and reproduction by you, or anyone authorized by you, of any and all photographs which you have this day taken of me, negative or positive, proofs of which are hereto attached, for any purpose whatsoever, without further compensation to me. All negatives and positives, together with the prints shall constitute your property, solely and completely.

I am over 18 years of age.   Yes __X__   No __________

MODEL _Keith A. Ha____________

Signature of Model

Address: _6____ KEITH HARING
611 BROADWAY
NEW YORK, N.Y. 10012

Witnessed by: ____________________

Signature of Witness

•   •   •   •   •   •   •   •   •

If the person signing is under 18 consent should be given by parent or guardian, as follows:

I hereby certify that I am the parent or guardian of ____________________

____

The model named above, and for value received I do give my consent without reservations to the foregoing on behalf of him or her or them.

DATED: ____________________

Signature of Parent or Guardian

WITNESSED by: ____________________

Signature of Witness

LIKE A FLIP-BOOK

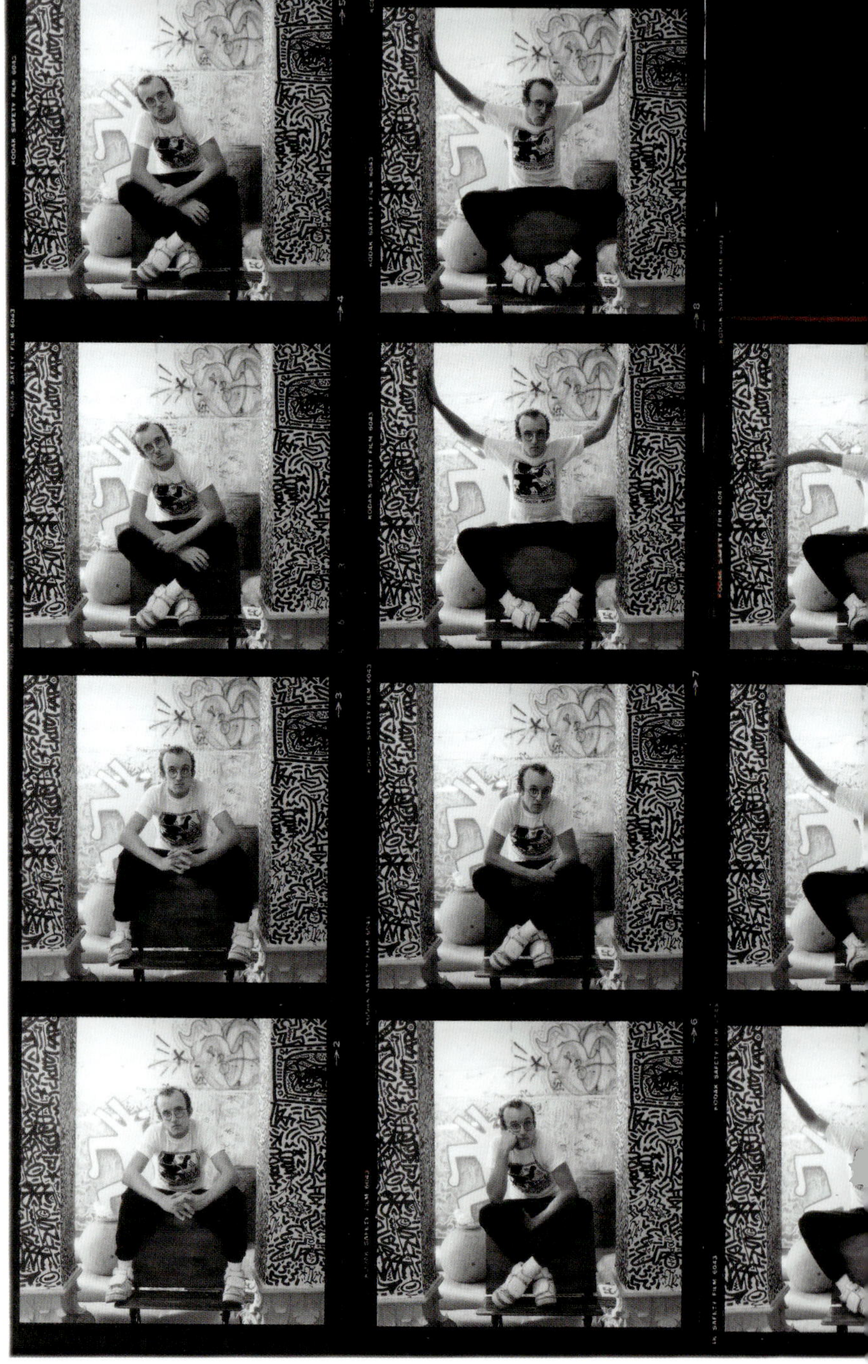

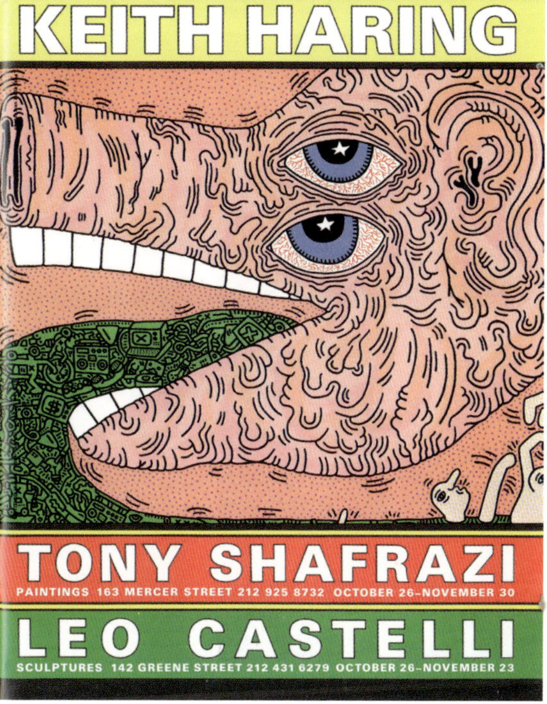
KEITH HARING
TONY SHAFRAZI
PAINTINGS 163 MERCER STREET 212 925 8732 OCTOBER 26–NOVEMBER 30
LEO CASTELLI
SCULPTURES 142 GREENE STREET 212 431 6279 OCTOBER 26–NOVEMBER 23

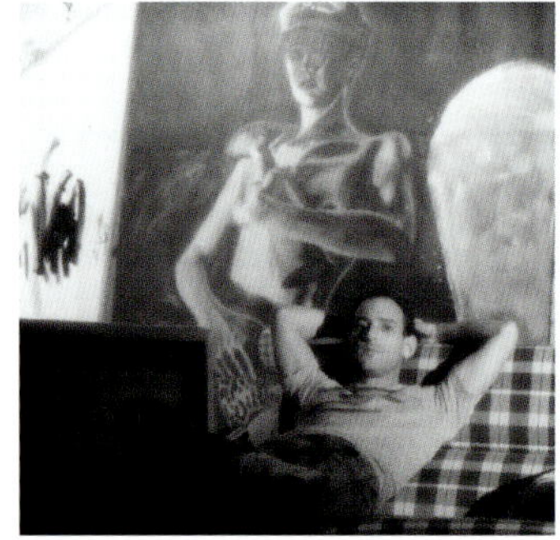 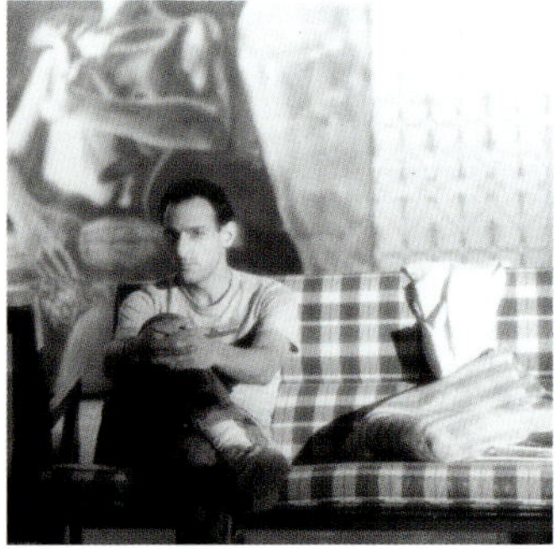

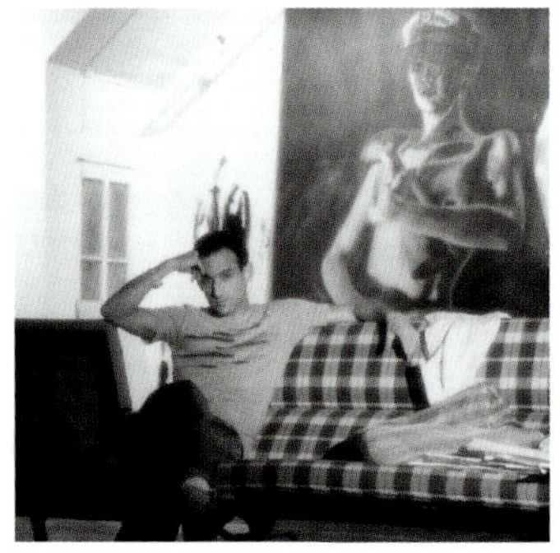 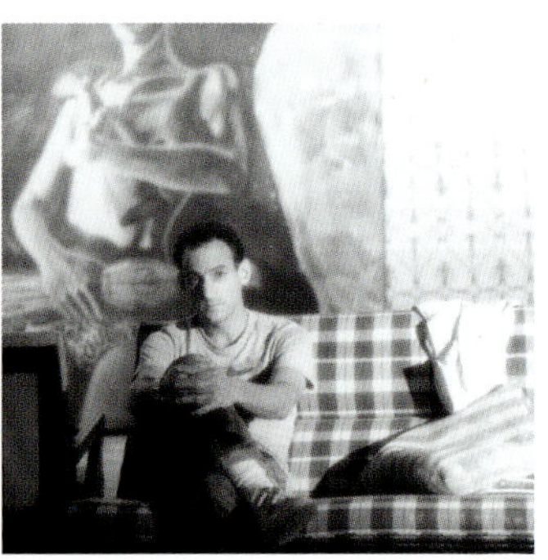

DAVID SALLE   NINE WHITE STREET, NEW YORK, NEW YORK 10013

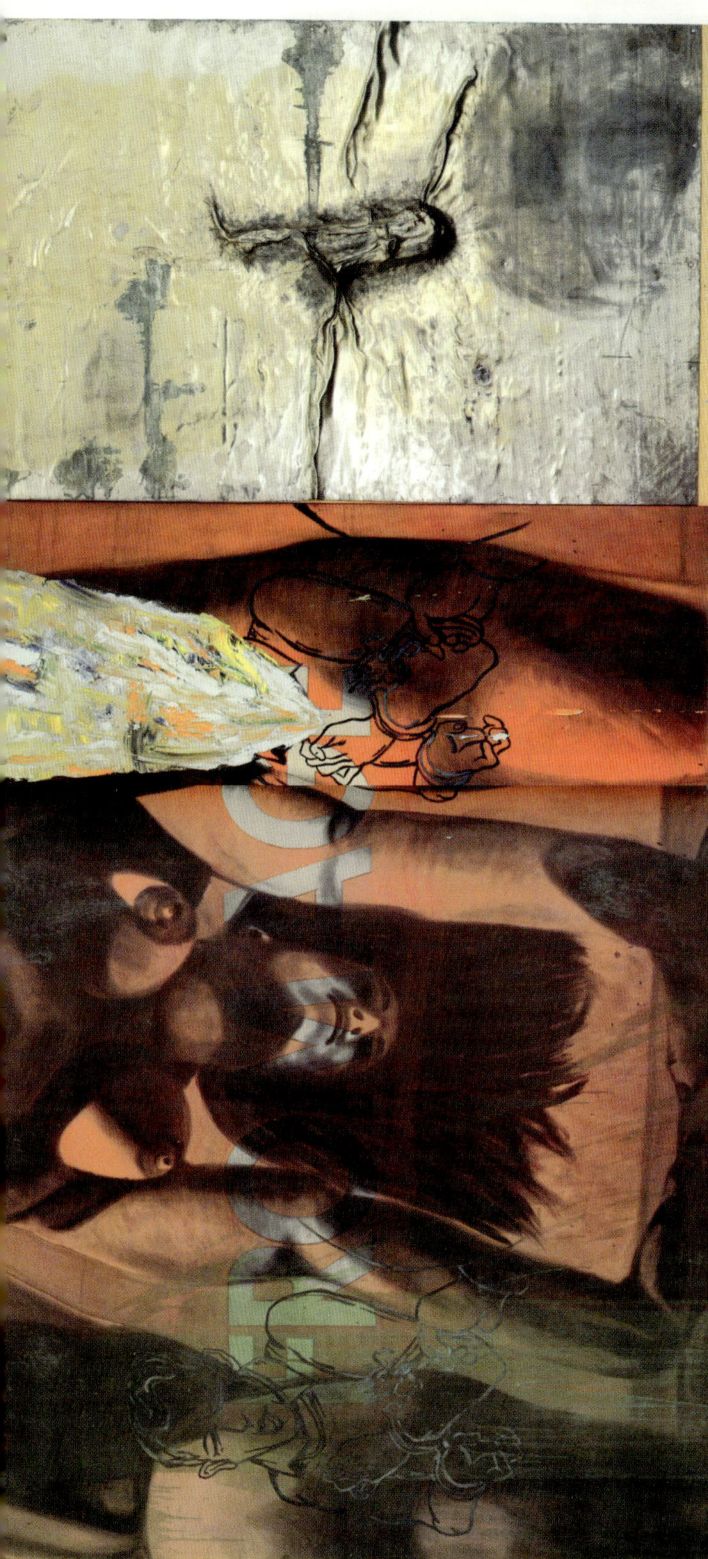

David Salle: What is the Reason for Your Visit to Germany?.. 1984, oil and acrylic on canvas and lead on wood, 96 by 191 ½ inches. All works this article Mary Boone Gallery and Leo Castelli Gallery.

The Real Salle

With a willful array of modernist, Pop and porno images, David Salle presents a provocatively subjective world where, according to the author, lust mingles with dread, sublimity with derision, adoration with contempt.

BY PETER SCHJELDAHL

To be despised proves nothing. Even minor artists have been despised. But a characteristic opprobrium salutes the appearance of a major artist, such as David Salle. People who agree on nothing else have been unified in loathing the young painter from Kansas. For the left, he is a reactionary renegade, traitor to the "post-studio" vanguard. For the right, he is a vile piece of goods—the "worst" of the new painters, in Hilton Kramer's forthright estimation. The smart line in Europe dubs him an abject plagiarist of Picabia and Polke. Other charges include cynicism (or sentimentality), crassness (or mandarin sterility), and sexism. The less articulate make do with mutterings of "hype." At least negatively, Salle has been something like all things to all parties, the avatar of each one's bogey.

Contradictory complaints typify the onset of a major art. Such art insults both necessity and freedom, disrupting the given and at the same time narrowing the range of what seems

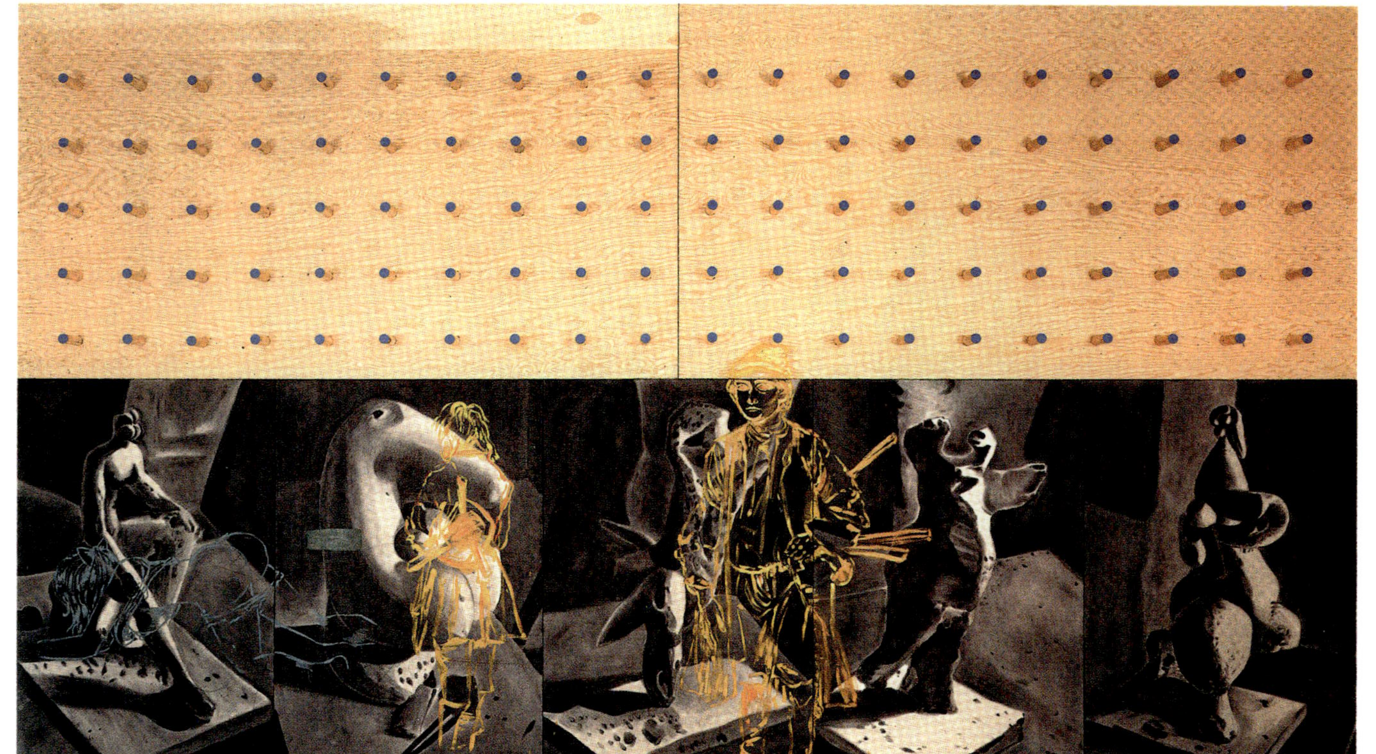

My Head, 1984.
Mixed media on canvas and wood, 120 x 210 1/2".

Interview with David Salle

"I don't think of things as references unless they really refer to something else."

Robert Pincus-Witten

Robert Pincus-Witten: *Are there important areas of issues, or perceptions of criticality, that should be addressed in the discussion around your work, but are not? Are there areas that you feel have somehow been misapprehended or insufficiently discussed?*

David Salle: No, it's not that there are big areas that haven't been addressed, it's that as the work takes on more characters and more specifically wears its sensibility, you can't expect commentary to keep pace with it. The lag is like a rubber band, the slack gets very great and we just take it out. The commentary advances, closes the gap, and the work advances, and there's a big gap. Maybe the work is different in feeling tone than it was a couple of years ago.

RPW: *In what sense?*

DS: Well, it seems to be classical.

RPW: *Too big a term.*

DS: It's the only one that comes to mind.

RPW: *Do you mean something like, the work is less immediately perceived in its connection to its conceptual origins?*

DS: I would say the work is less immediately perceived in connection to anything else around it.

RPW: *In other words, there's nobody working like you.*

DS: Right.

RPW: *But there are devices, pictorial, small, single devices out there in the world which in fact people are making a good deal of.*

DS: Dozens.

RPW: *They're making rather doubtful claims even. In a certain sense aspects of painting and drawing are now being legitimized through the critical issues embodied in your work.*

DS: Sure, sure.

RPW: *Aspects of pattern and decoration, at the Whitney.*

DS: It's an accident . . . overlaps things, images . . .

RPW: *Yes, it's that sort of thing . . .*

DS: But there is a murky, misunderstood area: the notion of popular culture. It's assumed my work is a commentary on popular culture, you know. For years

I've been saying the opposite. At least in my mind, my work has absolutely nothing to do with popular culture. Not only does it have nothing to do with popular culture in any kind of didactic, deliberate way, it simply doesn't have anything to do with popular culture.

RPW: *Is it because what is presented is not a reconstruction of popular iconography, but in fact is an aesthetic and autonomous abstract experience that is, that has always been available "to an elite," but has never been available to popular culture?*

DS: Something like that . . . since classicism can incorporate anything, or can be anything; but it's a different feeling.

RPW: *It's a kind of false signal, but what you're really getting is some kind of eternal, formal . . .*

DS: Yes.

RPW: *I'm beginning to see what you mean. One can look at your paintings and pick out recognizable references to popular culture, but in fact what one is dealing with is the creation of an authen-*

tic and isolated aesthetic world.

DS: Right.

RPW: *Something like that.*

DS: Something like that. The other thing that within that idea, there are very few real references in the work; and the references are not to popular culture or to art, but perhaps to artlike things. Look, I think there's confusion between an image that comes from somewhere and a reference. I don't think of things as references unless they really refer to something else.

RPW: *You're not speaking of the indexility of the work in terms of some sort of popular deconstruction?*

DS: I think that the way to look at my work is some other way.

RPW: *Can I suggest . . .*

DS: Yes.

RPW: *. . . these references. The information that one picks up, the references to art and references to the movies, whatave-you, are emblematic relationships; and an emblematic relationship to the movies as distinct from a lived relationship to them. Let's say that they are false clues as distinct from specific clues. If they were specific clues one might be able to construct a narrative layering in your paintings, whereas the lack of specificity of the clue means that one really cannot make a narrative out of your pictures.*

DS: Right. There's no narrative. There

really is none, there isn't one.

RPW: *There's no story.*

DS: Right. None at all.

RPW: *You see, my way of thinking keys into your notion of the autonomy of the work, its abstractness.*

DS: I think about a couple of different things that appear, that have lived their lives in the arena of popular culture, but I don't think of them as popular. One is a comedy, and the other is pornography. Those are two things that are important to me for themselves. Not as a comment on the society that produces them, but in their own mechanistic ways, you know, in a detached way.

RPW: *In a detached mechanistic way, I think that's what I was saying when I was calling emblematic . . .*

DS: Right.

RPW: *But emblematic suggests that it's an index, that it is an emblem of something.*

DS: I would say mechanistic.

RPW: *Mechanistic is better than emblematic. So, you know you have, say, the mechanism of comedy, the mechanism of eroticism, even pornography . . .*

DS: Yes.

RPW: *The art references are largely, it seems to me, references to ironic detachment. The movies would be another mechanism.*

DS: But the art mechanisms are always

about one thing. About how an image is simultaneously some molecules in paint that congeal in certain patterns that at a certain distance appear recognizable as a painting, are recognized as a painting.

RPW: *You know, that's an argument for pure painting somehow.*

DS: No, it's an image of reciprocity. You know, the French avant-garde.

RPW: *Which French avant-garde, like the early modernists, like Picasso, Matisse?*

DS: No, like Manet.

RPW: *Oh, like the 1860s, the 1870s.*

DS: Yes, early.

RPW: *The Manet-Monet.*

DS: Yes, the Manet-Monet. The wavering. You know, the just barely held together nature of Manet's paint. The fact that the paintings were always, I mean not to our standards but according to the standards by which they were painted, were always in danger of falling apart.

RPW: *You mean, falling apart as an image that coheres?*

DS: Yes. The ambiguity in the, in how the image is contextualized . . .

RPW: *Contextualized not socially, contextualized on the canvas, you mean.*

DS: On the canvas and how that represents its social dislocation. I think that's the art, I mean that *is* art, isn't it?

■

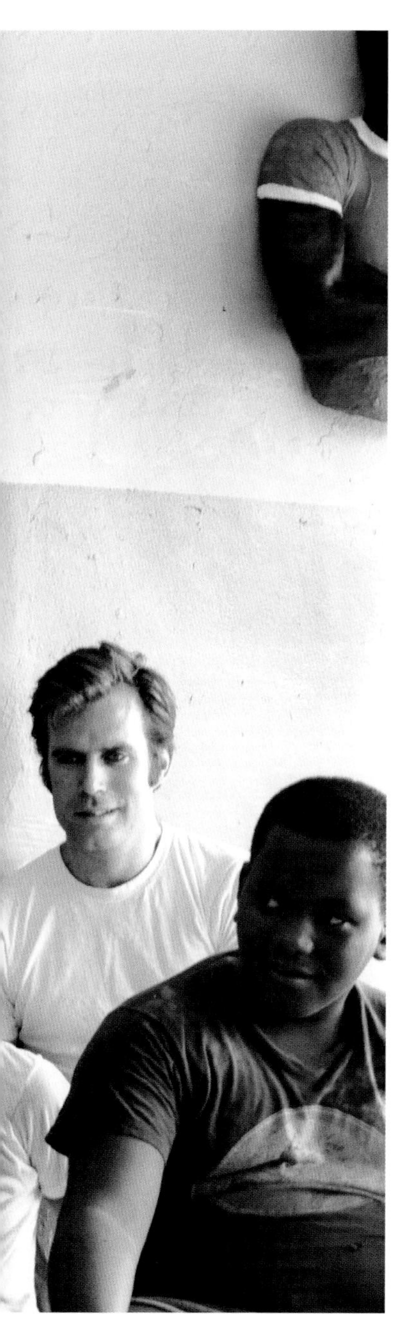

Rigoberto Torres and I have
worked together on art projects
for 35 years, but the day
Jeannette came to our Dawson
St. studio was one of our
happiest moments.
We had this busy storefront
workshop, the former KBA
Youth Center. It functioned as
another Social Club. We had
received a commission from
HUD's Art in Public Places
so now workshops focused
on installing permanent
neighborhood sculpture murals.
The little boy at the bottom of
Jeannette's group portrait, five
year old Thomas, was already
cast as the running boy for
the *Life on Dawson St.* wall.
Jeannette's amazing work
that day follows the casting
of lovely seven year old Janel,
surrounded by all her friends.

John Ahearn

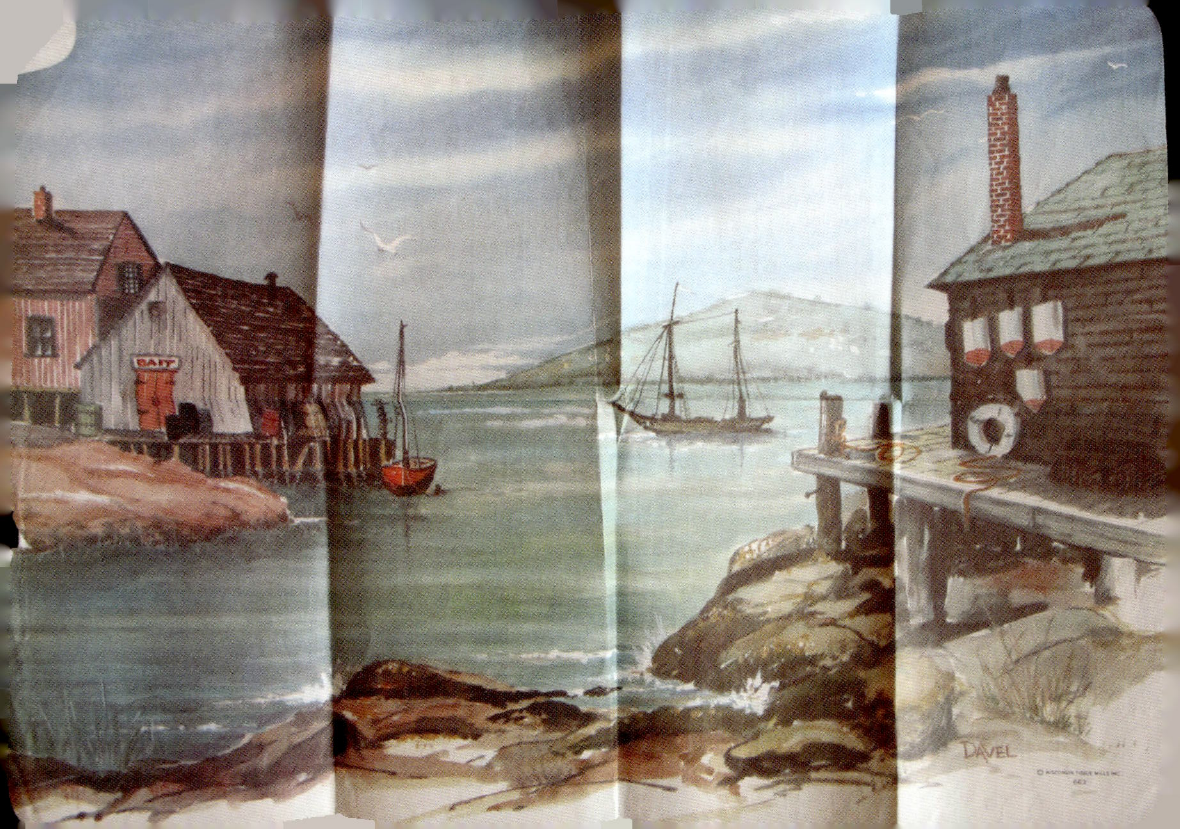

BAIT
DAVEL
© WISCONSIN TISSUE MILLS INC
663

Dear Jeannette, Well, Well, ... My, My ... I must say —
that sure was fun. Your opening!
I talked to ZéZé and met Peggy. They told me to stop
by the shop & pick up some tulips. I said "OK".. "OK".
I talked to Arnie and he said James, surprisingly so,
his approval immediately. I said "that must be a good
sign." I talked to James and told him about my trip (travel).
He said, he wants to know more! Met Ellen & chatted. She's
friends with Charles & Dominic. Although, I never met
them. Saw your Mom, stood nept to her and
listened to her beautiful southern accent. It made my
heart curl. I hope I get to meet her one
day just so I can tell her what a nice & talented
daughter she created! Waited around, forever, it
seemed for Monty. Told him I'd look him up this
June when I'm in L.A. for my girlfriend's wedding. He
said "great". He'd be looking forward to it. He said Eddie
took him down to Baltimore and showed him all the
low-life. I laughed! Met Niles — he's real special.
Then Bianca stopped by to say hello & left! I was
impressed but Niles said she was his enemy and to
watch out for her. I said that "Jeannette knows how to
take care of herself" and "not to worry".
Overall, it was a real nice crowd — some nice
fur coats and one good hairdo. Some looked like
serious collectors and loved the work. I know you will
"sell" from that show. I especially liked the one
of the guy infront of his canvas with the black
model in his underpants. Nice Buns! Peter thought it
a real good shot of Jean Michelle — liked the lighting.
Also, I was real happy to see a photo of one of my
favorites : William Edmonson. I recognized him because I
have his catalog from "Corcoran, Mississippi" or Black
Folk Art. Evidently, Louise Dahl Wolff met him through a
friend in Tennessee and she was instrumental in getting
him a show at the Modern. It was the first solo show
of a Black Artist at the Modern. He became a sculptor
because "God told him to start carving out of stone."
My favorite all time line ... Quote .. "I didn't know
I was no artist till them folks come and told me I
was." Unquote. That's why I adore him so. My second
all time favorite line .. Little Richard ... "The grass is
always greener, but you still have to cut it!"
                                        Love, Gina

DAVID SHAPIRO

FAILURE AND RESTORATION

Years ago I dreamed of an exhibition in which artists would
defend or explain their notions of what they keep and what and
why they throw things away: an essay on abandonment. A composer
had instructed me in my youth to destroy no exercise, because
at least I would discover after all a kind of Jungian map or dream
diary of generativity lodged in the patterns of this uncensored
heap. I have often told my own students that they must try to
maintain, despite all self-repugnance, a great deal of their work
and consider what poor critics they are at any given moment of
that which they are trying to repress. For this reason, our own
intonation must always be checked by another; for this reason,
we cannot hear or see ourselves clearly. It is a species of defense
of psychoanalysis, that we are not our own best hypnotists and
we everywhere resist those patterns that might let us grow. In
an age of perishability and throw-away art, we are probably still
repressing something like the notion of permanence. What can
a paradoxical exhibition of failure give us if not this thrilling
sense of the edge, of the allied concept of the unacceptable and
the tabooed? Kenneth Koch as pedagogue loved to make a metaphrasis
of Picasso that went as follows: If you like it, destroy it,
because then you are merely comfortable with it, an older beauty.
Is it possible that a show of self-confessed failure is the beginning
of a pluralist lesson in tolerance? William James, in his essay
"On a Certain Blindness in Human Beings," suggests that our greatest
failure is our habitual unwillingness to see how little we empathize,
either with others and their perspective or with our own creations.
Too often critics today think their business is proscription where
their truest task may be restorative.

(This essay on failure, moreover, will be a failure, to some
announcing itself too soon, too apologetically, for others too
loaded with quotation, too anti-Aristotelian, for one too incoherent,
for another not paratactical or personal enough.)

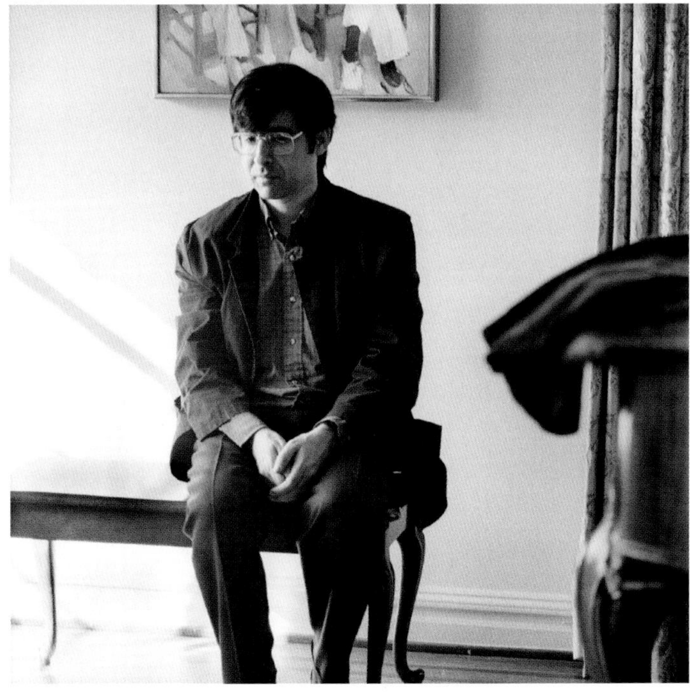

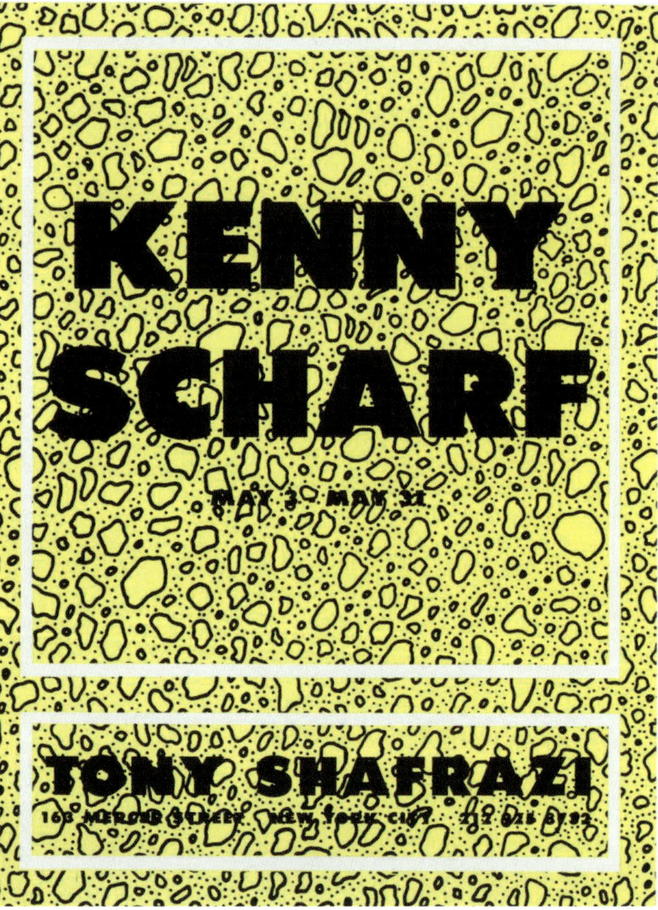
KENNY
SCHARF
MAY 3 - MAY 31
TONY SHAFRAZI
163 MERCER STREET   NEW YORK CITY   212 925 8732

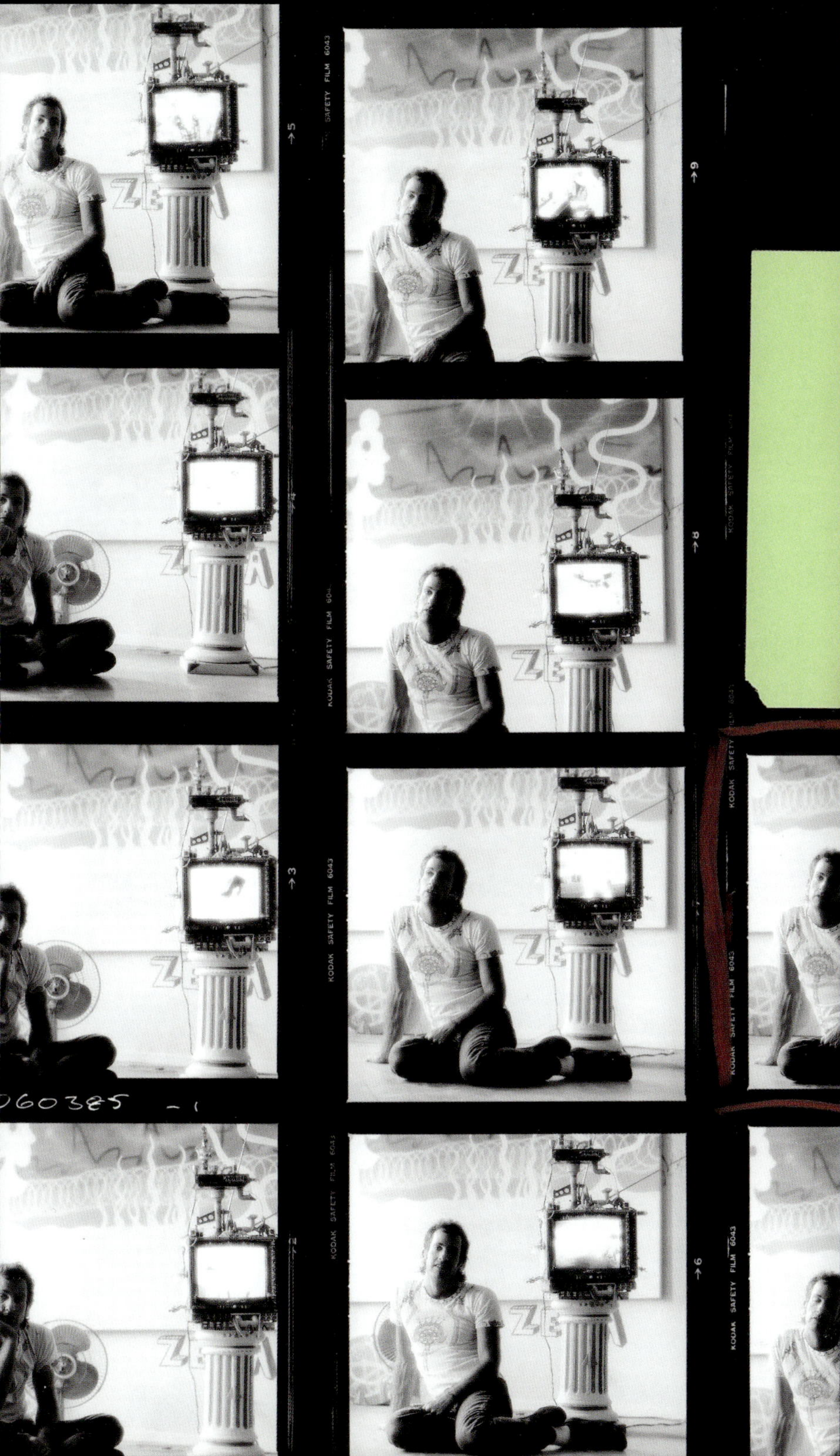

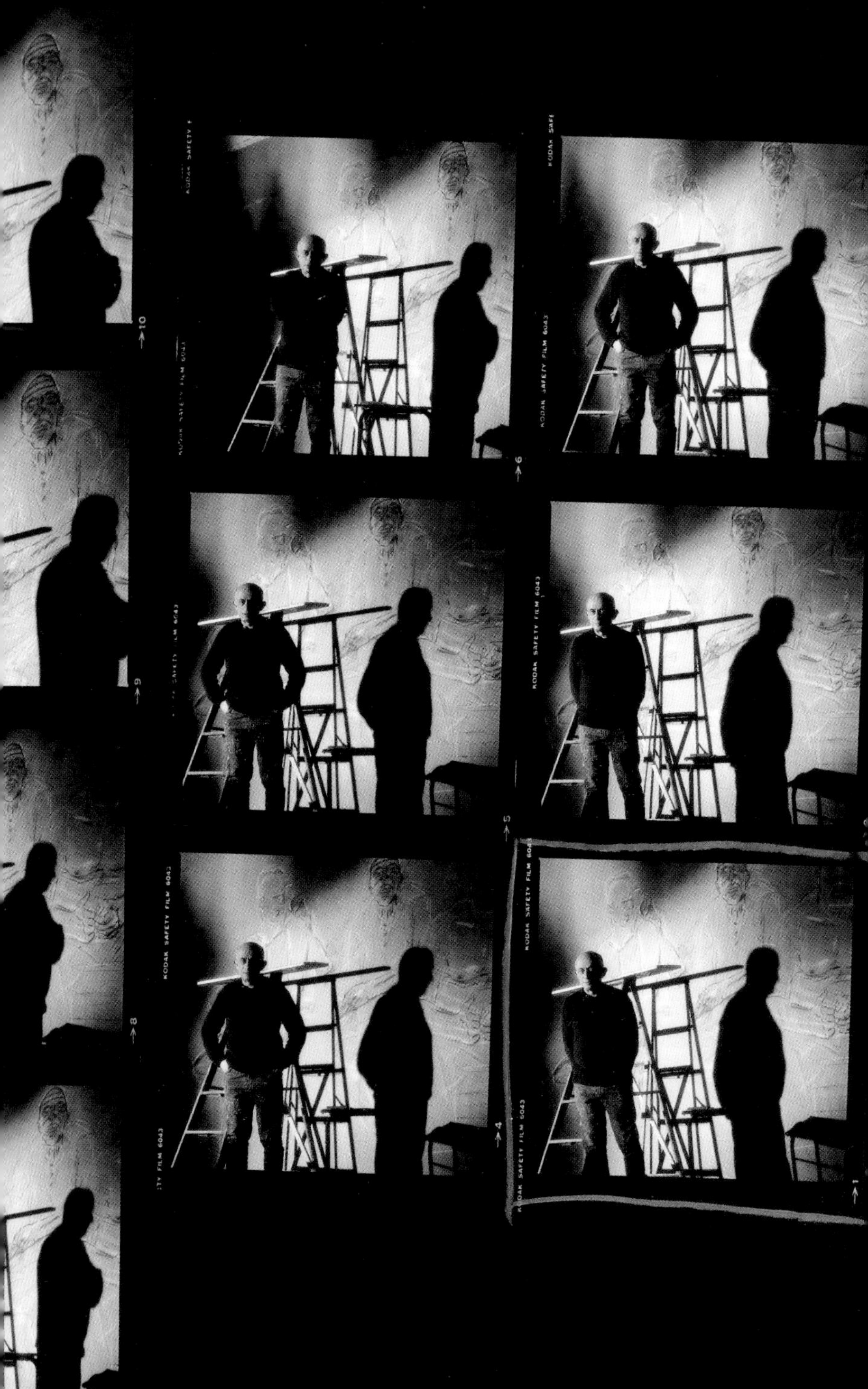

Artists Space
Barbara Gladstone
Cash/Newhouse
Tibor de Nagy

not to provide a critical position. Instead, these works function as glamorous illustrations of stereotypical metaphors for the cult of the beautiful male and the phallocentric. Peter Berlin's set of black and white 'treated' self-portraits depicts the artist in a series of assertedly macho poses, dressed in extremely tight-fitting bikini S & M leatherware that reveals a well-conditioned musculature. Berlin has accentuated his already amply endowed genital area by airbrushing the appropriate details, producing a somewhat grotesque caricature of phallic power/dominance. Yet there is very little parody contained in this image; it is a neutral and blank metaphor for the impossibility of contravening the overdetermination of sociological codes of 'deviant' sexuality.

George Dureau, another Mapplethorpe selection, produces elegantly restrained portraits of nude, deformed black men. In one shot, a naked midget reclines, like an art object, upon a white pedestal. In another, a black youth with half an arm stands in a classical contrapposto position, glowering suspiciously at us. These photographs could have built upon their quasi-documentary and socially realistic orientation, yet Dureau has suppressed this element in favor of an uncritical 'aestheticization' of the object. Invoking a humanistic empathetic reaction to the shock of the physical deformity, Dureau subsumes the connotations of the ugly under the rubric of a supposedly neutral cult of artifice.

Although Simmons has provided a somewhat less self-referential selection of artists, her choices nevertheless reflect an acutely self-conscious attempt to recycle and perpetuate her own strategies, as well as those of her colleagues such as Robert Longo and Allan McCollum. Alan Belcher, who enjoys considerable gallery exposure and critical attention, should never have been included in an exhibition at an alternative space which was originally created to service the needs of artists who are either underrepresented or unrepresented. Yet Belcher's photo-construction remains the most compelling piece in the show. Not unlike sarcastic 'commodity-advertisement' photo/sculptures, this work contains a series of blown-up Polaroids of various commodity products, their images blurred and distorted in order to displace the original viability of the referent of 'sign.' Belcher has fashioned these purposefully obscured photos into a glittery banner of commodity culture, transforming the 'promotional' codes of advertising into cryptic images of a collective consumerist memory.

The other artists selected by Simmons have adopted strategies of appropriation through image-manipulation that have become inscribed as conventions of certain types of post-modernist practice. Jerald Frampton borrows media imagery of generic violence and produces a simulacrum of the photographic 'original,' constructing photo-montages that unfortunately resemble a possible collaboration between Longo and Simmons. Lydia Panas offers an installation of a series of uniformly framed photographs of still lifes and various typed texts that operates along principles of 'radical undifferentiation' continually and redundantly utilized by Alan McCollum. Although Panas' work involves the interpenetration of textual signification and visual symbolism, the work is so blatantly based upon McCollum's formal and conceptual strategies as to make it theoretically, conceptu-

ally, and formally unsound. (Artists Space, *December 14-January 18*)

LEON GOLUB

The career of Leon Golub has been characterized by a problematic tension between the commitment to a tradition of Abstract-Expressionist painting and an engagement with certain 'radical' or 'left-wing' politics organized within the cultural sphere. Golub has been actively involved on a pragmatic level with various organizations including Artists' Call, yet on the level of aesthetic practice the integration of political/social contents has proven to be a more delicate and conflicted task. Emerging out of a tradition of Abstract Expressionism in the late '50s, Golub began to insinuate the viability of figurative narratives and allegorical structures into an aesthetic of cathartic expression. In a series of monumental works based upon the atrocities of the Vietnam War, Golub introduced elements of a humanistic didacticism which would inform his work throughout the later '70s.

Schematically basing his pictorializations upon media images of war violence and acts of torture, Golub managed to produce effects which often paralleled the neutrality of a photographic simulacrum. Golub modified his painting technique by reducing and essentializing the areas of muted pigment in order to foreground and reinforce the authority of the figurative elements. In such works, an awkward tension was produced between the monumentality of the painting (which referred explicitly to the scale and design of Clyfford Still and others) and the threatening images of violent acts about to commence or recently enacted. An uneasy balance was struck between the im-

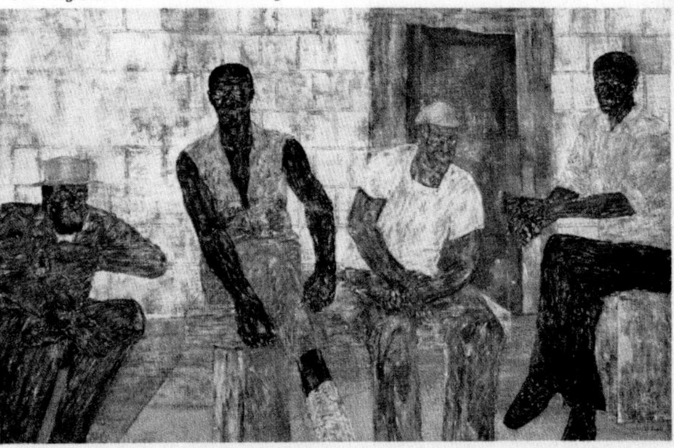

Leon Golub, Four Black Men, 1985. *Acrylic on canvas, 120 x 191".* *Courtesy Barbara Gladstone Gallery.*

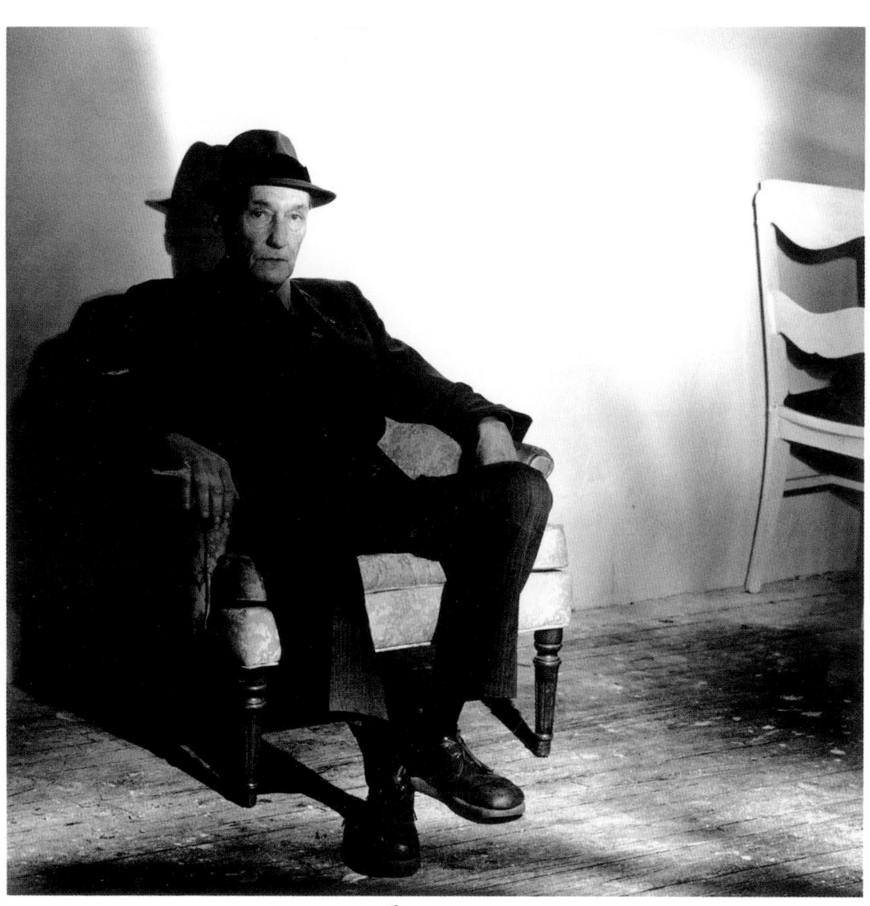

for Jeannette Montgomery all best
William S. Burroughs

1986

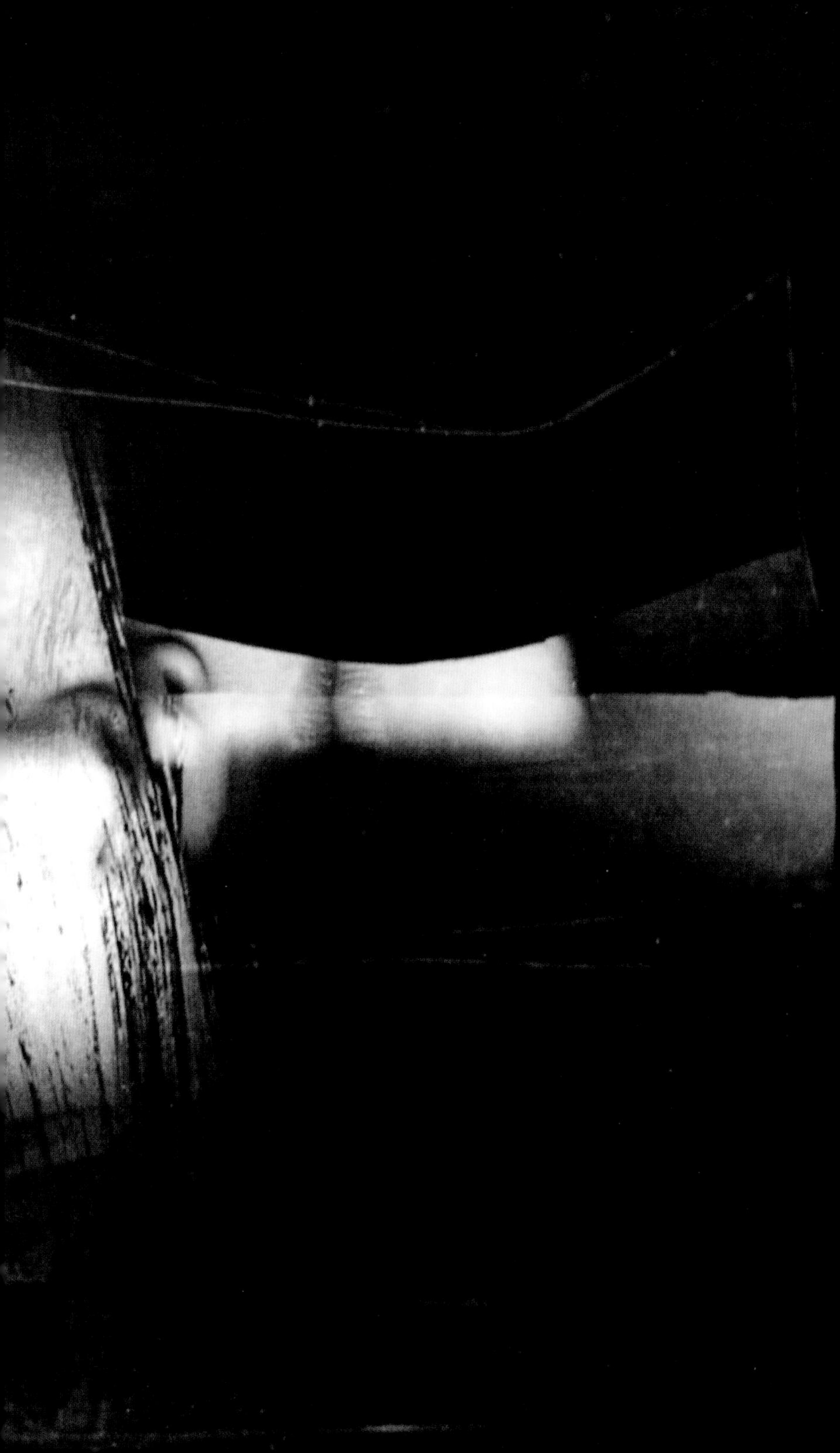

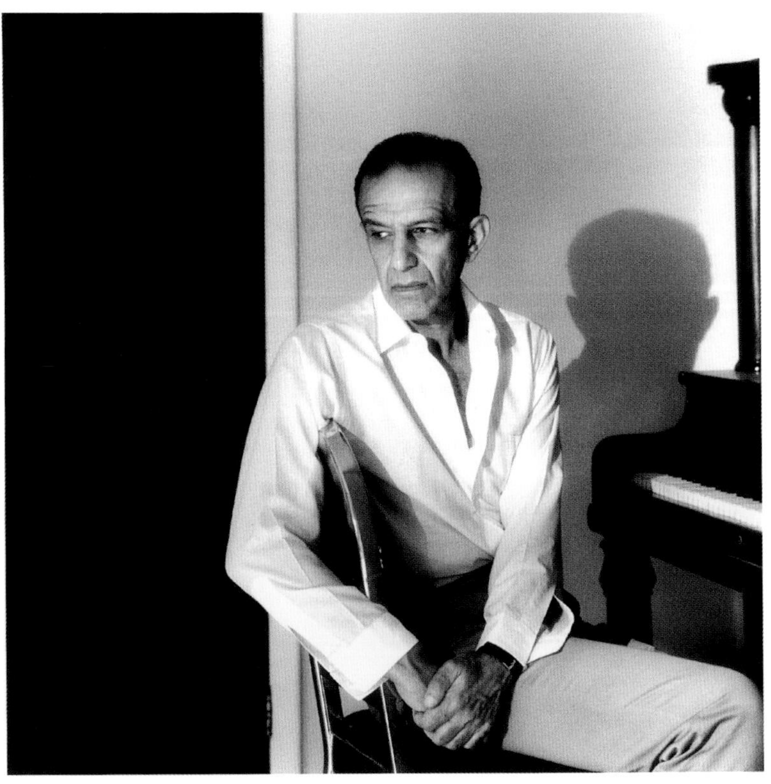

For Jeanette with love,

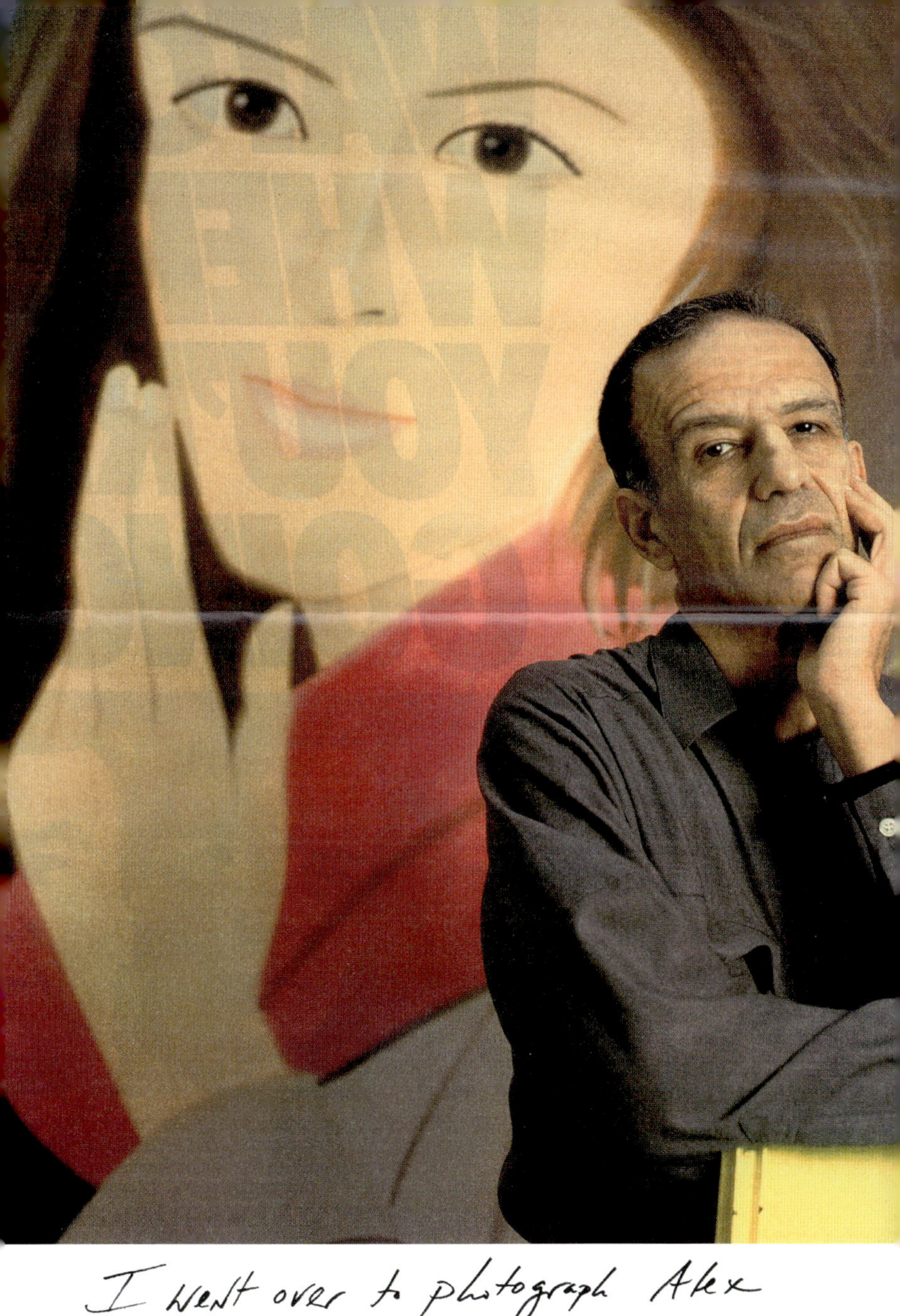

I went over to photograph Alex
Katz at his studio one day. He
asked me to model for him. I
did.

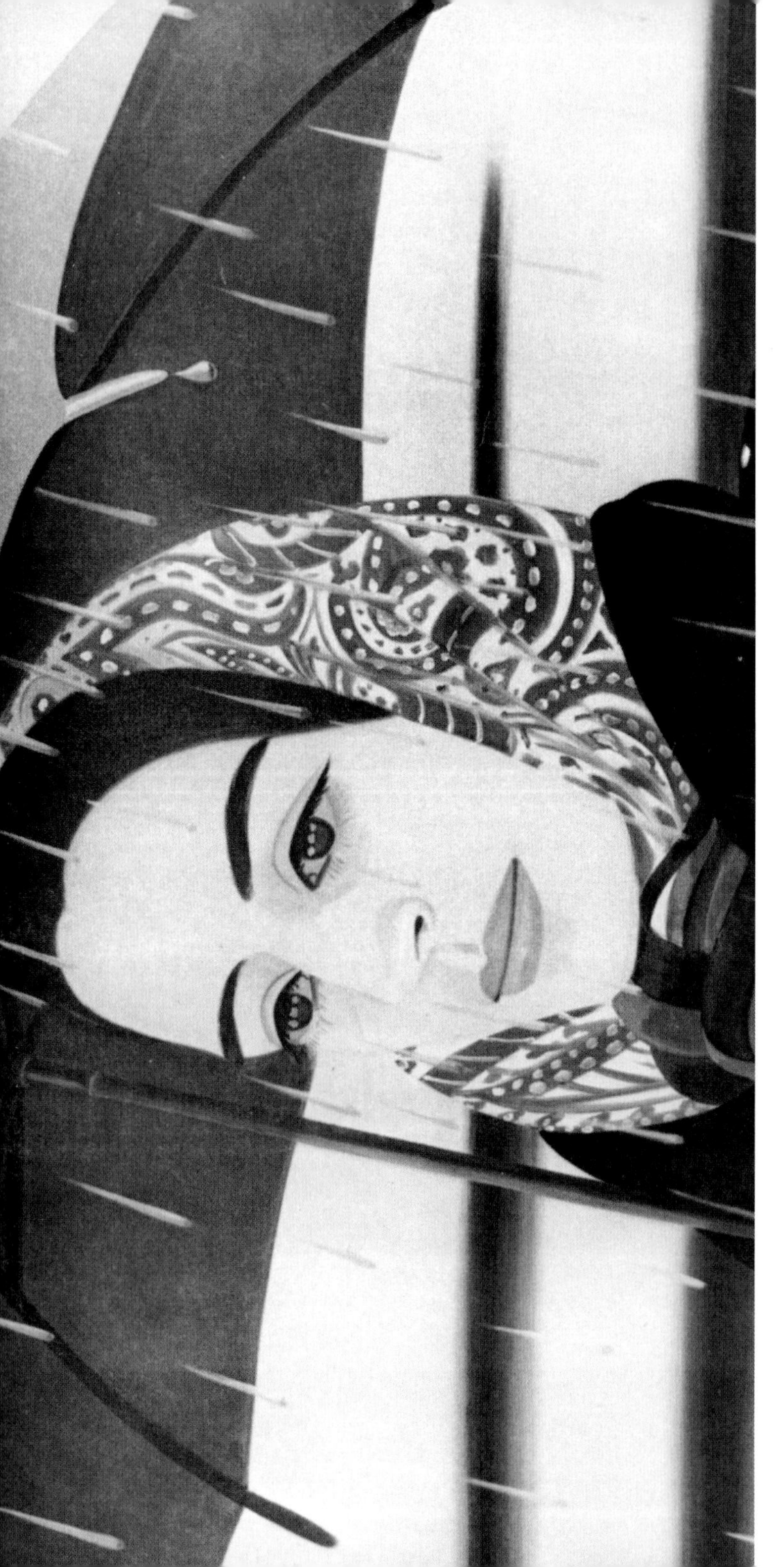

You are cordially invited to a reception for members of the Whitney Circle
and Friends of the Whitney Museum of American Art
for the retrospective exhibition

ALEX KATZ

Wednesday, March 12, 1986

9 to 11 pm   Black tie

Admission by invitation only   This invitation admits two

Whitney Museum of American Art   945 Madison Avenue at 75th Street, New York

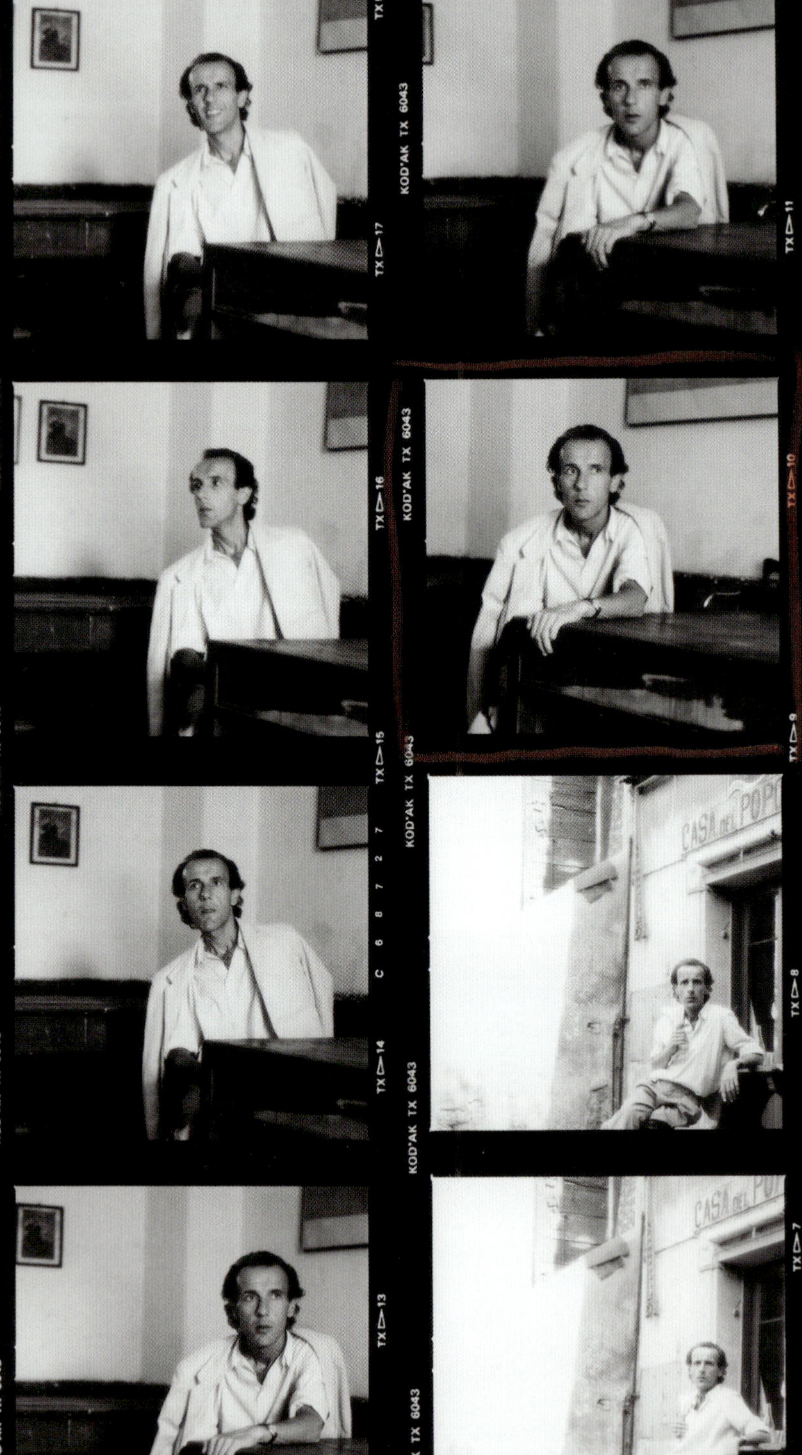

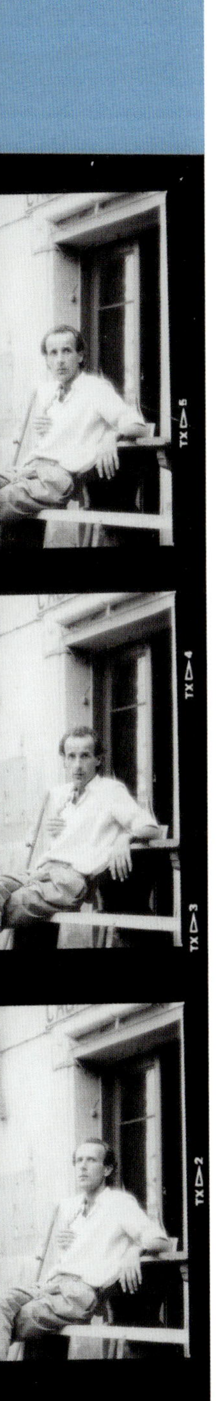

Ci siamo incontrati semplicemente
perché... perché siamo fortunati tutti e
due, semplicemente perché lei è venuta in
Italia, che è il paese più bello del mondo.
Stranamente io sono anche fortunato ad aver
incontrato una persona delicata e brava come
lei. Questa unione così bella è una fortuna per
tutti e due, per me che sono nato in questa
terra e per lei che è venuta da una terra molto
piu lontana.
Che altro c'è da dire, che lei è brava lo sa il
mondo!

Già nel 1985 io ero qui in via dell'Orso.
Nel laboratorio di Claudio di Gianbattista vado
tuttora ed è a Largo Preneste. In quella tua
foto molto bella c'è scritto Casa del Popolo
che è un bar lì nel quartiere Prenestino.
È il quartiere di Pasolini, un quartiere popolare
di Roma. Dopo tanti anni che sei qui non sei
più andata da Claudio? Lui è ancora lì anche
se è tutto molto cambiato: ora il giardino e
la casa sono sistemati e il suo laboratorio è
bellissimo, anzi al momento ci sono tre miei
nuovi affreschi che esporremo probabilmente
a fine maggio.
Jeannette io tutti i giorni faccio le stesse cose,
alla stessa ora, lo stesso minuto, come un
tonno! Ma questo non vuol dire che lavoro,
vengo in studio alla stessa ora tutti i giorni
però poi quando lavoro non lo so! Non sempre
lavoro, però il vizio assurdo, il pregiudizio, sì, è
lo stesso sempre.

Enzo Cucchi

15 - 5 - 1986

Janette, le tue
foto sono
vivamente belle -
grazie -
devi telefonarmi
quando vieni in
Italia --- lavoriamo.
Ciao Enzo Cucchi

Jeanette
MONTGOMERY
425 East 51 Street
NEW YORK - N.Y. 10022
U.S.A.

Nº 31   GOYA
El espejo indiscreto. El hombre oso.
MUSEO DEL PRADO. MADRID

Depósito Legal: B. 30.616 - 1964

Barcelona, 1969 - Seix Barral

1986 *ultimi giorni di ottobre a Roma,*

CUCCHI ABITA SOLO VICINO ALLE PORTE, IN UNA CASA CHE SOPPORTA
UNICAMENTE L'ARREDO SPOGLIO, NATURALMENTE OLIATO,
DI UNA CERNIERA CHE SEMBRA PROMETTERE MOLTE AGNIZIONI, EPIFANIE E
ILLUMINAZIONI INVECE DA QUESTO PUNTO NESSUNO ARRIVA. ALLORA
L'ARTISTA SI BUSSA DA SOLO, CREA UN'ASPETTATIVA INCOMBENTE E
CONFINANTE COL SILENZIO. NON ABBANDONA MAI LA POSIZIONE D'ATTESA,
NON MUOVE MUSCOLI, MA SI PREMUNISCE ASSUMENDO UNA POSIZIONE,
QUELLA DEL COLLO LUNGO, DI UN MOVIMENTO RETRATTILE CHE GLI
PERMETTE DI SOLLEVARSI DA SÈ, D'INTRAVEDERE E
CONTEMPORANEAMENTE DI STRAVEDERE.
SI SA, ED È PROBABILE, CUCCHI È UN UOMO CHE NON HA LA TESTA SULLE
SPALLE, QUINDI NEANCHE IL COLLO, TUTTI SE NE AVVEDONO: TALE
EVIDENZA VIENE INSEGNATA ANCHE AI BAMBINI NELLE SCUOLE, E QUESTO
È DENUNCIATO COME SEGNO DI IRRESPONSABILE ASOCIALITÀ.
L'ARTISTA, COME DICE THOMAS MANN, NON È UN BUON RIFORMATORE, IN
QUANTO HA UN AMORE PARTICOLARE PER LA VOLGARITÀ E LA VITA, CHE
POI SONO LA STESSA COSA.
CUCCHI NON SI ORGANIZZA SCORTE, NON PRATICA ACCUMULI DI VIVERI NÉ
ASPETTA QUALCUNO CHE GLI PORTI DONI ADATTI PER LO SCAMBIO, PERCHÉ
NON HA OCCHI PER VEDERE NÉ ORECCHIE PER SENTIRE PERCIÒ SI BUSSA
DA SOLO, INTRODUCE COSÌ OLTRE LE PORTE DI ROMA IL FANTASMA DELLA
CITTÀ CHE ENTRA ED ESCE SUI CARRI DELLE IMMAGINI AMATE DI RUOTE E
DI UN MARGINE LUCENTE DI MOSAICO D'ORO.
COME LA TARTARUGA CUCCHI SI FA CARICO DELLE PORTE, SI CARICA LE
IMMAGINI SULLE SPALLE, CORAZZATO CON QUESTE, CIRCUMNAVIGA CON IL
COLLO INTORNO E FUORI, PRONTO A RITIRARSI APPENA EFFETTUATO IL
COLPO D'OCCHIO.
IL COLPO D'OCCHIO TERMINA INEVITABILMENTE NEL SUO PUNTO INIZIALE.
L'ARTISTA CON IL COLLO LUNGO FA LA RUOTA DI PAVONE E SI TROVA CON LA
VISTA A SCOPRIRE MOLTI PAESAGGI CHE AFFONDANO SILENZIOSAMENTE
LUNGO LINEE OBLIQUE CHE SONO POI LE TRAIETTORIE DELLA STORIA. ROMA È
UN SIMULACRO IN ATTESA DIETRO LA PORTA. INSOMMA L'ARTISTA NON
ASPETTA MAI VISITE, COSÌ SI CONSOLA APRENDOSI E CHIUDENDOSI DIETRO E
FUORI LA PORTA CHE FUNZIONA IN TAL MODO DA SPECCHIO. È LÌ, SUL
GUSCIO CONCAVO E SPECULARE, CHE IL PASSATO SEPPELLISCE IL PROPRIO
FUTURO, CHE IL COLPO D'OCCHIO FONDA LA PROPRIA SVISTA E
L'ALLUCINAZIONE PERVERSA DI MOLTE UBIQUITÀ.
I GEMELLI ROMOLO E REMO SI PERDONO NELLA COSTELLAZIONE DEL MITO IN
UNA DIMENSIONE CHE RESTITUISCE L'INFANZIA DELLA CITTÀ ETERNA,
PICCOLI E SOLITARI PRESI DAL GIOCO DELLA SIMMETRIA E FORSE DELLA
LOTTA. IL SUOLO È UNA NUVOLA INCOMBENTE ED ANCHE GEOLOGIA DI UN
SUOLO OSCURO, ABITATO DA MOLTE CAVERNE E CITTÀ ULTERIORI INVISIBILI.
COMUNQUE CUCCHI SI CARICA IL COLLO SULLE SPALLE E CONTINUA LA
PROPRIA PERIPEZIA, PONENDOSI IN ASCOLTO DI ALTRE APPARIZIONI, PRONTO
AD ALTRE COGNIZIONI, SOLLECITO NELLO SPALANCARE LE PORTE DI ROMA
SULL'ASSENZA DEL PRESENTE.
COSÌ IL CIGOLIO SI MISURA CON IL RUMORE SOMMESSO DELLA RISATA
QUELLA DI ZARATHUSTRA, CHE SA COME APRIRE SIGNIFICHI SOLTANTO
SPOSTARE ARIA E PORRE INEVITABILMENTE LE PORTE SOTTO IL SEGNO DEL

ENZO CUCCHI

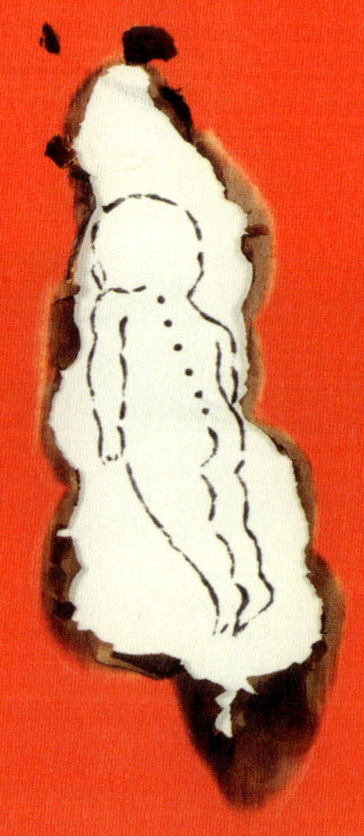

Enzo Cucchi
Solomon R. Guggenheim Museum

Enzo Cucchi broke with tradition in three major ways for his exhibition this summer at the Solomon R. Guggenheim Museum, New York—two of them ruptures of museum conventions (and, in one case, of this space in particular), and a third having to do with the meaning and content of the show. Most obviously, Cucchi discarded the Guggenheim custom of having the public ascend by elevator from the ground floor to a higher gallery and then return to the bottom via the spiraling ramp. His show was to be seen from the ground up, by ascending the incline. This could have been seen as a disruption of the public's established viewing patterns, but I believe that it was actually a reflection of the complex symbology underlying Cucchi's work, and we shall see how. Second, the show was not the usual retrospective in which a span of works from different stages of the artist's career succeed each other in chronological order. It reflected no particular dating, and most of the works were quite recent. Cucchi conceived the show as a whole, specifically designing it for the Guggenheim. It was a kind of gigantic installation in the Frank Lloyd Wright space, though to label it like this is reductive, for its meaning—and now we have arrived at the third break with convention—lay in its articulation of a unified expression across all formal or other boundaries. The Guggenheim's and Cucchi's initiative in risking this show, in which the artist was left free to make the decisions that would govern its form, is to be applauded. Curator Diane Waldman did not so much mount an exhibition as allow an event to take place, a creative interaction of artist and environment. Instead of considering the artwork as a discrete object to be classified, inventoried, and assigned a place in history, it was permitted to become verified as part of a larger whole, overturning the modus operandi of the museum show but enlarging the possibility of a new work of art, the exhibition itself.

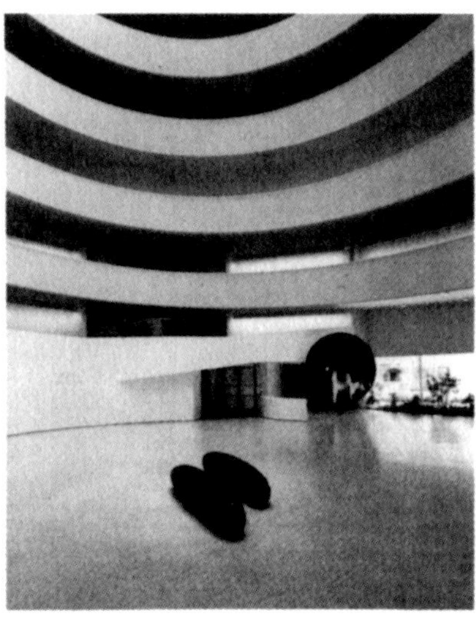

Enzo Cucchi, untitled, 1986, bronze, in two parts, each ca. 24 × 79 × 24". ***Preistoria* (Prehistory), 1986,** oil on canvas, iron, 135½ × 118⅞ × 12½".

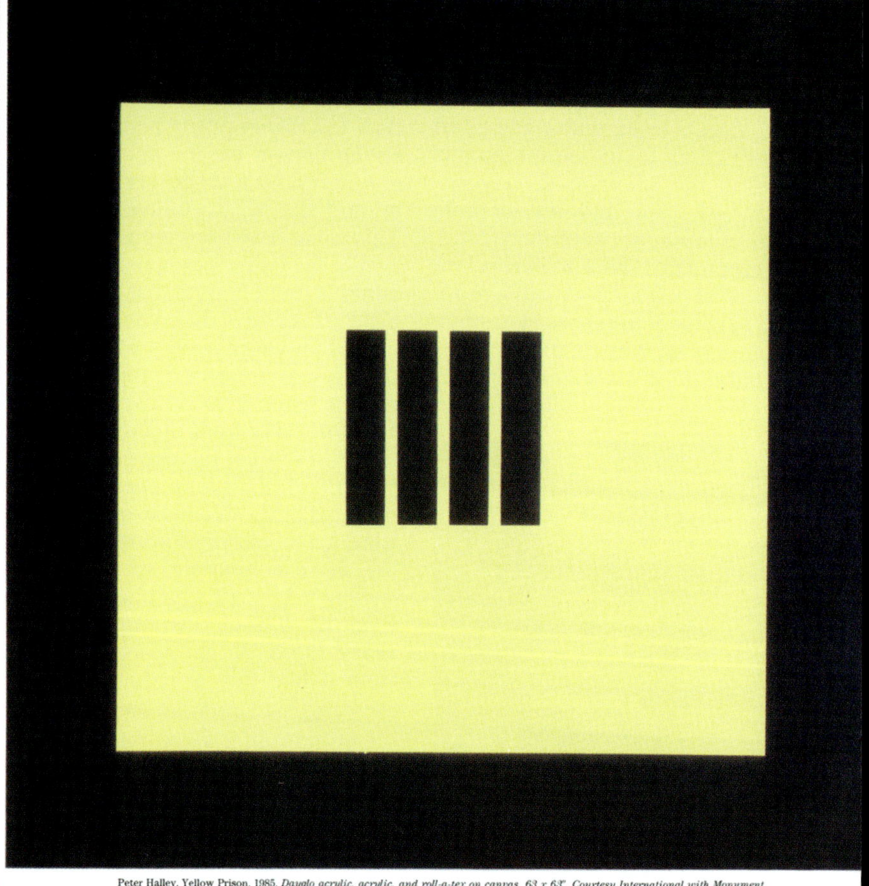

Peter Halley, Yellow Prison, 1985. *Dayglo acrylic, acrylic, and roll-a-tex on canvas, 63 x 63". Courtesy International with Monument.*

earlier works. In her show "1917," she juxtaposed copies of Malevich's and Chasnik's geometric paintings with a group of expressionist works by Egon Schiele to expose the modernist myth of linear development in art. Recently, she extended this idea by combining a series of small stripe paintings that rely on geometry with others that rely on accident. These, no longer appropriations, despite a familiar look, are "original accumulations of classic modernist idioms."[4] Geometry here represents the mental or culture strain in modernism as opposed to the organic or nature strain. The works allude to every painter who used stripes from Rozanova through Marden to Buren, pointing up the role of seriality and presentation.

Like other '80s artists countering formalism, Levine infuses geometry with meaning beyond itself. She now comes closer to Halley in her more generalized references to earlier art through painting, although by remaining within the parameters of art and art history, she reveals herself increasingly as a late modernist.

Spiral: the path of a point in a plane moving around a central po while continuously receding from or approaching it.

I'm interested in a synoptic experience and this refers to circles a kind of structure that has a uniformity to it.

—Ellen Ca

In Ellen Carey's large silhouetted self-portraits, geometry intera with the body. Her head and shoulders, sometimes arms or hands, veiled or camouflaged by geometric designs derived from patte books. Repeated patterns of squares, circles, triangles, and diamor are blown up and combined. The degree of anonymity or specific in the features depends upon her choice of patterns, their amount a

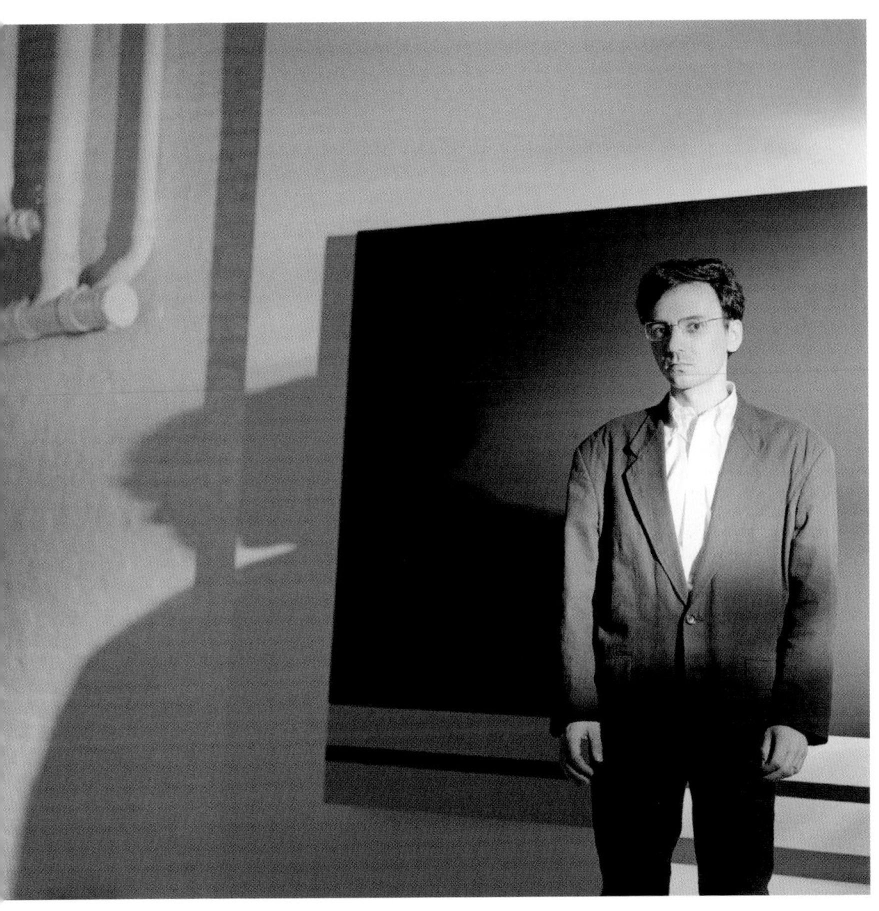

There I am in front of one of my bleakest most minimal paintings
—it's almost all black—wearing a suit by Rei Kawakubo. I love the
shadow in the picture. It reminds me of a Warhol painting.

Peter Halley

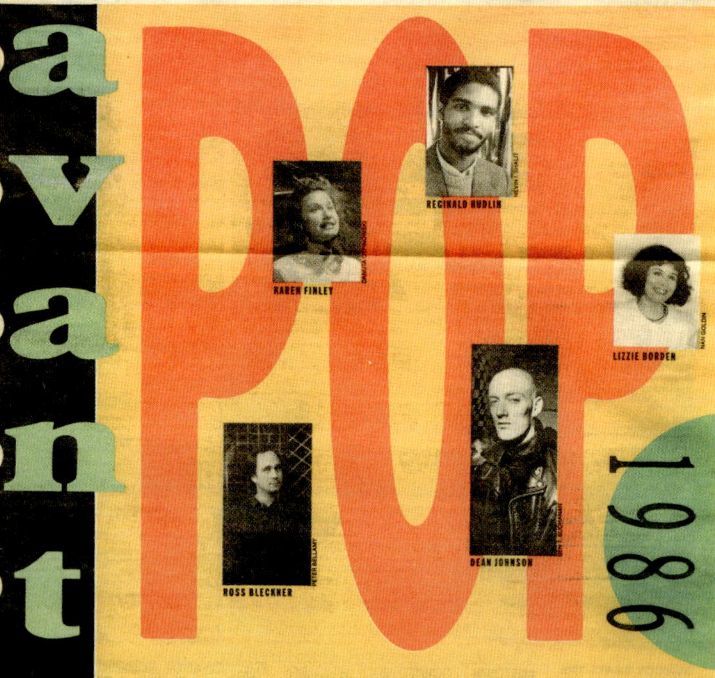

DON'T BAN THE BUTT (ELLEN WILLIS, P. 31)
the village
VOICE
Rate Our Critics
Their 10 Best Lists vs. Yours (Sarris, Hoberman, Edelstein)
VOL. XXXI NO. 1 THE WEEKLY NEWSPAPER OF NEW YORK JANUARY 7, 1986 $1.25
Plus Musto's Felix Awards
avant
POP
1986
REGINALD HUDLIN
KAREN FINLEY
LIZZIE BORDEN
DEAN JOHNSON
ROSS BLECKNER
BREAKING OUT—FROM CULT TO CULTURE:
A Bald Rapper in Drag, a Chicano Comic Book, a Harvard Hip-Hop Filmmaker, a Space Condo, and a Mutant Typestyle. Predicting Tomorrow's Mainstream from Today's Vanguard (P. 21)

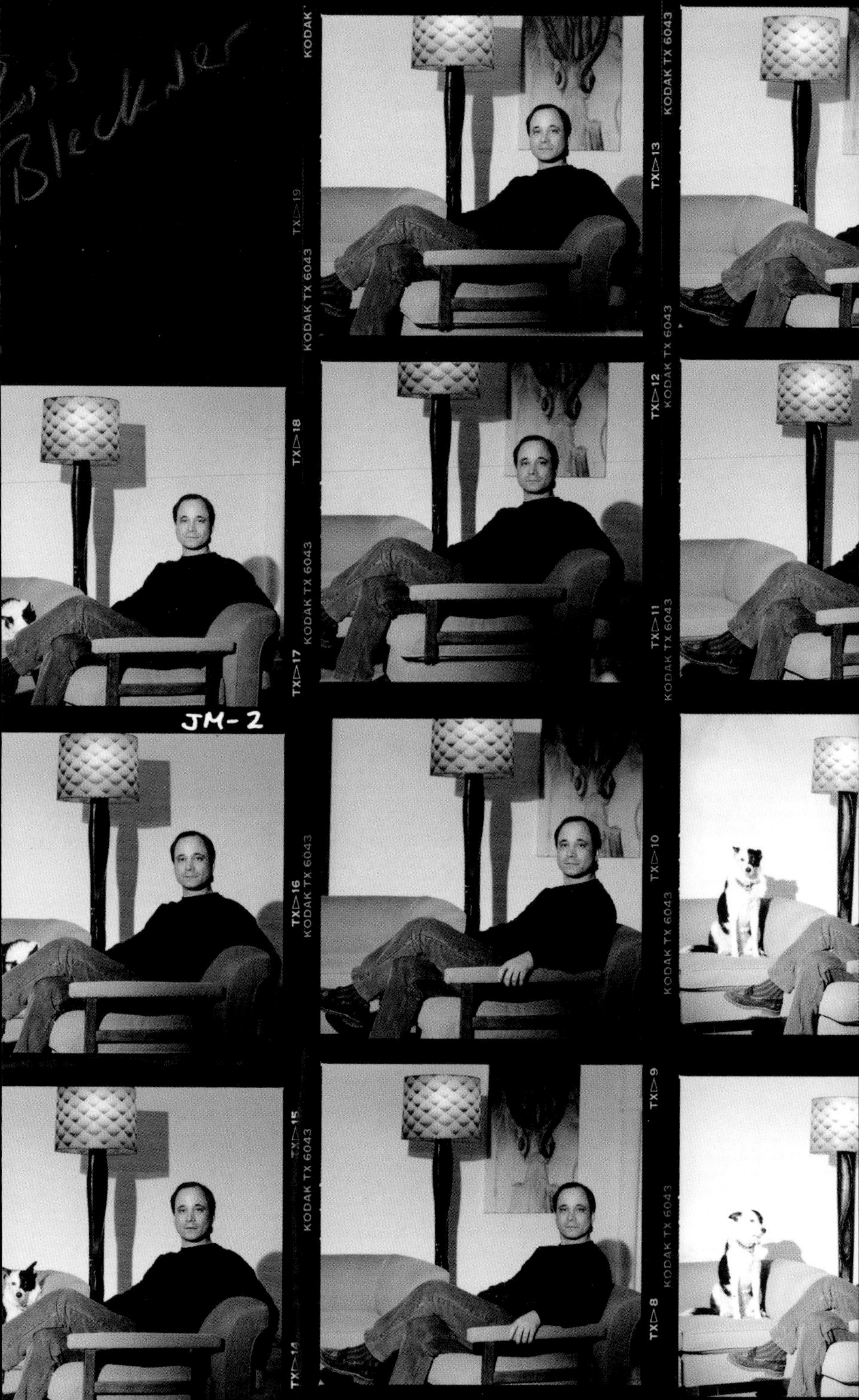
Bleckner
JM-2
KODAK TX 6043
TX→19
TX→18
TX→17
TX→16
TX→15
TX→14
TX→13
TX→12
TX→11
TX→10
TX→9
TX→8

<u>Untitled</u> (We don't need another hero), 1986

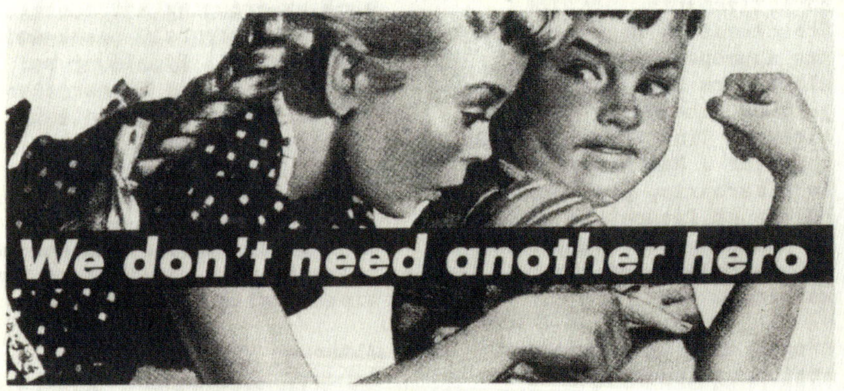

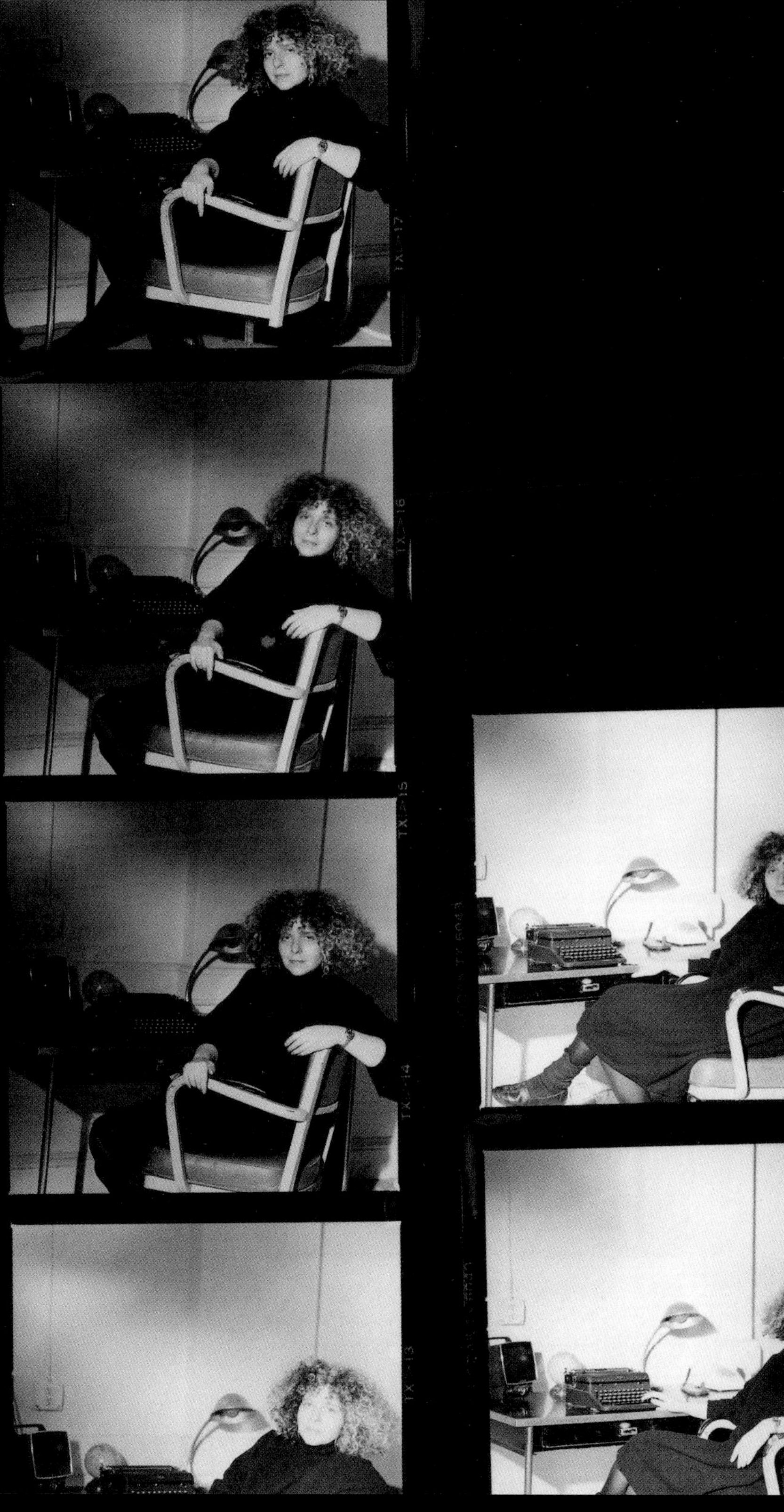

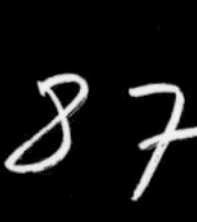

1987

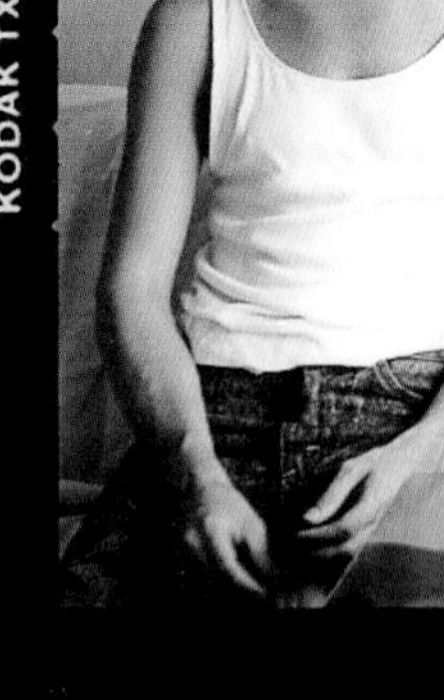
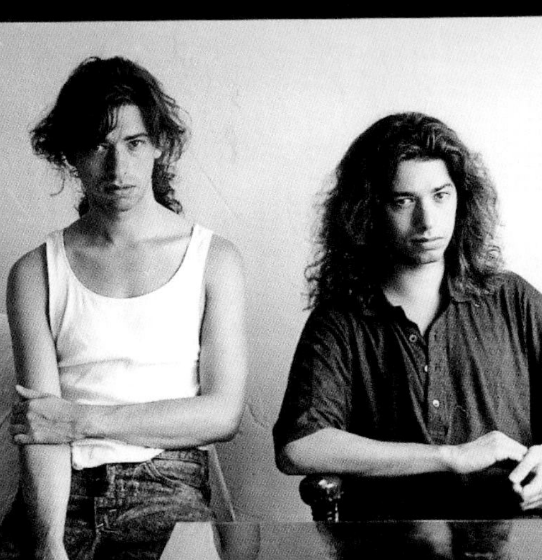
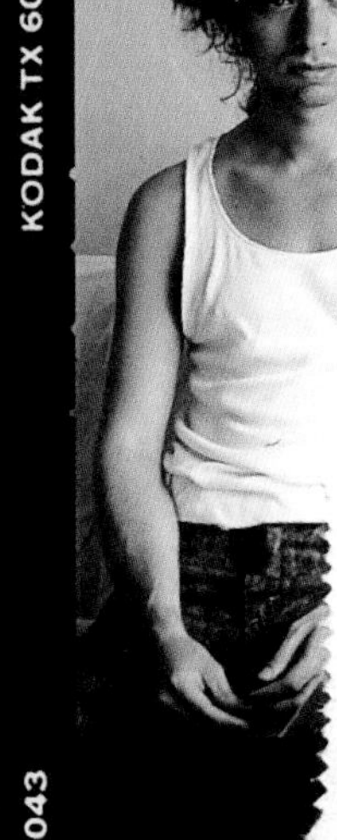
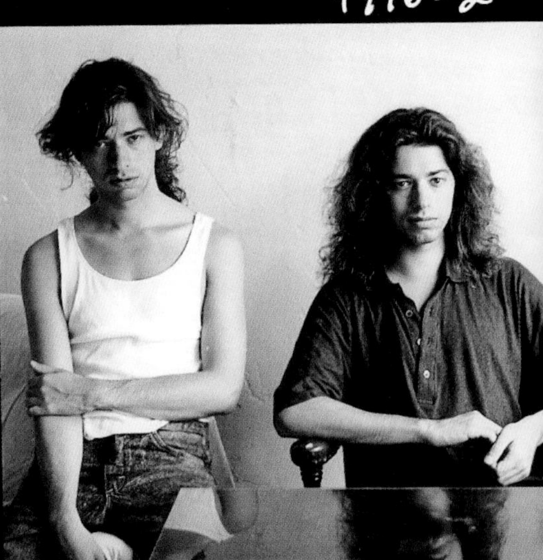

4496-2

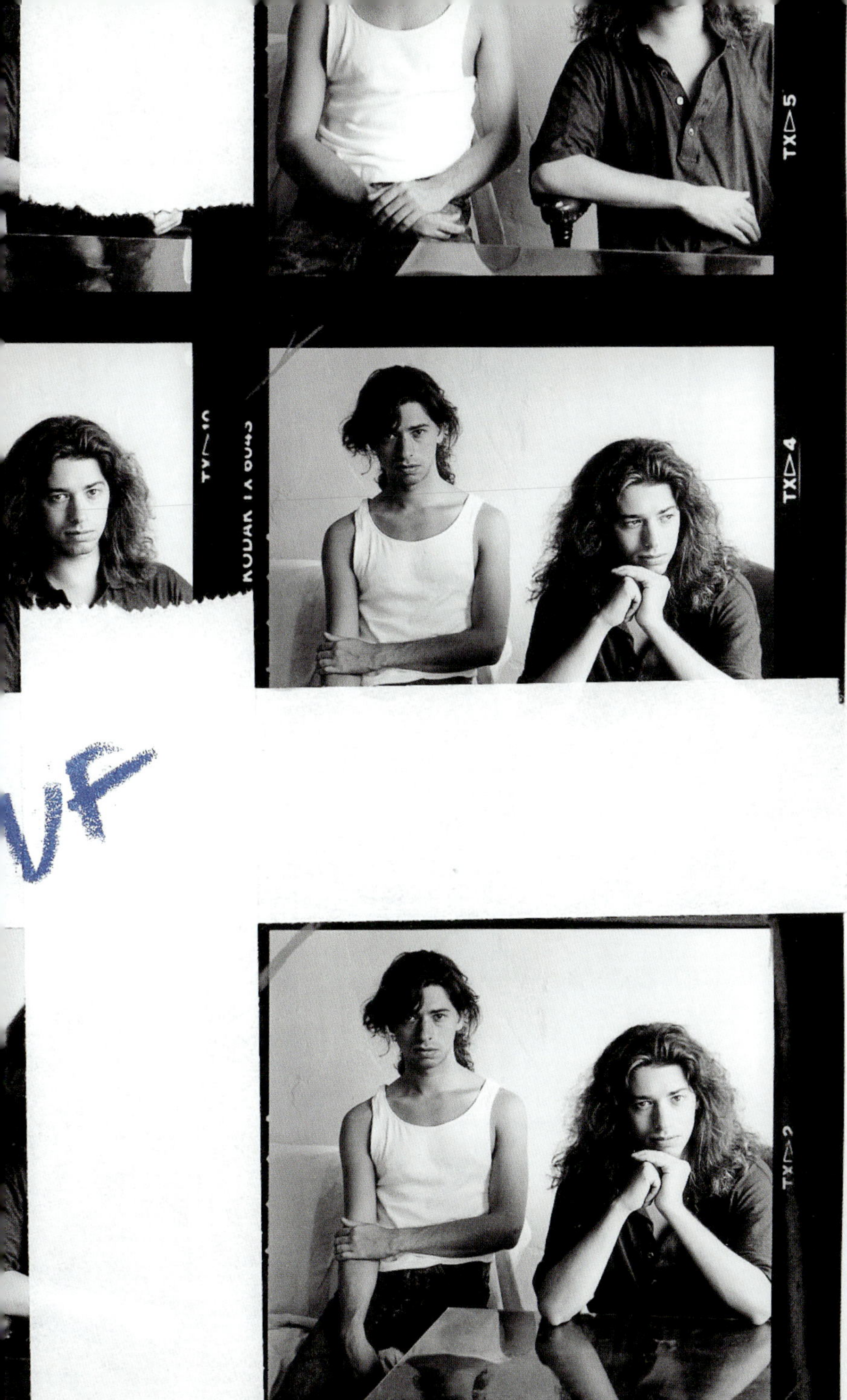

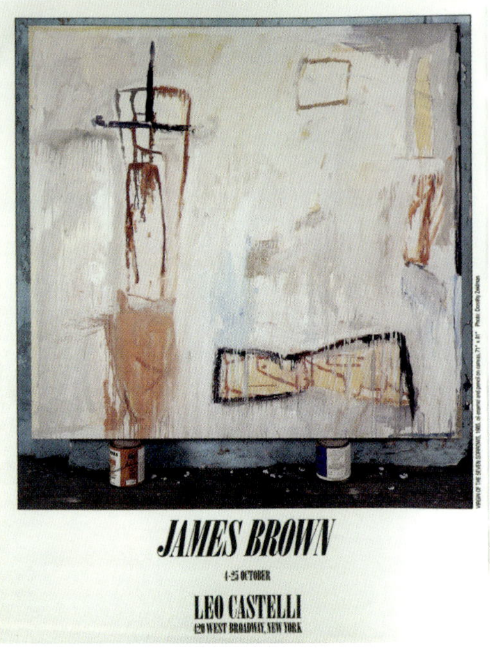

Jeannette Montgomery: the gentle touch in all ways and always.
How could one not be open and willing to sit for Jeannette.
There was a fine and subtle aura that surrounded that woman
who so casually needed to take your picture. It seemed that all the
South was knocking at your door and that she might have just as
well arrived with Eudora Welty–thus was her charm and power.
We all flocked around Jeannette and wanted to be complimented
and embraced by her lens, by her eye, her presence. We wanted
to be completed by her. I think of being phoned up for a portrait
session with Jeannette: a wonderful exciting R.D.V., Ludlow below
Houston, sometime next week, some sunny afternoon.
I look forward to the day. I like the simplicity, the friendliness.
I like enigmatic beings, the ones who have perfume and mystery
about them. This is how I remember my encounters with Jeannette
Montgomery Barron.

James hd Brown
Merida, Mexico
January, 2014

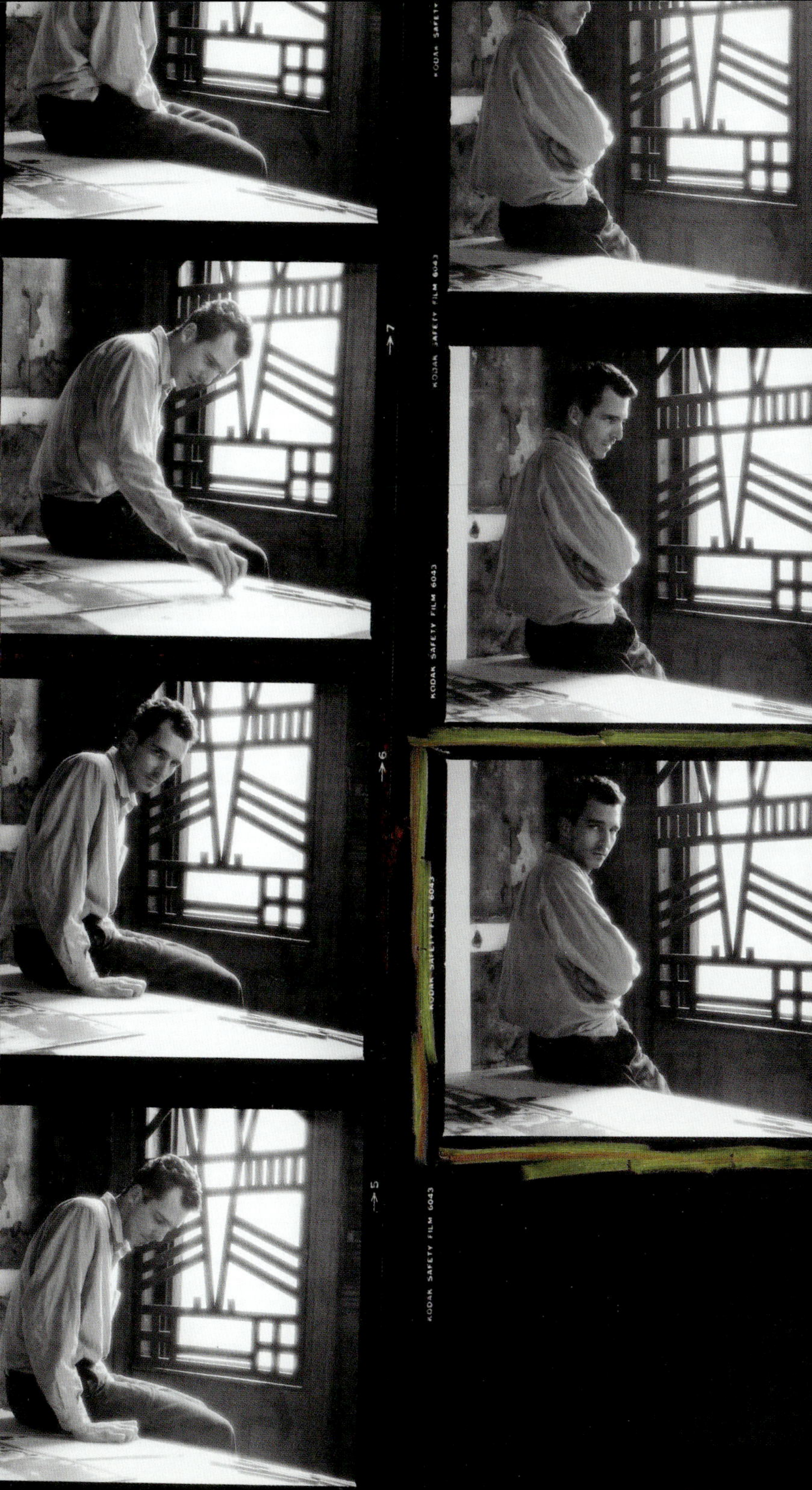

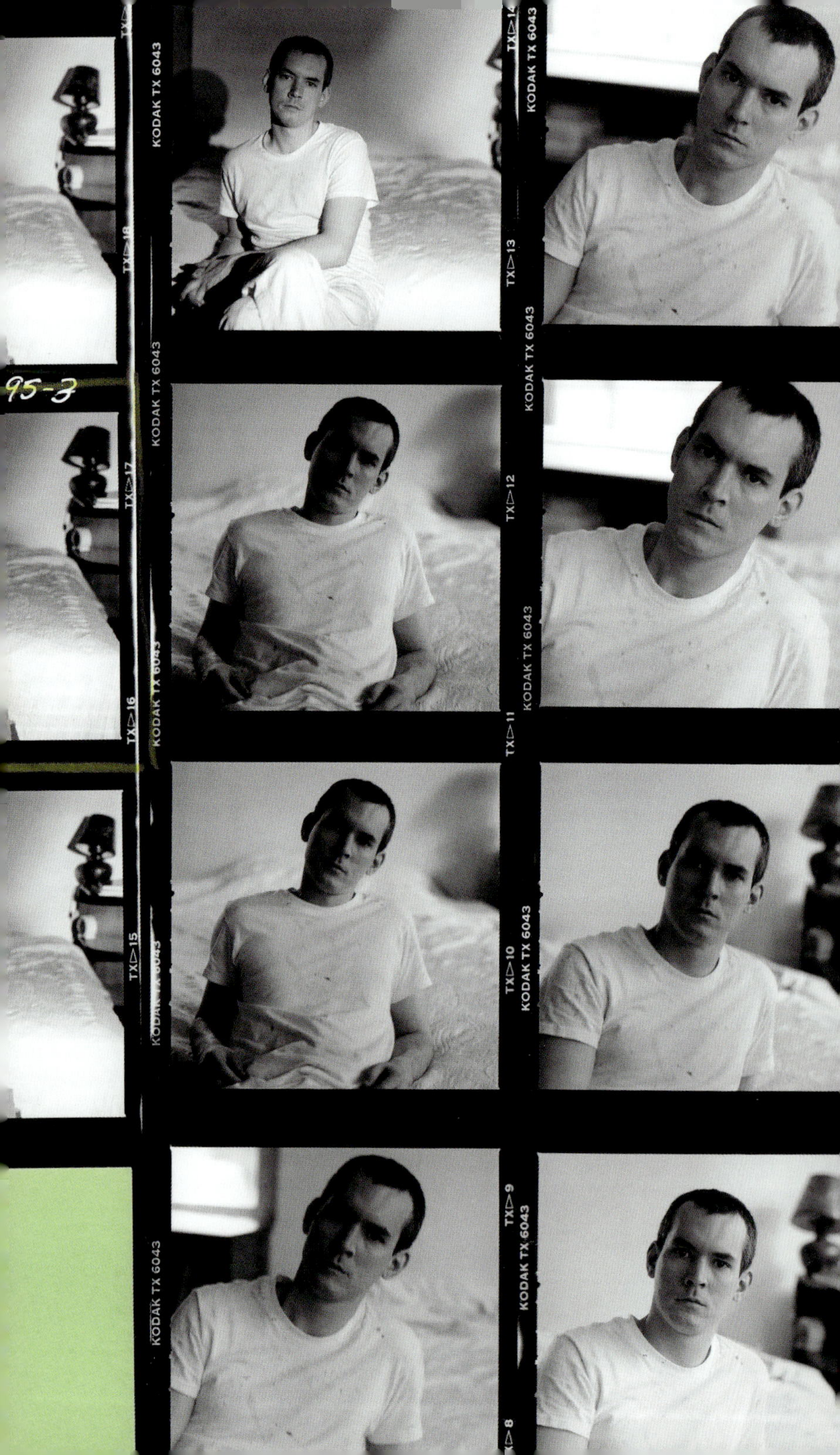

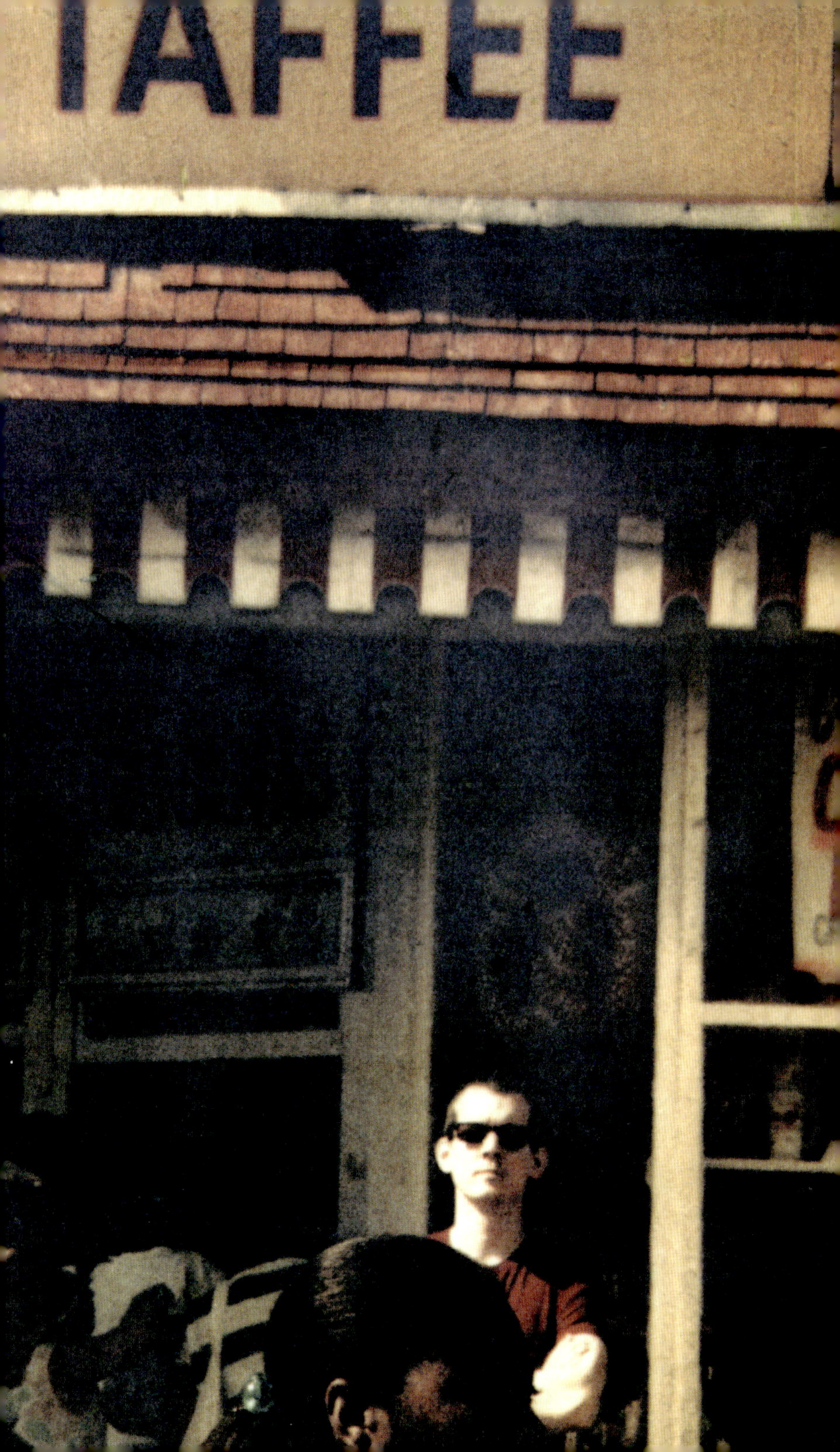

TAFFEE

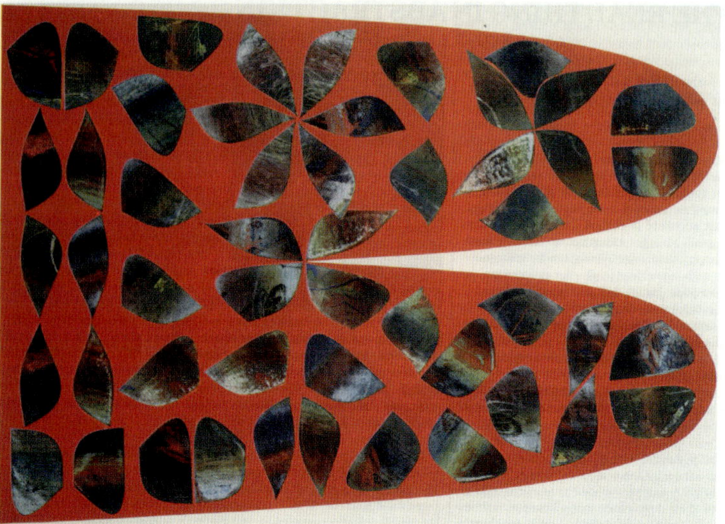

Philip Taaffe, Nativity, 1986[...]
*screen collage and acrylic [...]
canvas, 65 x 90". Courtesy [...]
Pat Hearn Gallery.*

led: to hideous, gargantuan "decorations" on Wall Street and on Third Avenue; to Jules Olitski's cake frostings on Plexiglas. From this vantage, Halley's Baudrillardian terminology begins to look suspect; perhaps it should give him pause.

Halley has one measly idea, and he's serving time on a self-imposed esthetic death sentence, playing at another fake dead-endgame position for those who can't seem to get enough of them. But many formula painters have begun from zero, from a virtuous, superior position acclaimed for its extreme, constricting "discipline." If one takes Stella and Judd as examples, the reductive approach can be seen historically to be one of a *loss* of meaning, either through a retreat from the confines of the original concept, or by a pigheaded repetition mania. And the loss of the first serious impulse not-so-coincidentally ends up as deeply involved not with what the art object *means* but *how it is used*; that is, with function, and, again not coincidentally, with decoration.

By 1966, Stella openly admitted a desire to reformulate abstraction in terms that relate directly to Matissean concepts of decoration. And Judd's boxes—without developing in any significant way since 1966—have long passed to the stage where it is impossible to overlook their functional/decorative component: they read as tables, shelves, chairs. This historical shift has not gone unnoticed: witness the revival (totally justified) of Richard Artschwager, the ubiquitousness of Mark Stahl and John Armleder and a whole host of others whose work is indebted to functionalism, decoration, interior design, and Scott Burton. The point is that when art loses its "serious" credentials, when times change, what we are left with is an object as period piece, as token of style, and then its decorative component becomes apparent.

How is it that every writer has failed to mention that Philip Taaffe's large-scale collages extend precepts first laid down by Matisse's late, decorative cutouts? Everything about them—physically, procedurally, and pictorially—points to this reference. Are people really that unaware? (Is Taaffe unaware?) When he redoes *Vir Heroicus Sublimus* by adding collaged, twined tassels, is it possible to overlook the fact that Newman was himself redoing the *Red Studio*, right down to the "drawing" that was a band of unpainted canvas, and which was itself an inventory of a personal history of painting? In Taaffe's most audacious painting to date, he ties up entire episodes of modern art in one

joyous ribbon: a green Kelly arrow becomes scaffolding for R[...] undulations in orange, and pasted all over the background, a flur[...] fun-flower decals are scattered like the blossoms on Matisse's *Int[...] with Eggplants* and painted like Lee Krasner's, with neutral-t[...] collaged bits that are scraped away, reused and recycled from ea[...] paintings. When Taaffe's on top of things, his paintings move outw[...] expand in multiple directions of reference, sometimes incompa[...] often startling. He is not engaged in an emptying-out of the reso[...] of painting or its history, but in a filling-up of the space with mem[...] of modernism—not to mourn modernism's passing, but to ret[...] the pieces, to synthesize the fragments into a generous, optim[...] rhapsodic crazy-quilt of styles, meshing and crisscrossing and i[...] weaving sources without appearing derivative.

When Taaffe gets lost, overwhelmed by the possibilities, he may[...] control of those resources and paintings become a muddle of s[...] intentions, misfired connections, a confusion of visual ideas that ca[...] each other out. But one always respects the attempt, which co[...] from the admirable effort to try something different in each w[...] Because collage allows him to construct imagery in layers, the[...] paintings look like recombinations, constellations of styles where [...] is given equal emphasis without levelling their differences. If he [...] Arp or Riley or Newman or Kelly or Paul Feeley, you never feel [...] levelling them out, and you don't feel he's resorting to diversi[...] score little art historical points.

It is the less pronounced effects that win you over: a sensitivi[...] material reminiscent of Dorothea Rockburne's use of the complex[...] of paper's double-sidedness; the mirrored imagery that suggests [...] Johns of the crosshatch paintings; the introduction of architec[...] structure, the balustrade and wrought-iron work; the limpid, ge[...] flow that rushes your eyes over a surface. When he sets up a pa[...] and then just lets it blow away like dry autumn leaves, when he [...] up a field with waves and funny amoebalike forms and irregularly[...] black spots, he's like a great, young jazz musician taking the histor[...] basics and improvising, embellishing with discordant detail, jug[...] and mixing old tunes and coming up with a style of his own. Ma[...] reinvented collage with *Jazz*; like Matisse, Taaffe reinvents co[...] and pulls it all off effortlessly, airily, without any ponderous posir[...] attitudinizing. Perhaps it risks not looking "serious," but isn't seri[...] like heroic and tough and raw, a little too limited as a descriptio[...] great art?

the attention to detail, the commitment to craft, the painstaking
[ ]ique (not simply *labor*) that draws you in. The great failure of
[abstra]ct painting since Abstract Expressionism has been that it
[gi]ves the *thinness* of the mural-size painting without its *grandeur*,
[bre]adth that, as Rothko said, made the experience intimate. Taaffe's
[detou]r through Newman may have allowed him to learn how to seduce
[the vi]ewer into this kind of intimacy. The red that wraps around the
[bound] edge of *Nativity* pulls you close, pulls you over to view the
[elong]erated, double blimplike shape from an even more foreshortened
[angle.] Fingerprints and smudges trace the activity of laying down the
[silks]work. Symmetry is interrupted in *Yellow, Grey* by a mirror inver-
[sion t]hat doesn't anchor the bottom of the painting but gives it a lift,
[as if t]he whole thing was suddenly understood as floating on an ara-
[besqu]e. Four central black dots, the four voids of the spirals in *Quad*
[Corn]*na* are multiplied and dispersed to activate the remaining space,
[mak]ing the novalike negative space that pulsates pleasurably, humor-
[ously.] A black-and-white work is, on close inspection, showered with
[paste]l blush. Fungible shapes grow little whip-tails, turn into leaves,
[tadp]ods, pinwheels, cutting through and into the authority of the
[clea]wed abstract "background." If Matisse's stylized natural forms
[alw]ays on the verge of turning purely abstract, then Taaffe's abstract
[form]s are always threatening to go natural, organic. Everywhere is
[the d]ominance of predetermined scaffolding undermined by quirky
[sing]ulars, signalling that something was discovered, *learned*. Taaffe's
[pecul]iar range of scuzzy browns and grays veined like marble with
[wor]ries and laid against dizzyingly "off" prismatic hues isn't safe,
[it]didn't come from heaven: it was learned, invented, discovered.

[Th]e following passage comes not from Anouilh, and not from Baud-
[elaire]; it's Greenberg writing about Milton Avery, with an aside on
[Matis]se.

[If d]ecoration can be said to be the spectre that haunts modernist
[pai]nting, then part of the latter's formal mission is to find ways
[of]using the decorative against itself. It is as though Late Impres-
[sio]nism and Fauvism have come on the order of the day again
[pr]ecisely because being so much more antisculptural and there-
[fo]re exposed to the decorative than Cubism, they dramatize the
[pr]oblem by increasing the tension between decorative means
[an]d nondecorative ends.

[There] are two striking ideas here. First, the phrase "using the decorative
[again]st itself" echoes every so-called radical theoretical premise not
[only o]f modernism but of "post-modernism": using advertising against
[itself,] commercial culture against itself, the commodity against itself,
[the o]riginal or author or whatever against itself. The simple "using X
[again]st X" is the critical recipe of every intellectual defense of art
[pract]ices wherein what is purportedly critical looks way too much
[like]what is being criticized. It is indispensable to all evaluations of
[the a]esthetics of Duchamp and his progeny up to and including Jeff
[Koon]s and Haim Steinbach.

["U]sing X against X" as modernist criticality is modernism's greatest
[sca]m, one that has ceaselessly been exposed as mere fiction, as
[ideo]logical pretense. As soon as it is invoked as a value, the "critical"
[artis]t is absorbed into the "resisted" culture. (The realization of this
[has]led to the "new complicity," which for all intents and purposes
[is]dropping the fiction that artists are subversives and replacing
[it]with the equally posturing fiction of the artist as a good whore.
[It's]such complicity that links Peter Halley not to Mondrian but to
[Keith] Haring.)

[The] second and more extraordinary idea offered by Greenberg is
[that t]he "tension" between the (decorative) means and the (serious,
[high]art") ends is analogous to the Marxist revolution: the decorative
[is,]to speak," the communist threat haunting modernism. I'm more
[than]willing to accept this view that decorators are the workers keeping
[the c]apitalist artists fed with new products to exploit. Decoration in
[its va]rious forms is *still* the artist's haunt. When David Salle dismembers
[image]s and sticks them into big swatches of fabric, he's still agonizing
[over t]he tension between decoration/design and "real" art. The whole
[recent] crop of artists who shop for readymade knickknacks and then
[try to] force something "conceptual" on them, are feeling the same
[pressi]on. At another point, Greenberg, hiding in a footnote, insists that
[even]though Matisse absolutely thought of his cutouts as decorative
[ensem]bles, they *had* to be pictorial, otherwise they couldn't be the

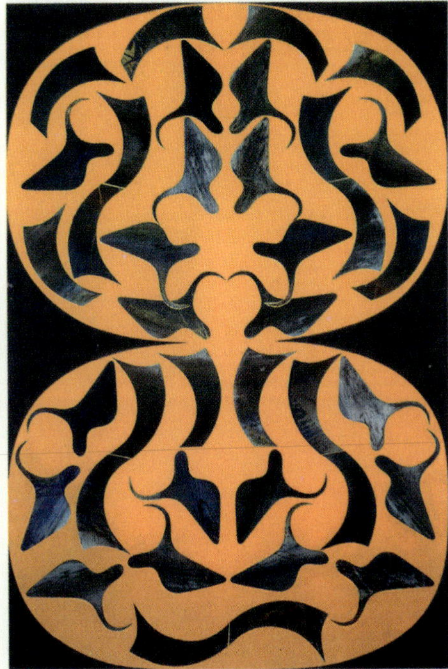

Philip Taaffe, Yellow, Grey, 1986. *Silkscreen collage and acrylic on canvas, 84 x 55¼".
Courtesy Pat Hearn Gallery.*

"supreme achievements" Greenberg thought they were, and, of course,
are.

Matisse obviously felt comfortable with the word "decorative" and
did not consider it to be a devastating slur. Earlier in this essay I called
Taaffe a populist, and what I meant was that he doesn't make the
mistake of thinking that the decorative component of art must be
contradicted by its serious intentions; that is, he doesn't use the decorative against itself. His *work* doesn't as a consequence, look *defensive*
or point-making the way everyone expects "serious" art to look; rather,
a Taaffe is lightfooted, decorative in the sense of open, flexible, demo-
cratic, equal-minded—what might be called communist with a small
"c." He uses modern abstract art as a sort of communal pool of visual
knowledge, and he doesn't use the pleasure of that knowledge against
the viewer, or use it to "criticize," i.e., feel superior, to the guests he
invites into his house.

There is something rather liberating about Taaffe's acceptance of
Newman or Kelly or Riley as his pre-designed underpinning, as decorative backdrop. He has replaced the all-encompassing, rigid, timeless
grid of modernism with the *styles* of modernism—and he only uses
them as jumping-off points. They help him, as Matisse wrote, "jump
the ditch." The idealized prison of the grid has made another comeback
and I hope Taaffe has the strength of conviction to ignore the pressure
of its "seriousness." For now he's pursuing a path of options, of the
accidental correspondences of sensibility and style; the road to a
heterogeneous, freewheeling, freely-circulating art: that vision of our
culture that's shall we say racially mixed, an esthetic hybrid, a mulatto.
And the end of the anxiety of influence.

1988

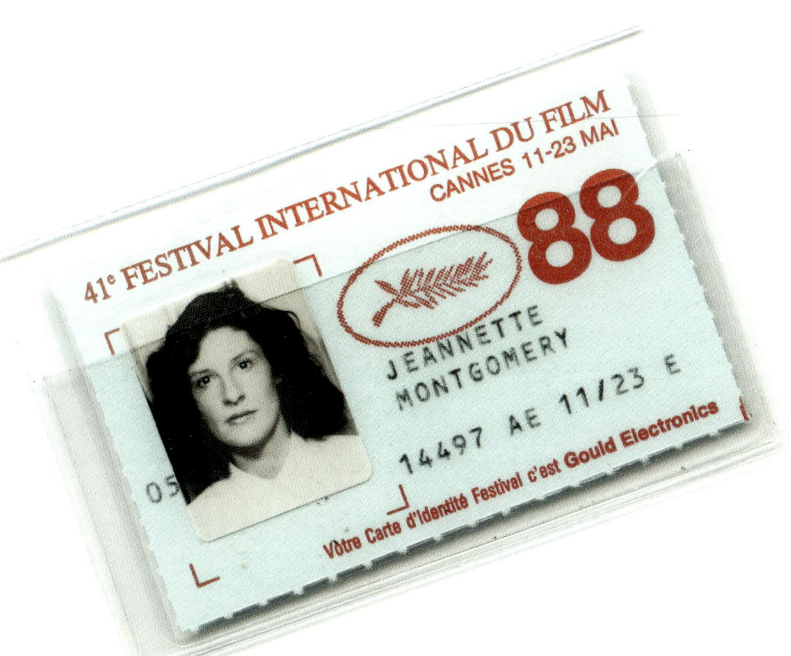

41e FESTIVAL INTERNATIONAL DU FILM
CANNES 11-23 MAI
88
JEANNETTE
MONTGOMERY
14497 AE 11/23 E
Votre Carte d'Identité Festival c'est Gould Electronics

VISUAL OBSESSIONS
How to Talk

Updating the painted word: a beginner's guide to the ins and outs of postmodern parlance

BY WILLIAM GRIMES

ABSTRACTION: Mode of painting whose practitioners persist in believing is avant-garde.

AMMANN, THOMAS: Swiss dealer whose collection of modern art is fast approaching the quality of his wardrobe.

ANGST: Suffering of white suburban artists who, upon checking their bank balance, begin to regret not having gone to dental school. Found chiefly in the work of the American neoexpressionists. *See* Irony.

APPROPRIATION: 1. The use by one artist of an image created by another (formerly known as plagiarism). 2. Borrowings from television and advertising that constitute a criticism of those media; no one has yet figured out where the criticism part comes in. 3. A way to make realistic art without having to learn how to draw.

ARTE POVERA: Italian version of minimalism that uses such "poor" or humble materials as discarded wood, metal, and glass. Baffling to Americans. Needs marketing strategy.

ARTFORUM: Like Great Brita[in], an imperial power fallen upon ha[rd] times. The art magazine for crit[ics] who think they can write.

ARTNEWS: Art magazine m[ore] likely to be found in a dentis[t's] waiting room.

ART OPENING: 1. Bad party w[ith] artist present at which inferi[or] wine is drunk out of plastic cu[ps] amid enough leather to fill an S&M bar. 2. A testi[ng] ground for insincere congratulations.

AVANT-GARDE (colloquially, "cutting edge") In the past, art no one understood; today, art everyo[ne] wants to buy. Believed by artists to no longer ex[ist] except in their own work. 2. Marketing strategy [of] certain downtown dealers (in real estate, known as [the] "you're buying a little piece of history here" pitc[h].

BAUDRILLARD, JEAN: Cryptic French sociolog[ist] and media star, known for his theories on the sta[tus] of images in modern culture. Indifferent to art, he [has] nevertheless become a cult figure for artists

Art

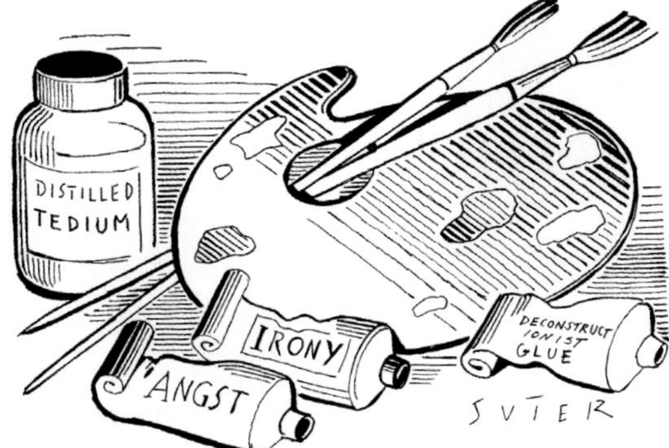

esperate search of a theory that will explain their own work to them. Hotly debated, little read.

OONE, MARY: Wicked Witch of West Broadway. vengali to Julian Schnabel, David Salle, and Eric ischl. Has more shoes than Imelda Marcos.

ASTELLI, LEO: Art dealer. Once defined the cutting edge. Would now be grateful for any hints as to here it might be found.

OLLECTOR: Moneyed individual with inexplicable rge to have Peter Halley over for dinner.

ORPORATE COLLECTING: Private-sector subdy program for Frank Stella.

ECONSTRUCTION: 1. A critical method that leases the genie of irrationality from the bottle ithin every text. 2. Intellectual's equivalent of MSG: nrow it on anything to perk up flavor. 3. Trendy nonym for "analysis." *See* Derrida, Jacques.

ERRIDA, JACQUES: French philosopher, father f deconstruction. Influence has been in direct proortion to his unintelligibility. Hotly debated, little ead.

OCUMENTA: Art-world trade show held every ve years in Kassel, West Germany.

DRAWING: Obsolete skill much in vogue during the Renaissance.

DUCHAMP, MARCEL: French artist (1887–1968), spinning in his grave. Would never have placed urinal in a museum if he could have foreseen the consequences.

EAST VILLAGE: Urban wasteland where middle-class kids live the fantasy of being proletarian artists while selling their work to surrogate parents, otherwise known as collectors.

ENDGAME ART: Post-death-of-painting painting. *See* Painting, death of.

FAB FIVE: Neo Geo artists Ashley Bickerton, Peter Halley, Jeff Koons, Haim Steinbach, and Meyer Vaisman. *See* Neo Geo.

FISCHL, ERIC: Neoexpressionist painter, known for scenes of nuclear family at sexual play. Succeeded in making U.S. suburbia the world capital of angst, displacing Kafka's Prague.

GALLERY: Art boutique; owner now referred to as "gallerist."

GRAFFITI ART: Briefest artistic movement on record; art-world equivalent of the Nehru jacket. High-

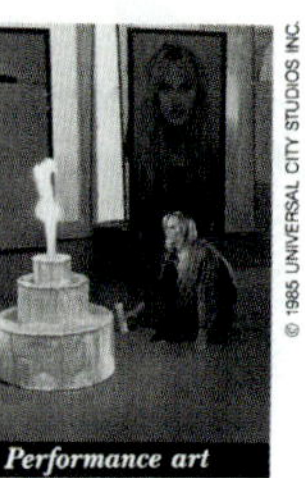

Performance art

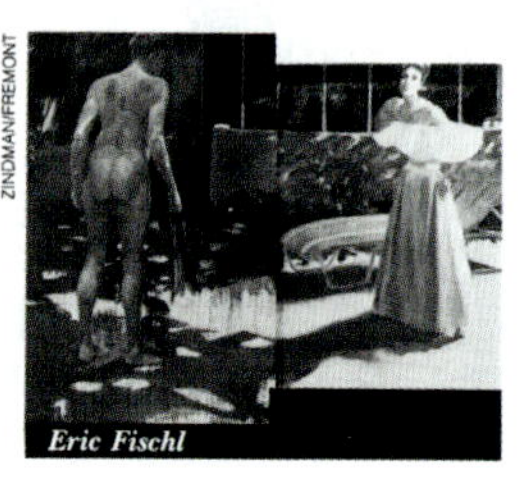

Eric Fischl

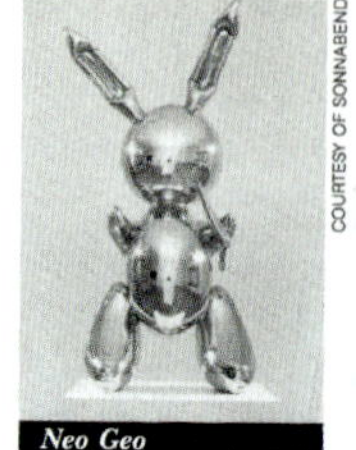

Neo Geo

water mark: Keith Haring's Absolut vodka ad.

GREENBERG, CLEMENT: Great White Father of modern art criticism. Like Lear, despised and rejected by his children.

IRONY: 1. Opposite of angst. 2. Face-saving tactic for artists who continue to paint after the death of painting. A series of winks and nudges to indicate that the artist does not take the work seriously, although collectors are supposed to. *See* Neo Geo.

LEVINE, SHERRIE: Appropriationist moll whose career has been floated on an ocean of theory only dimly understood by the artist herself.

MEMOIRS: Meandering thoughts published by artist simultaneously with retrospective exhibition. Mercifully brief due to extreme youth of author. *See* Schnabel, Julian.

MINIMALISM: Less is more, with several volumes appended to explain why.

NEOEXPRESSIONISM: Style of painting that flourished 1980–1985, now obsolescent. Too remote in time to have any influence on current art.

NEO GEO (also, Neo Pop, commodity art, smart art): 1. Any work by an artist under thirty that sells for more than $20,000. 2. A way to expose the commod[ity] status of art under late capitalism while cashing [in] big—hence the term smart art. 3. Marketing strate[gy] of certain downtown dealers.

PAINTING: Officially pronounced dead, desp[ite] glut of painters and galleries showing their work. *S[ee]* Painting, death of.

PAINTING, DEATH OF: Marketing strategy [of] certain downtown dealers. *See* Endgame art.

PERFORMANCE ART: 1. Visual art's impositi[on] on theater. 2. *The Gong Show*, but with a smaller a[u]dience. 3. Last refuge for the artistically impaired, r[e]quiring no specialized talent or technical abili[ty] whatever. Role model: Daryl Hannah in *Legal Eagle[s]*.

POSTMODERNISM: A term in search of an a[rt.] Everyone agrees we need it, no one can find it.

REALISM: Basis of Western art. Considered unim[portant] by contemporary artists and critics.

RETROSPECTIVE: 1. In the past, the capsto[ne] to an artistic career: an exhibition surveying a lifetime['s] work. Today, the payoff for five years of solid sale[s]. 2. Marketing strategy of certain major museums.

SAATCHI & SAATCHI: British advertising mogu[l]

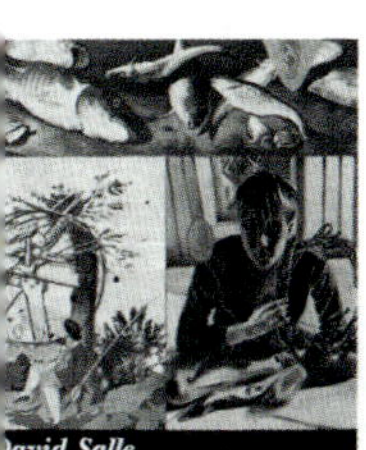

David Salle

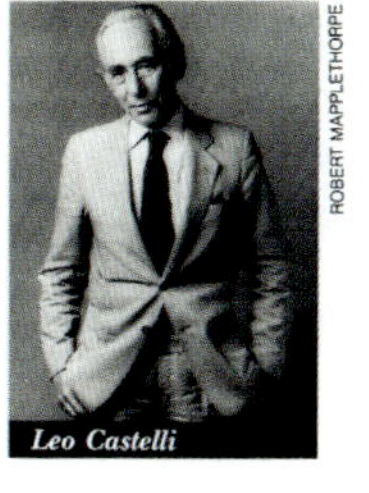

Leo Castelli

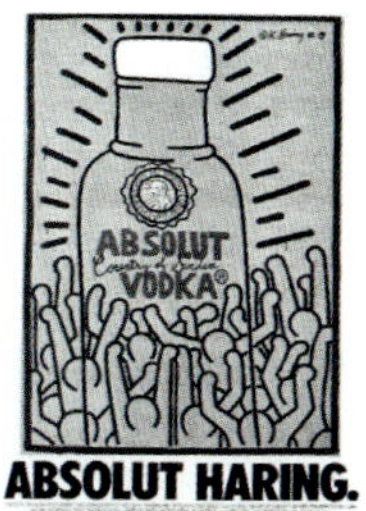

Graffiti art

...d megacollectors. The art world's Dow Jones In-
...strial Average.

...ALLE, DAVID: Neoexpressionist princeling,
...own for his uncanny ability to make provocative
...d erotic imagery boring. The most serious Western
...tist since Charlton Heston in *The Agony and the
...stasy.*

...CHNABEL, JULIAN: Neoexpressionist giant.
...rmer short-order cook, known for broken-plate
...intings, who traces aesthetic lineage through van
...ogh back to such well-known but lesser talents as
...ıccio and Giotto.

...HO: Former factory district in lower Manhattan.
...ow thought of as an artists' district, although no art-
...has been able to afford a loft there since Alan Bates
...*An Unmarried Woman.*

...RUCTURALISM: 1. A critical method, derived
...om linguistics, that replaces "What does it mean?"
...th "Why does it mean?" and "How does it mean?"
...Precursor of deconstruction and, of course, post-
...ucturalism. America dimly became aware of its ex-
...ence just as Jacques Derrida declared it dead. Still
...ay to put "structure of" before any stray noun (for
example, "structure of meaning," "structure of
feeling").

TELEVISION: Seminal aesthetic experience for current generation of artists. Modern equivalent of the
Renaissance's rediscovery of classical sculpture. Years
of squatting in front of tube now called "learning to
think in images."

VIDEO ART: And you thought commercial television was bad.

WARHOL, ANDY: Pop artist, officially canonized
as patron saint of fame and wealth after his death in
1987. Deprived of his sanctifying presence, young artists now burn incense and chant money mantras in
front of bewigged statuettes.

WHITNEY BIENNIAL: The art world's senior
prom, held every other year at the Whitney Museum.
Despite excruciating pains taken to avoid controver-
sy, the curators are routinely burned in effigy after announcing list of invitees.

YALE SCHOOL OF ART: The Academy. Proving
ground where young artists hone the nasty character
traits necessary for art-world success. Considered a
bad school by everyone who didn't get in. ■

GRETA GARBO, 1955
PHOTOGRAPH BY GEORGE HOYNINGEN-HUENE

YES TO EXTENSIVE TRAVEL.

fotofolio

MISS JEANNETTE MONTGOMERY
425 EAST 51ST STREET
APARTMENT 4D
NEW YORK, NEW YORK 10022

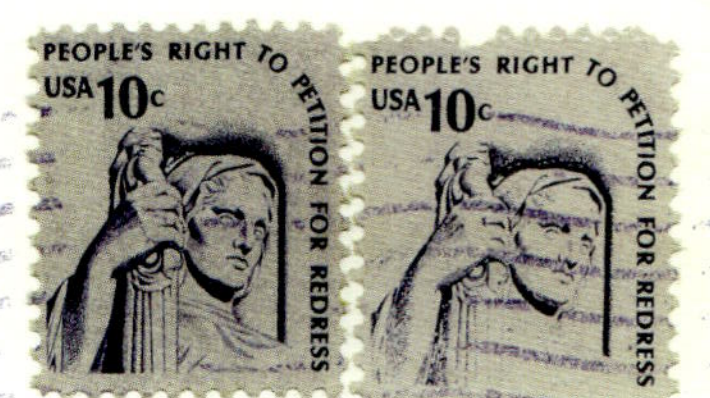

© HORST P. HORST
PRINTED BY RAPOPORT PRINTING CORP.
© 1979 FOTOFOLIO, BOX 661 CANAL STA., NY, NY 10013
HH14

GRAND CANYON NATIONAL PARK, ARIZONA

Lipan Point, elevation 7,250 feet, is one of the best views of the Colorado River and San Francisco Peaks. The Grand Canyon National Park is visited annually by more people than any other scenic attraction in the United States.

Pub. by Petley Studios, Inc., 4051 E. Van Buren, Phoenix, Ariz. 85008

LET'S GET BACK THERE.

M

JEANNETTE MONTGOMERY

425 E 51ST ST

4D

NYC 10022

dp MADE BY DEXTER PRESS.

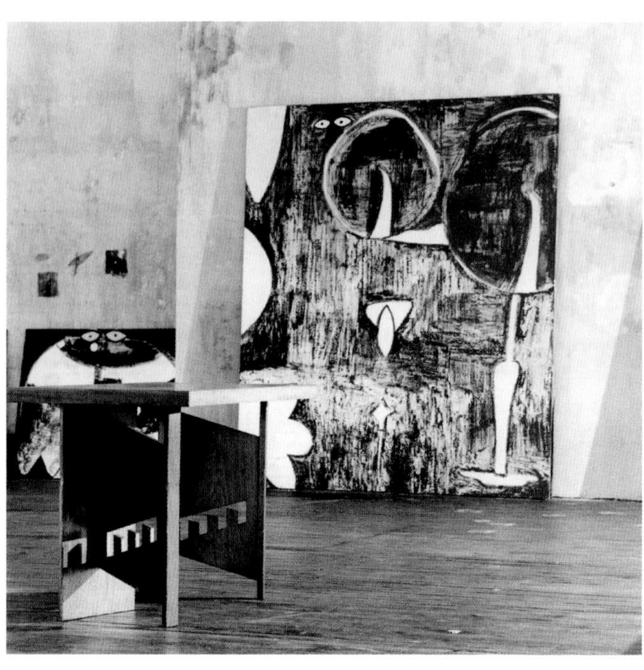

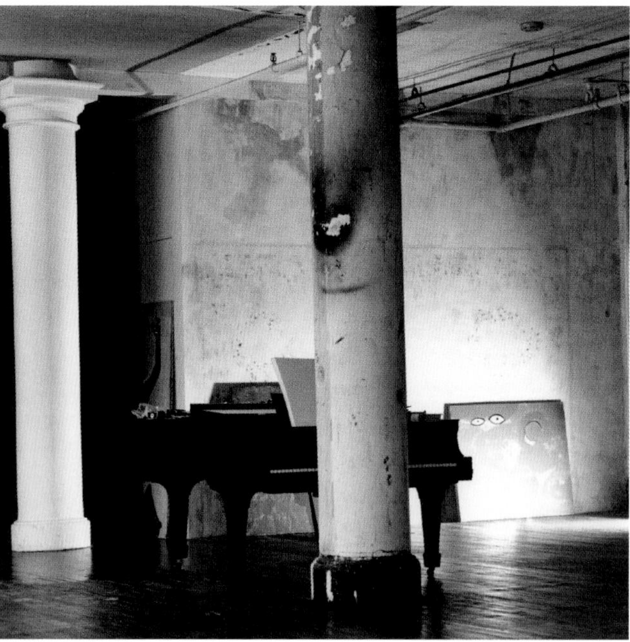

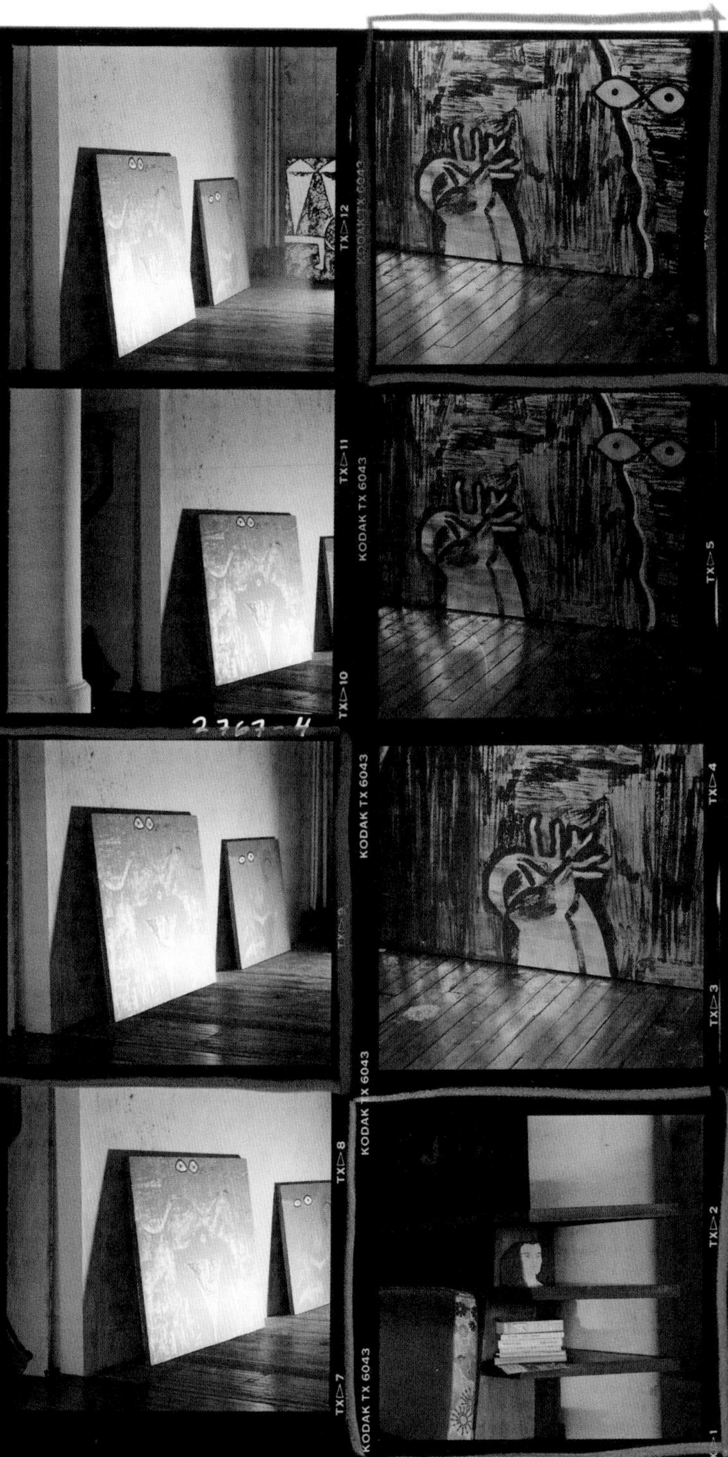

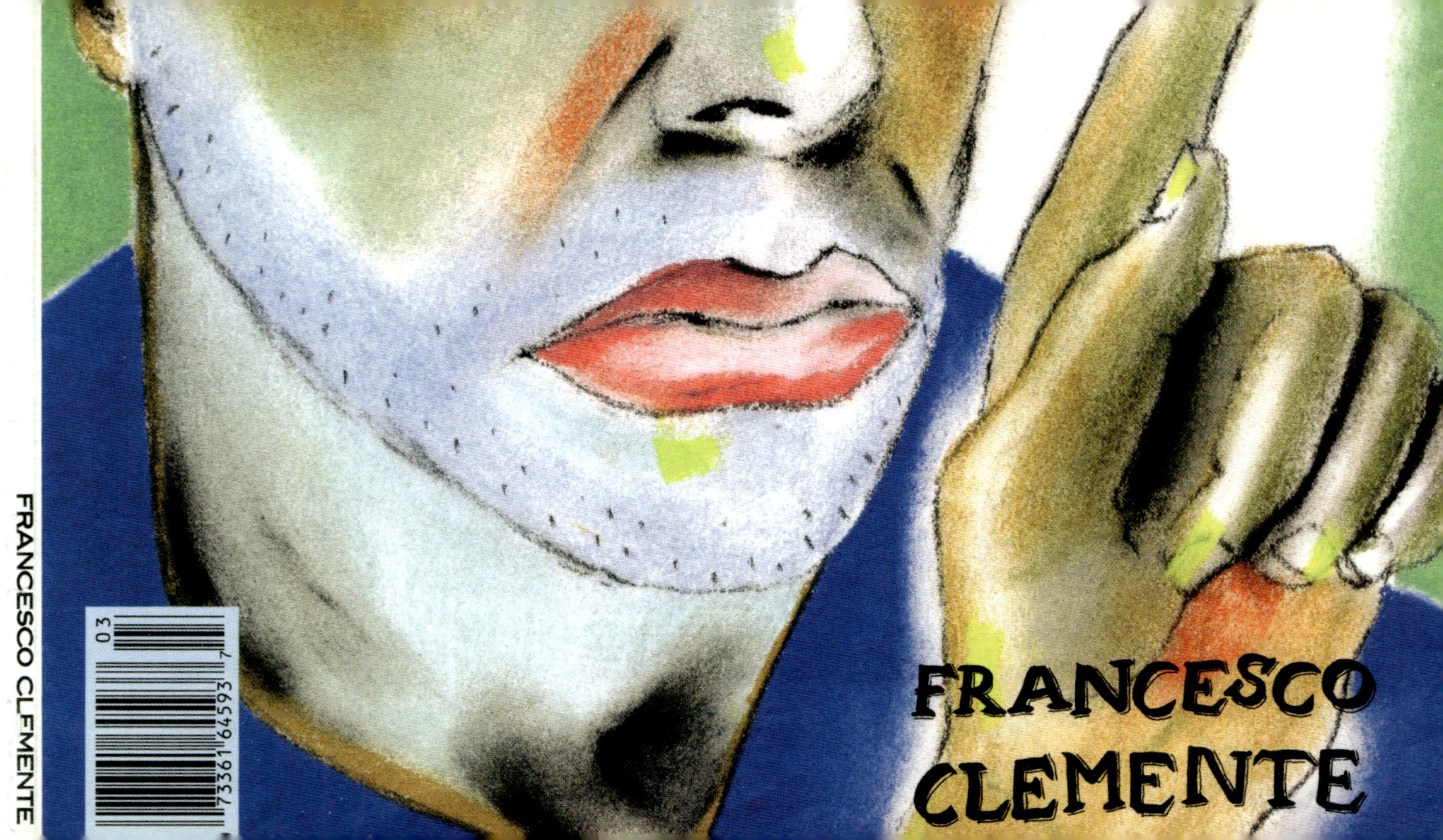

FRANCESCO CLEMENTE
03
73361 64593 7
FRANCESCO CLEMENTE

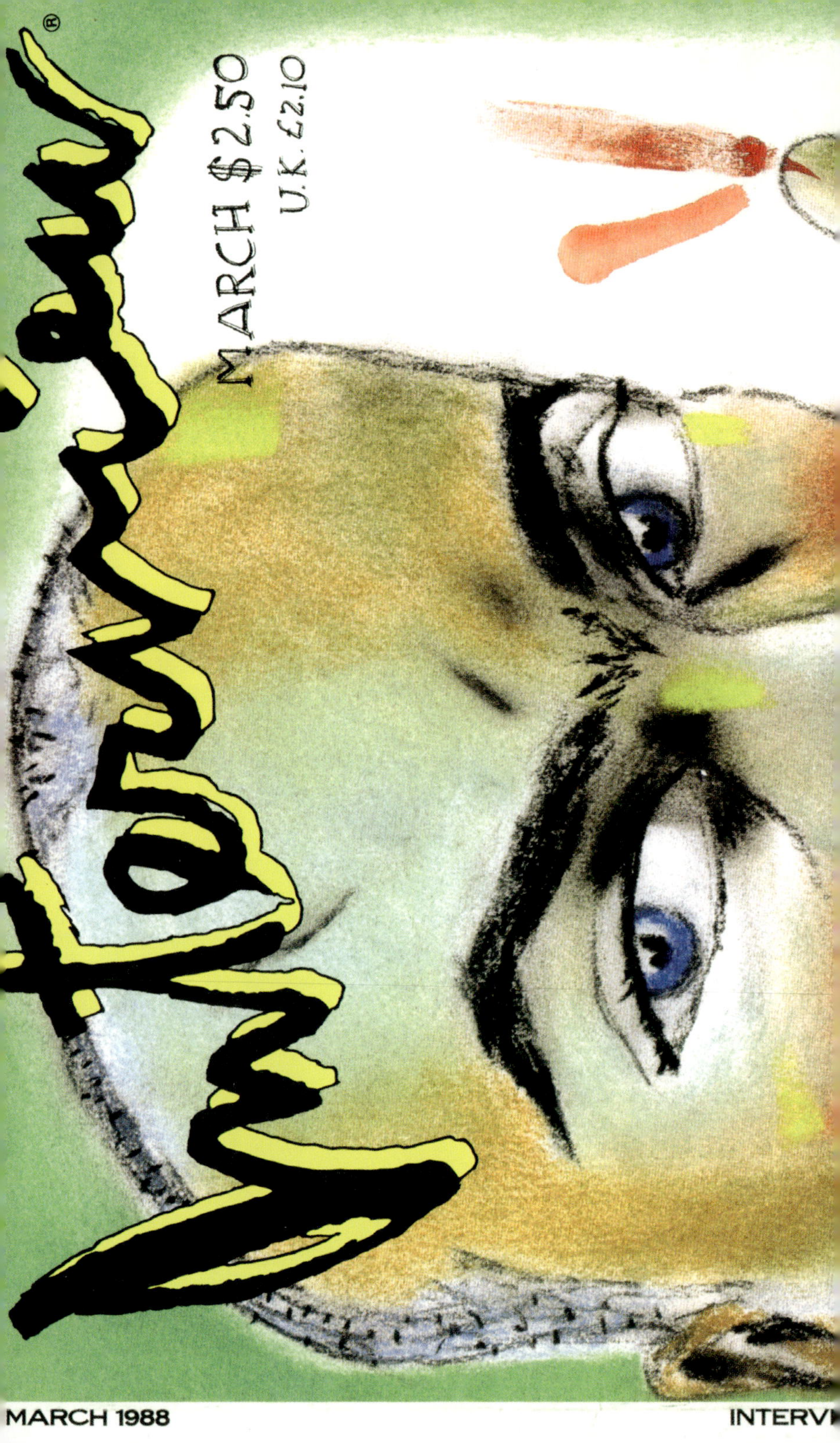

MARCH $2.50
U.K. £2.10
MARCH 1988
INTERVI

1989

* ZCZC PZB432 ZTH457 TTH33
* PARIS 026/024 01 1005

* JFB5437
* JEANNETTE MONTGOMERY
* C/O GALERIE SUSAN WYSS
* DIENERSTRASSE 16
* 8004/ZUERICH

* BEST WISHES FOR YOUR EXHIB
* NNNN

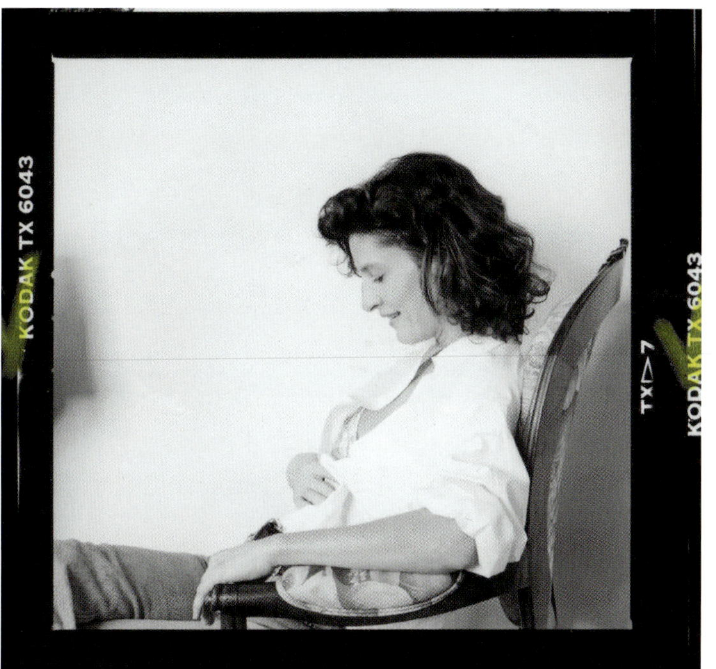

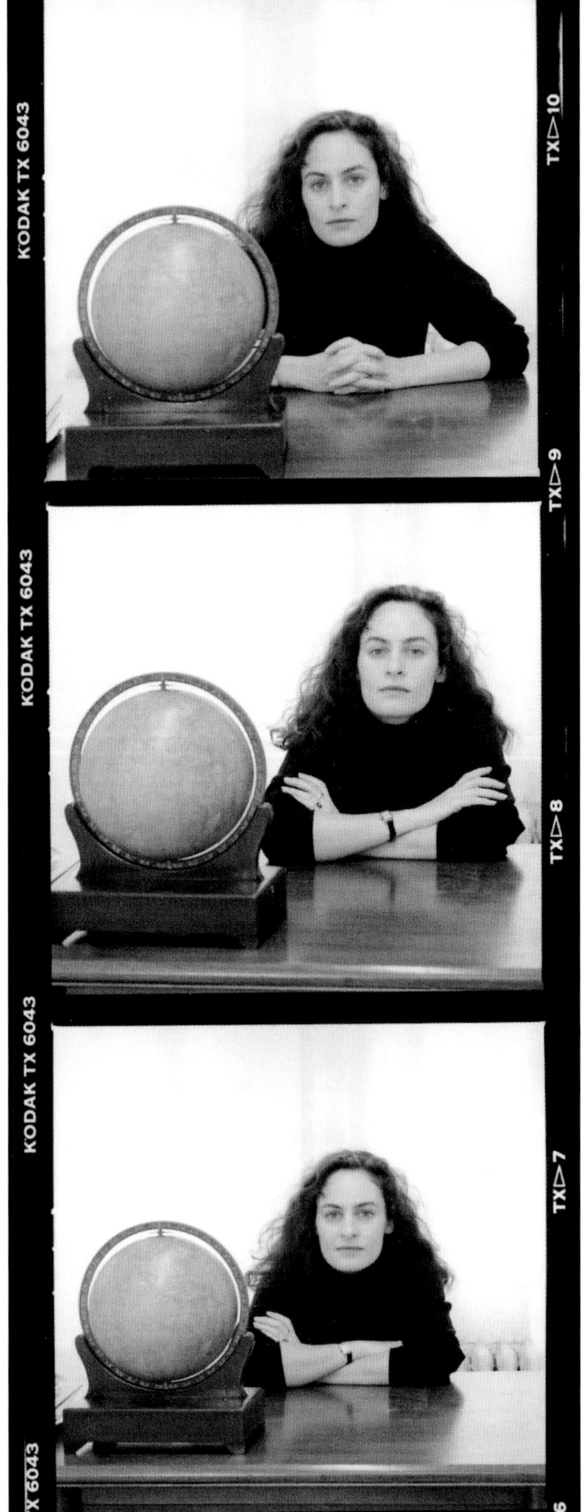

4/22/89

Dear Graneth—

Thanks so much for the photo. I am pleased.

There was a bill in envelope which is also enclosed.

Sincerely
Annette Lemieux

[A]nette Lemieux
[1]3 West 27th St. #1005
[N]C NY 10001

560 HARRISON AVE
4th FL·
~~59 Wareham St.~~
Boston MA 02118

After I got my BFA I went to New York and had a job with Jack Goldstein that didn't work out and then I called David (Salle) and said, «You know, I need work. Do you know anybody that wants an assistant?» And he said, «Yeah, me!» So I started working with him and probably most of the Mary Boone Gallery artists. As their assistant rather.
I learned a tremendous amount, you know, about being an artist, what it takes, what it isn't, what it is, I mean, it was a great education. Better than any MFA you could get.

… Me and Ross were, or are, friends. I haven't seen him in a while. It was a great experience. I don't' really know how to describe it, but you know I did other stuff, the other ridiculous stuff when I couldn't be an assistant, you know? I was a waitress, a bookkeeper, I did.
…It was a colorful beginning.

We all introduced each other to whatever dealer, etcetera. I mean, I think that's how it works. You know, artists say to their galleries, «Hey, you gotta check this out». You know, I don't think you get anywhere by sending your slides. It's a tribe and we all help each other because you believe in their work or their friendship or whatever.

What happened was—in the 1980s, the East Village, which was fantastic in terms of artists creating these tiny little storefront galleries, you know, I was hanging out with the gang and they knew my work and then one day, Cash/Newhouse asked me if I wanted to do a show, and I said yeah! So my first show was in '84 and everyone thought it was a group show because the work tends to be a bit eclectic for everyone's taste. It's nonlinear, you know?

And when I was in New York in the '80s and doing really well... You know, there's like a *zeitgeist* or a buzz in the air and everyone comes flocking.
But in the end, Emilio Mazzoli was my connection to Europe.

Annette Lemieux

Annette Lemieux
THE APPEARANCE OF SOUND

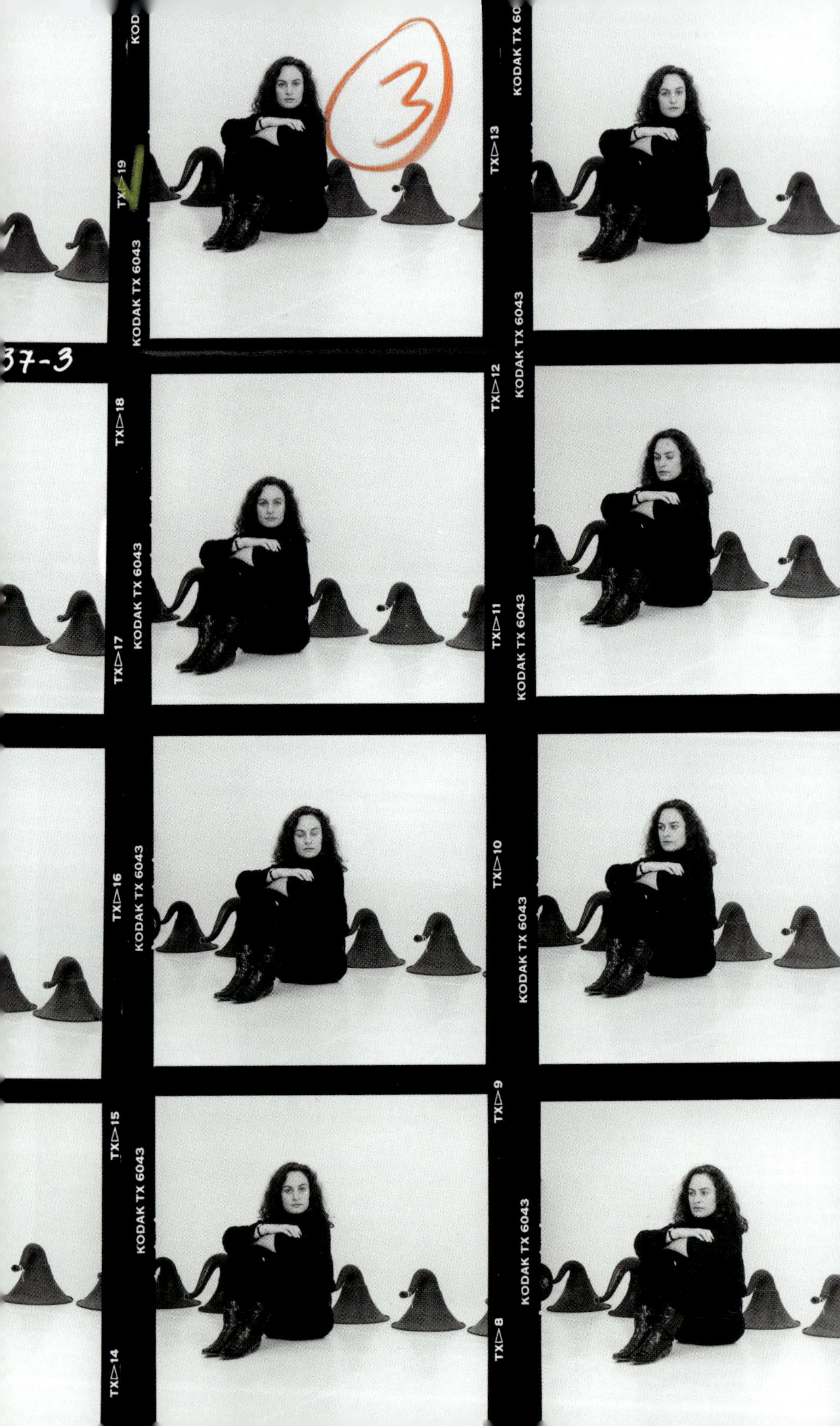

I was just inspired to finally write looking at one of the portraits
that Jeanette took of me, the straight on one in front of my
phonographs that would be later an installation work entitled
Tongues (I think that is the title, not sure). That day I was probably
feeling—how the hell did she hear about me?
Still feel the same, when someone calls they want to make contact
to take a photo or to discuss your work for a show, or for what
ever. To be included is *mirinda.*
I come from nothing, well, not completely, but you know what I
mean. I still feel this way when someone makes contact. What a
world I be in. And thankful that I am, and once again included.
Thank you Jeanette

Annette Lemieux

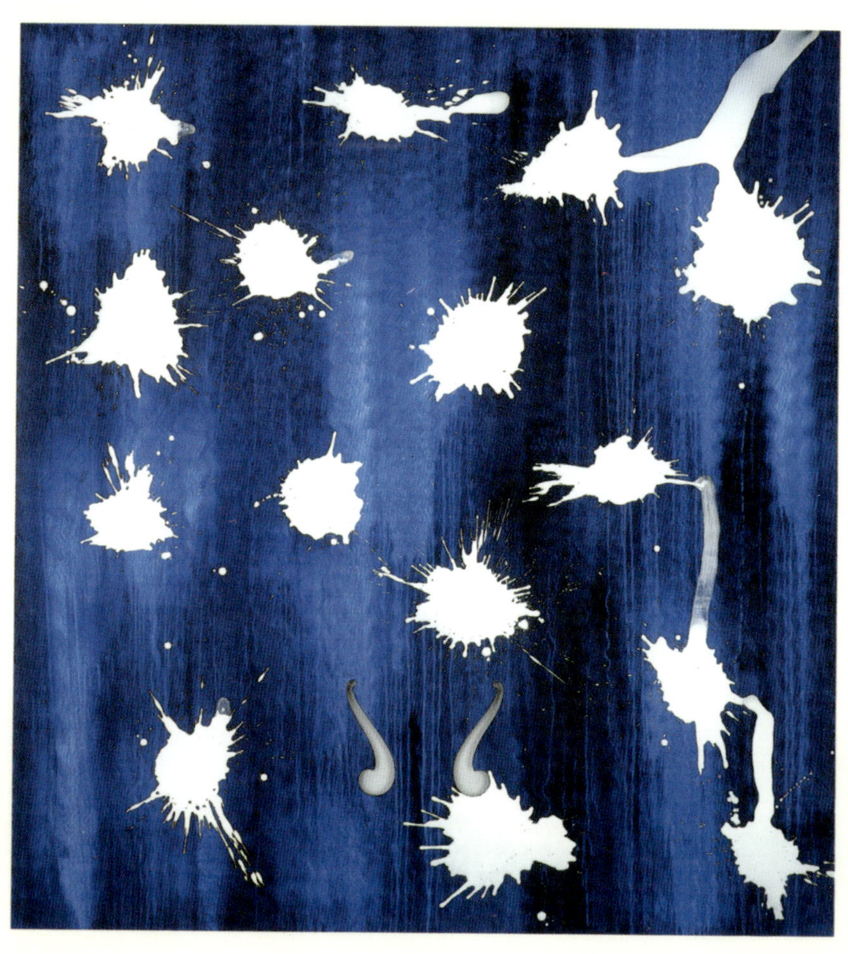

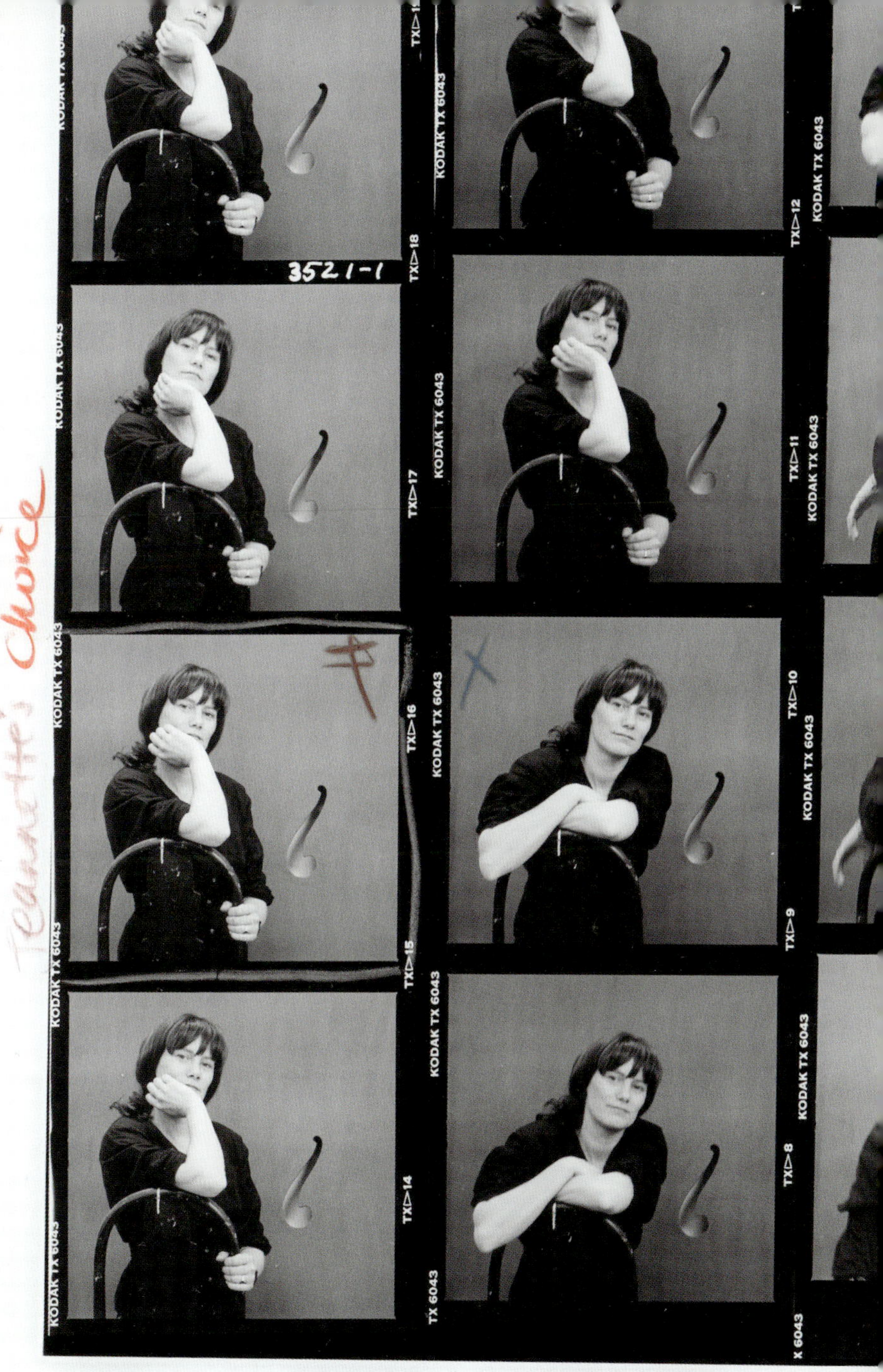

Jeanette's Choice
3521-1
KODAK TX 6043
TX▷18
TX▷17
TX▷16
TX▷15
TX▷14
KODAK TX 6043
TX▷12
TX▷11
TX▷10
TX▷9
TX▷8
KODAK TX 6043

Thomas Ammann

Dearest Jeannette,

Congratulations on your most wonderful book!
It really came out phantastic and I was thrilled
to receive a copy with your dedication.
Thank you very much!

Lots of love,

Also to James + baby!

Thomas

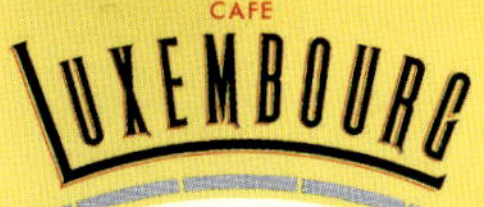

DINNER

IN HONOR OF
JEANNETTE MONTGOMERY BARRON

****

APPETIZERS

PEA SOUP WITH GARLIC CROUTONS

MIXED GREEN SALAD: Boston, romaine, chicory, arugola,
radicchio, endive, mache and frisee with a balsamic
vinaigrette

*****

HALF ROASTED CHICKEN, with steamed spinach and garlic
mashed potatoes

PASTA DU JOUR

SAUTEED JUMBO SEA SCALLOPS, with orzo and a piquant sauce

STEAK FRITES

*****

CREME BRULEE

APPLE AND DATE CRISP, with a vanilla and Calvados sauce

FRESH FRUIT, with either whipped cream or creme fraiche

COINTREAU

espresso, coffee, tea, cappuccino

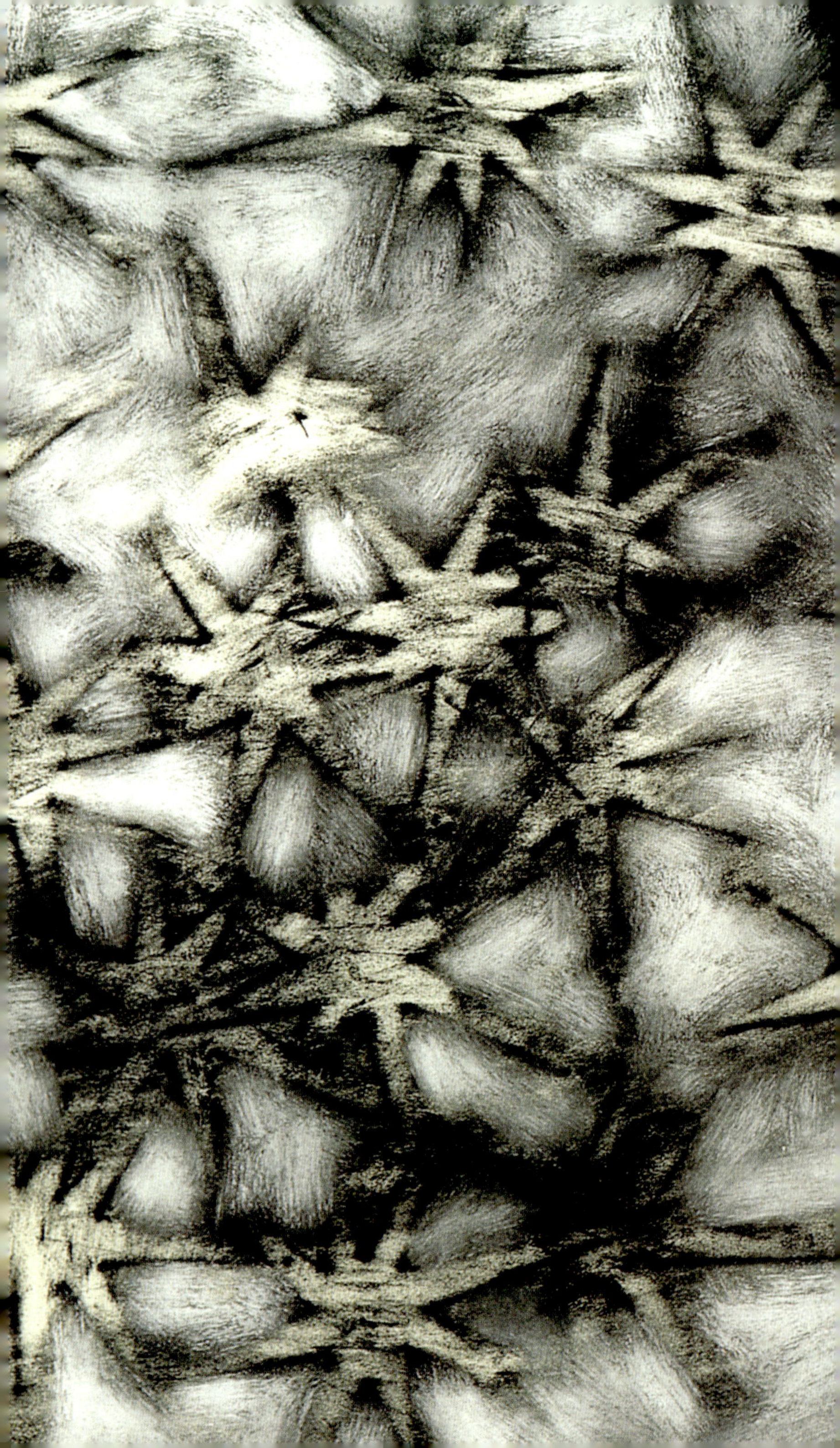

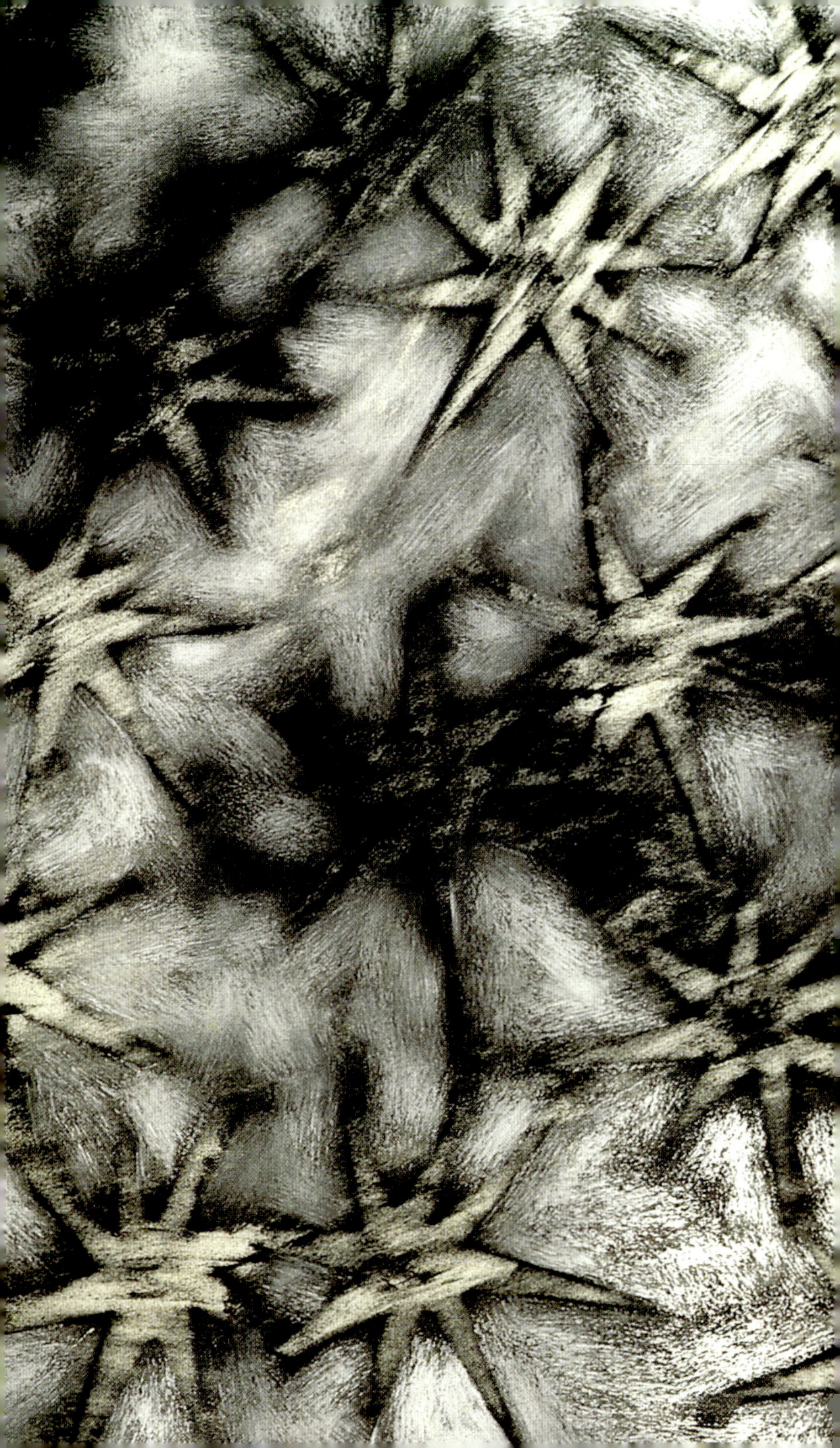

BY ELEANOR HEARTNEY

f us would have believed
Ginzel. When he and his
was working with elastic
ms within architectural
orate constructivist col-
lved, traveling to Italy
and unofficially sharing a
interests converging and
oving beyond advice and
5 Art Galaxy presented
as a team. It was an
was transformed into a
uous cycle from darkness
d lightning, and back to

ell known for their mys-
voke, through bursts of
and cascades of water, a
formation. The materials
markably prosaic—large
g fans, dry ice—mostly
Canal Street.
l expression seems less
about the death of the
sense of the artist as
sisted of closed systems
nlightenment God whose
Two recent works broke
d "Pananemone" (1987),
rom trees and 45 spheres
n downtown Manhattan;
ld and Figures," which
ere there was necessary
es, the effect was not of
er.
ature of their approach.
plicated and elaborate,"
here are two people."
s. "The pieces are based
situation and an under-

lationship that draws on
n has a more developed
. "She is concerned that
centrate on the concep-
why that glass vessel is

e less glamorous aspects

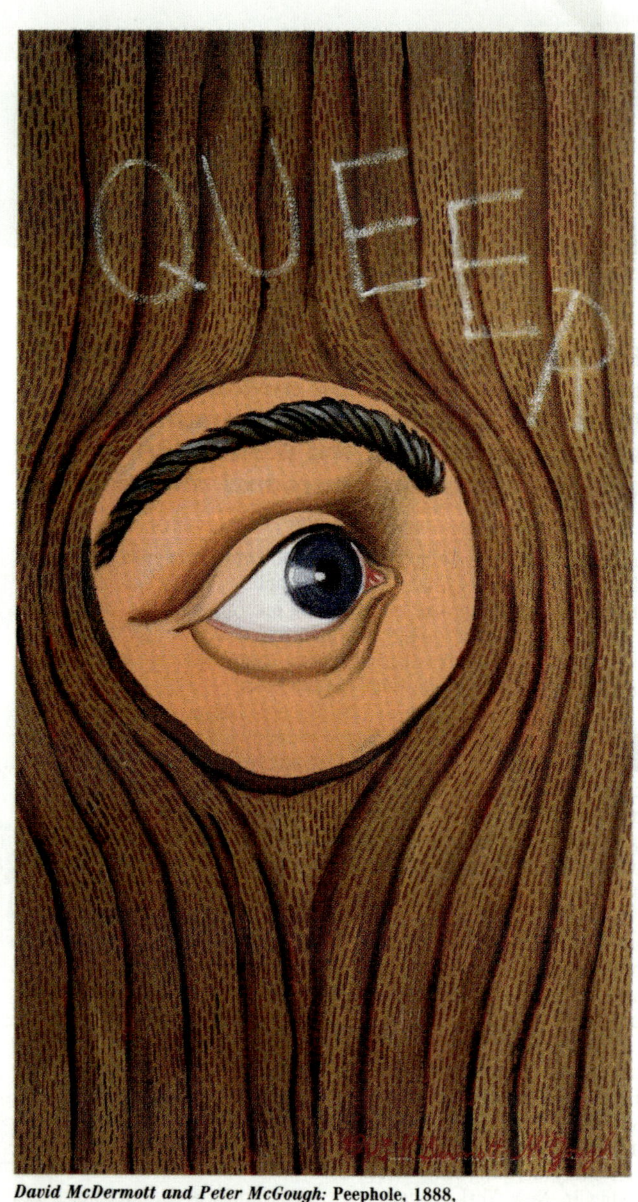

David McDermott and Peter McGough: **Peephole, 1888,**
1988, oil on linen, 24¼ by 13 inches.
Courtesy Galerie Bruno Bischofberger.

1

We needed a place to live. We had been forced out of our studio/
living space on the Bowery (half the roof leaked when it rained) by
our landlord Bradley Field, a well know musician/persona on the NYC
punk scene of Teen age Jesus and the Jerks, The Contortions, etc.
We found through our friend, the artist Nicolas Moufarrege, that
there was an apartment above him on Avenue C and 7th street in the
East Village-alphabet city.
The east village in the 1980's was a run down neighborhood that
resembled Berlin after the Second World War with bombed out
blocks of buildings. Ave C between 9th and 10th Street was flat dirt,
a full city block of emptiness.
People lined up on 7th street in the summer to buy drugs from a man
standing in a doorway. In the winter drugs were sold from and ice
cream truck playing the repetitive jingle outside our window through
out the night.
This is where we set up house. The first year no one visited.
Avenue A was OK to visit. Avenue B was a bit dicey. Avenue C-no
man's land, Avenue D- do not enter.

We took the two floors, lying to our landlord we had the money for
the rent and begun "de-vinylization," removing all modern elements.
Gone went the modern heaters (there were two fireplaces) out
with the modern kitchen. We built fireplace mantles with blue
police barricades we found in the street and marbleized them. We
wallpapered each room with "dollar a roll" 1930s reproduction of
Victorian patterns and then decorated with furniture from the trash
or antiques from flea markets. The furniture had to be kept from our
dreams of a mid 19th century "time machine/experiment" 1835 till
1865.
We read period books by candle light in front of the burning hearth.
We slept in night shirts and caps in foot high feather mattresses
made by Ishkabibble Iskowitz, the feather man of Ludlow St. He said
we were his best customers.

As our success grew from the sales of our paintings and
photographs we rented the Kings County Savings Bank in
Williamsburg Brooklyn, a Second Empire edifice on Broadway at
Bedford complete with a walk in safe.
First floor: offices. Second floor: painting studio. Third floor:
Photography studio.
We gave a grand ball (a recreation—well, our version—of Louise
Comfort Tiffany's Egyptian Fête) with a hand delivered invitation

stating «Only those dressed as in the time of Cleopatra will be admitted». An 18-piece dance orchestra was hired to play popular music from the 1910s. On another floor was an Arabic band complete with a belly dancer and 4 roaming peacocks. A 7-foot tall blackamoor in turban greeted guests standing between two burning urns of fire. They were really two city garbage can with wood from the street. "Anything Goes" was the theme of these two neighborhoods. No rich white person from the Upper East Side was coming here, unless for a "fix"–of many kinds.

Upstate we had our 1790 brick house that was never modernized. No heating, plumbing, or electricity. We went driving in our horse and carriage. Drove in our 1913 Model T Ford. Bathed in the creek behind the barns in the summer.
All this and more. Invites to sumptuous dinners, glittering celebrity and financial gain. We danced all through it. A never-ending champagne fountain of wonderment.
And then the financial crash of 1987 "Black Monday" came, followed by a visit from the IRS. A three day auction of our country house along with our cars, carriages, saddles, furniture, and our personal effects. Our own *Gone with the Wind*. Cut- end scene. That's were I'll end my story. It didn't kill us. It may have put a limp in our "two step" for a while. We regrouped, moved to Dublin, Ireland and are still working together after 33 years.
A lot of memories arise looking over Jeannette's photographs. So many young faces now older.
So many stories. Some with happy trails, and others, dead ends. I remember it well.

Peter Mc Gough

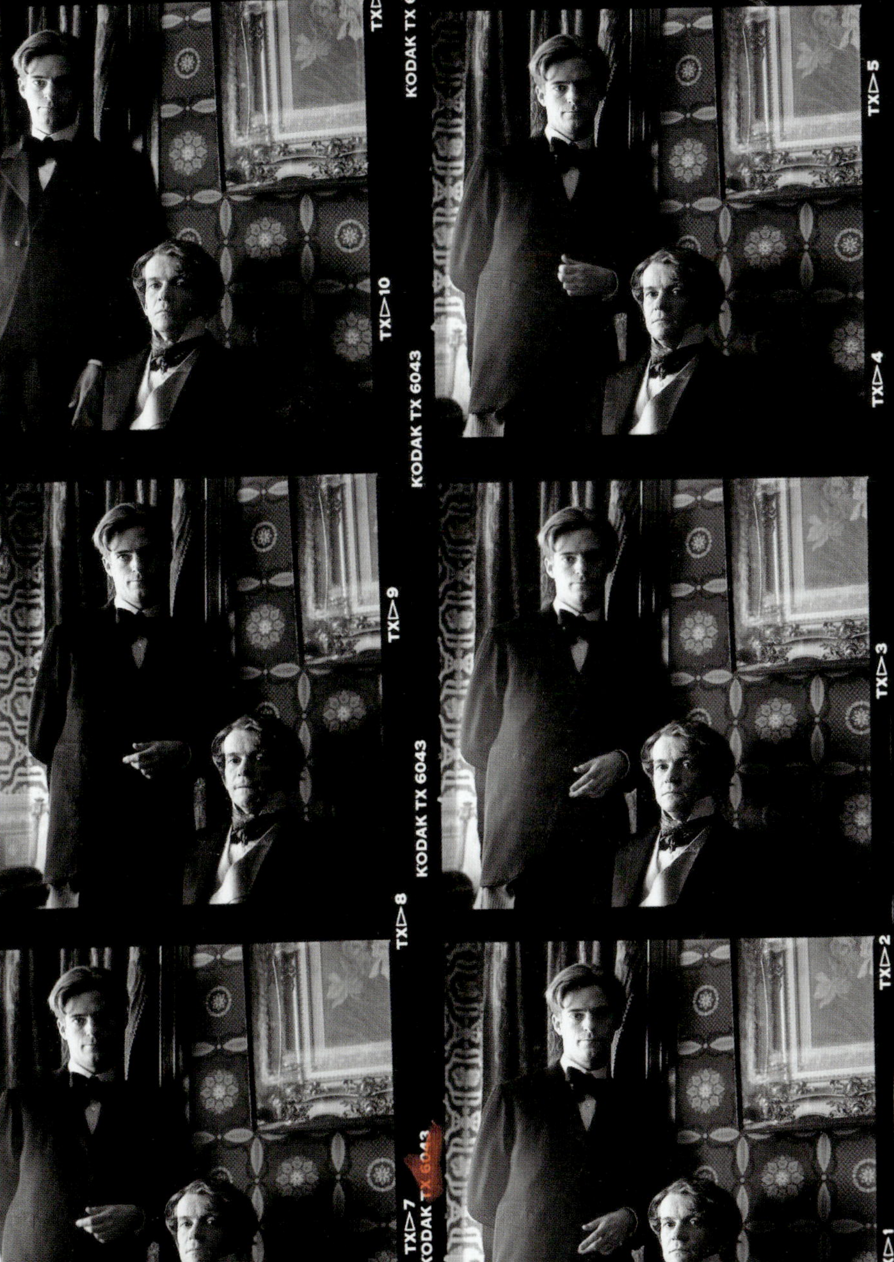

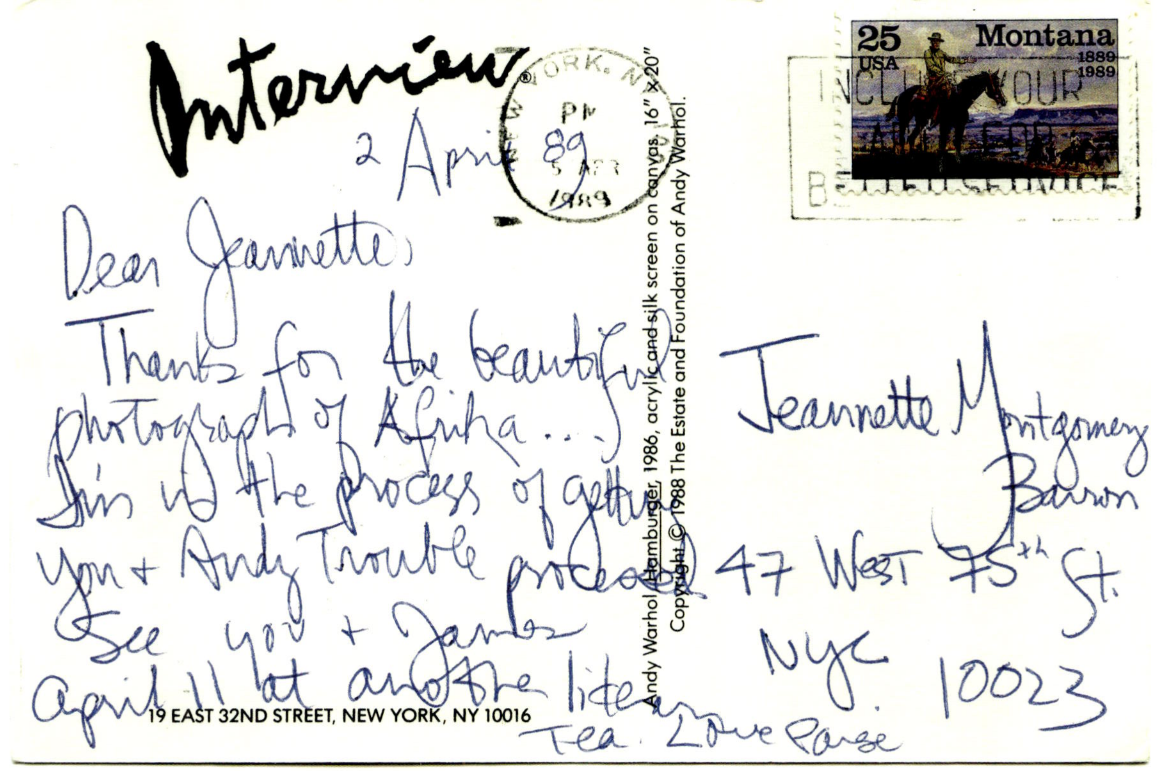

Andy Warhol, Hamburger, 1986, acrylic and silk screen on canvas, 16" x 20"
Copyright © 1988 The Estate and Foundation of Andy Warhol.

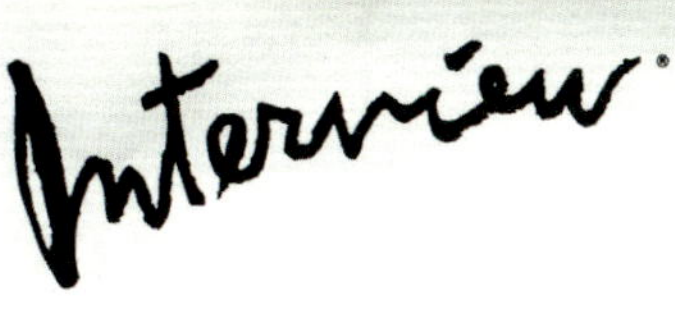

gust 31, 1989

anette Montgomery
W. 74th Street
w York, NY 10023

ar Jeanette,

think you should have these gloves; they were given to me by
e artist Dale Chihuly, who I think you should photograph. I
ught the gloves would make an appropriate part of your Western
llection.

ve,

ige

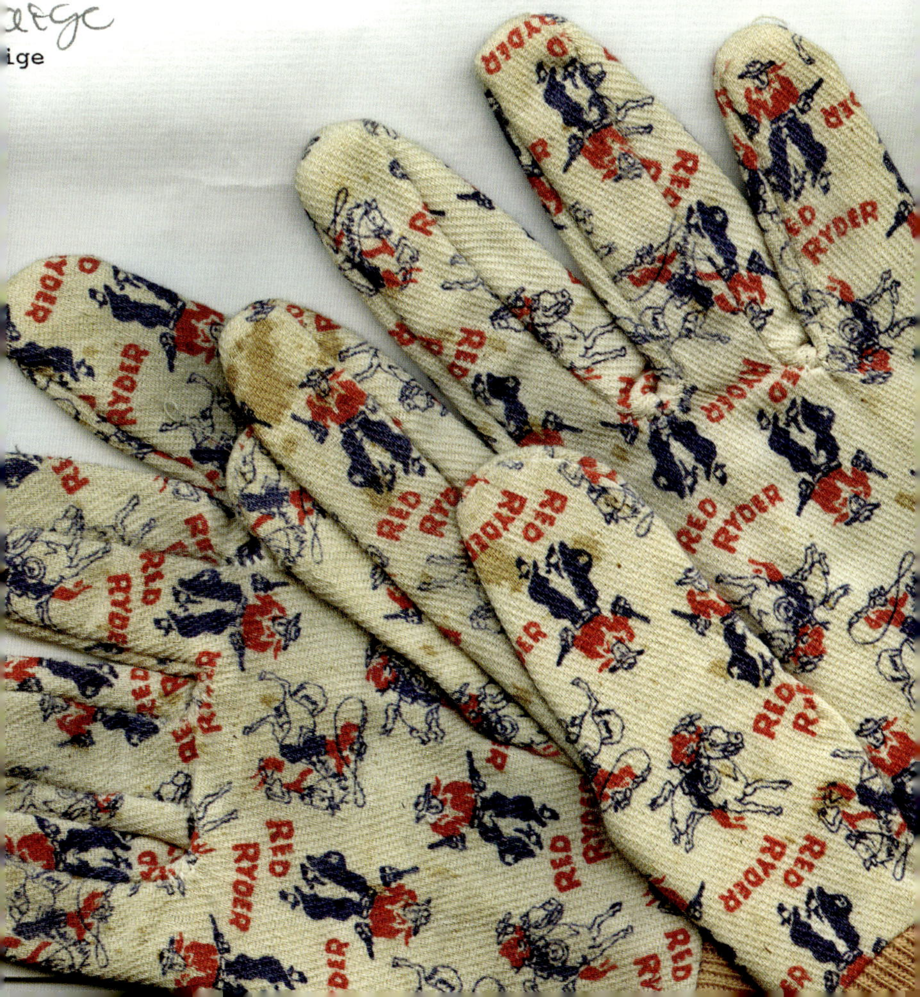

3606-2

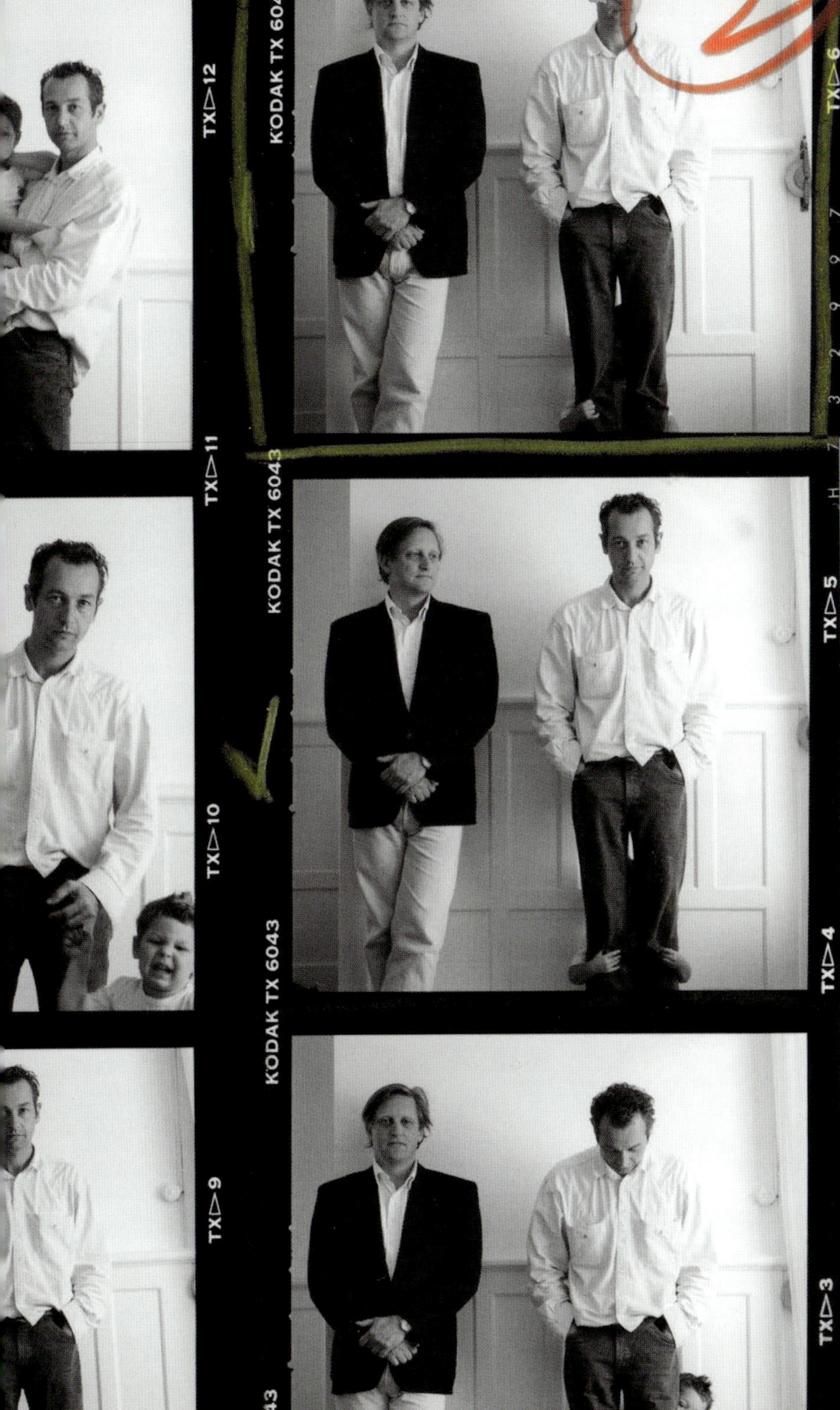

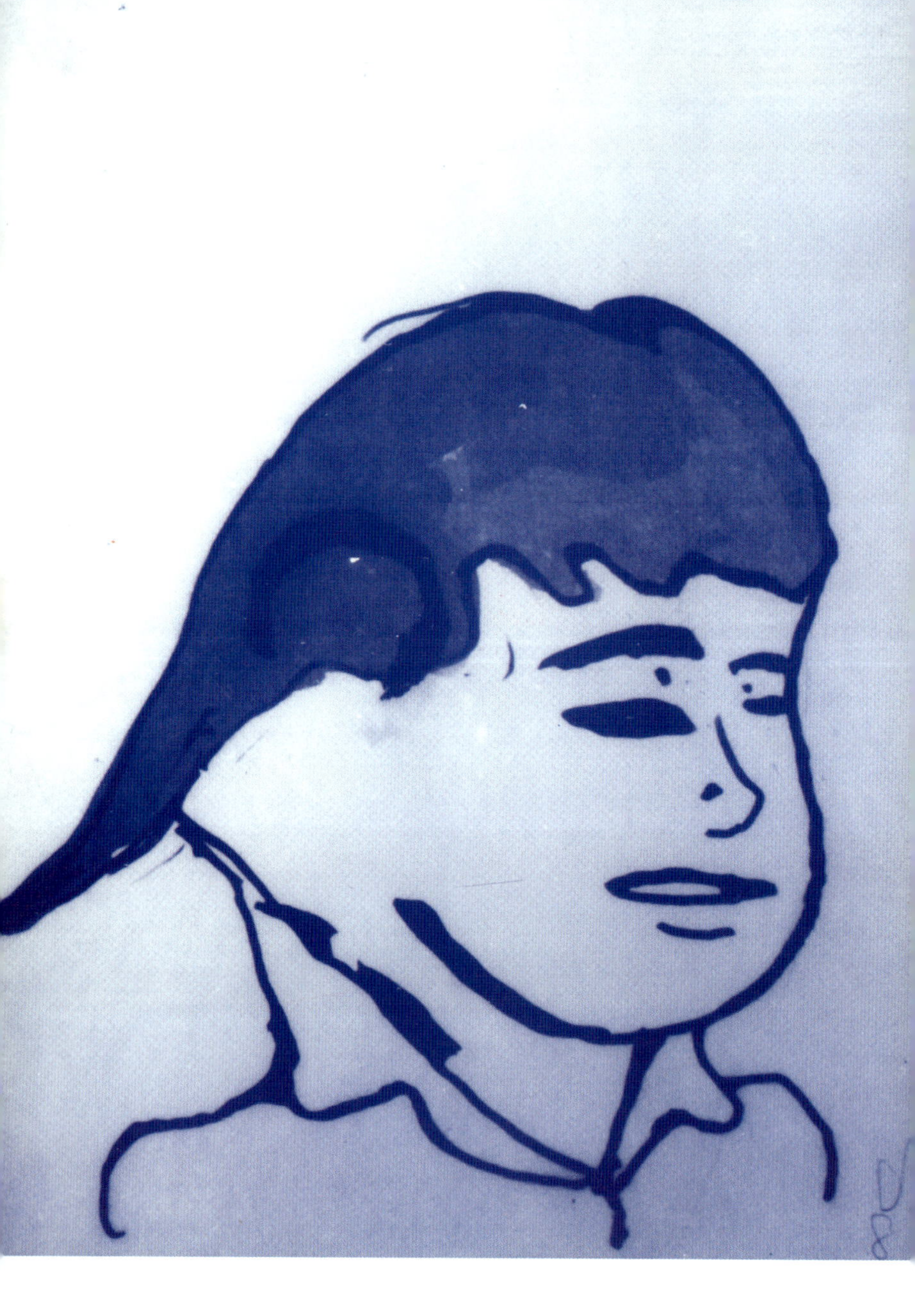

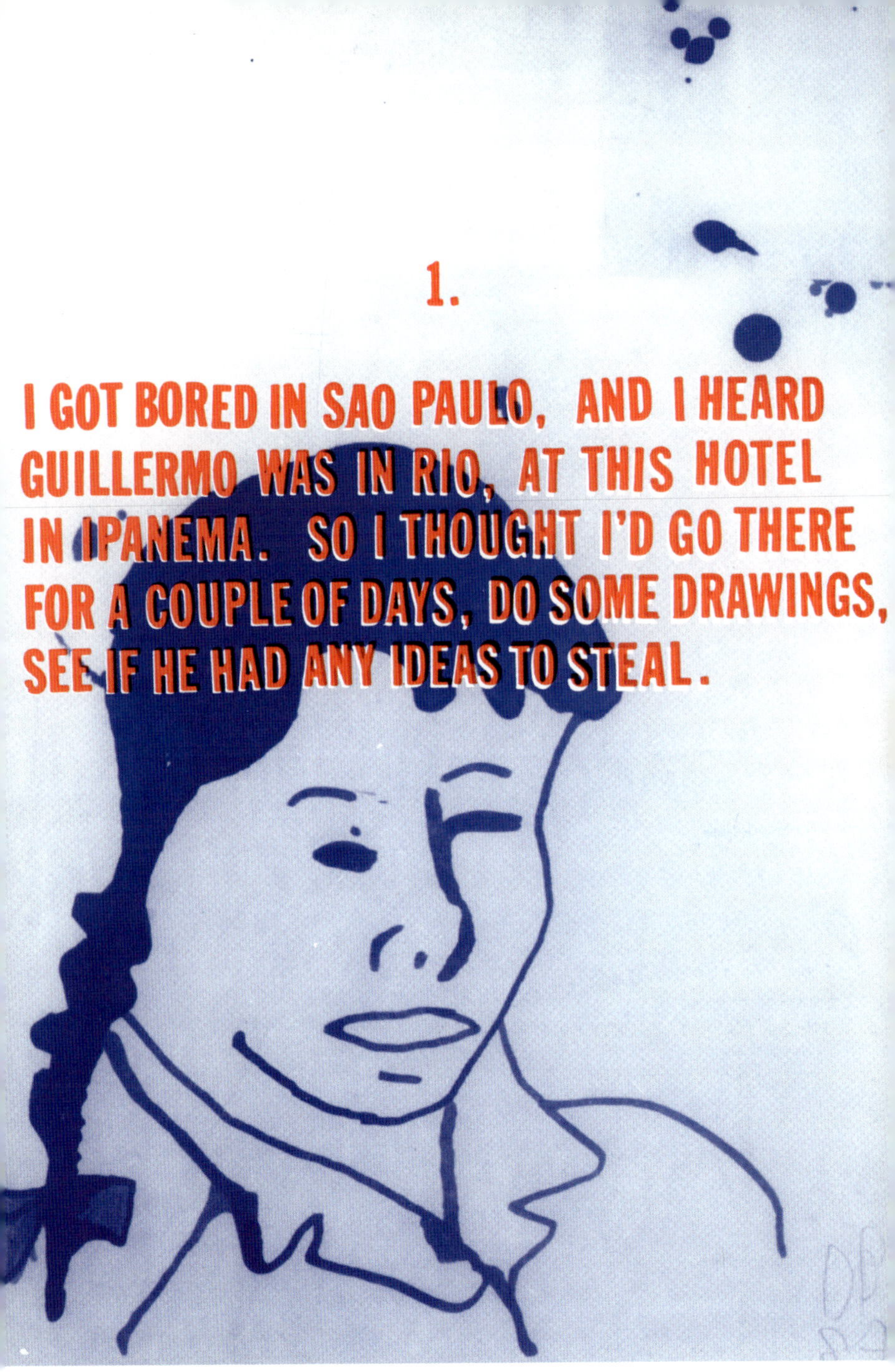

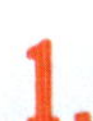

1.

I GOT BORED IN SAO PAULO, AND I HEARD
GUILLERMO WAS IN RIO, AT THIS HOTEL
IN IPANEMA. SO I THOUGHT I'D GO THERE
FOR A COUPLE OF DAYS, DO SOME DRAWINGS,
SEE IF HE HAD ANY IDEAS TO STEAL.

TOMPKINS PARK

Four skin heads stand
in the streetlight rain talking
under an umbrella

-Allen Ginsberg

GRANDMOTHER

Her hands, blue roadmaps
veins of the white tulip
are braiding my hair.

-Kathryn McDonald

TELEGRAM TO MYSELF

Congrats on death of lover   stop
making of history   stop
walking away

-Jennifer Joseph

said no to six panhandlers-
        lonely sneakers
down the steps of the Bart station

-Jim Vallely

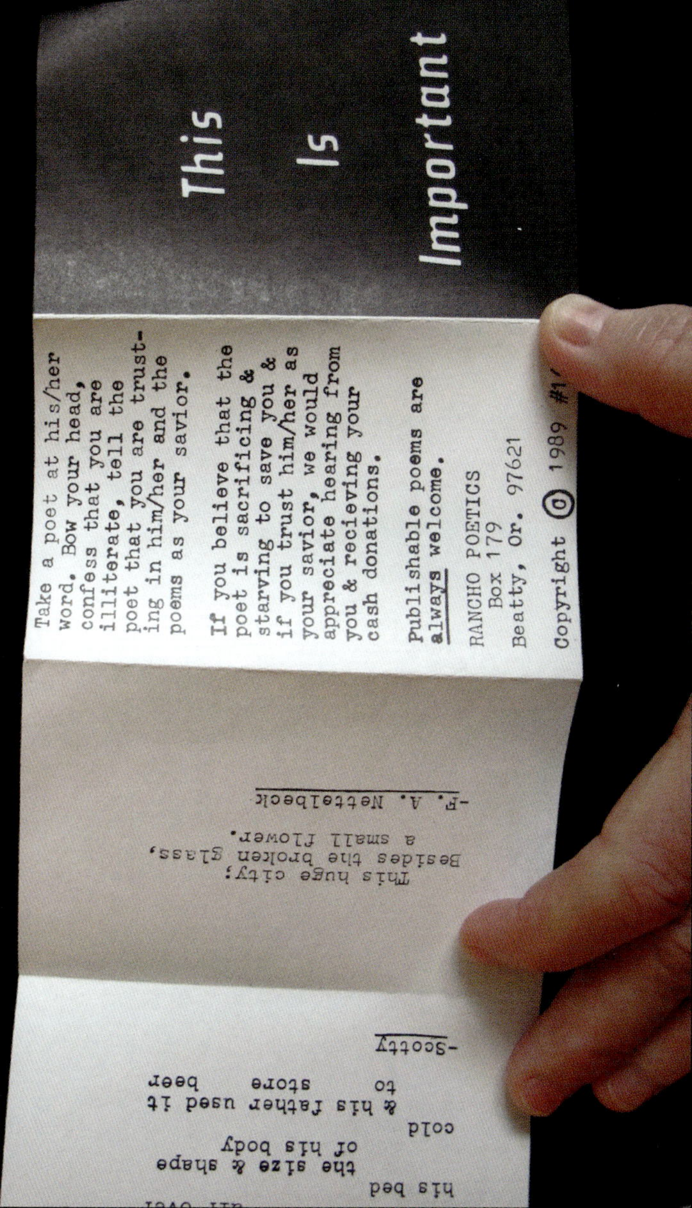

his bed
        the size & shape
        of his body
cold
        & his father used it
to   store   beer

        -Scotty

This huge city;
Besides the broken glass,
a small flower.

                -F. A. Nettelbeck

Take a poet at his/her
word. Bow your head,
confess that you are
illiterate, tell the
poet that you are trust-
ing in him/her and the
poems as your savior.

If you believe that the
poet is sacrificing &
starving to save you &
if you trust him/her as
your savior, we would
appreciate hearing from
you & recieving your
cash donations.

Publishable poems are
always welcome.

RANCHO POETICS
    Box 179
Beatty, Or. 97621

Copyright © 1989 #1

This

Is

Important

1990's

KADDISH

AND OTHER POEMS

1958-1960

ALLEN GINSBERG

'— Die,
If thou wouldst be with that which thou dost seek ! '

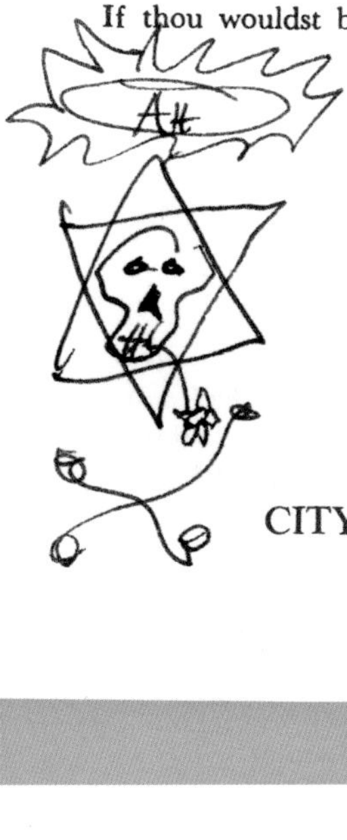

CITY LIGHTS BOOKS

San Francisco in the mid-1950's
Photo by Arthur Winfield Knight

2/4/91

Dear Janet —
Here's some photos
from the visit — drugstore
prints! —
Allen Ginsberg

© 1986 the unspeakable visions of the individual
P.O. Box 439, California, PA 15419

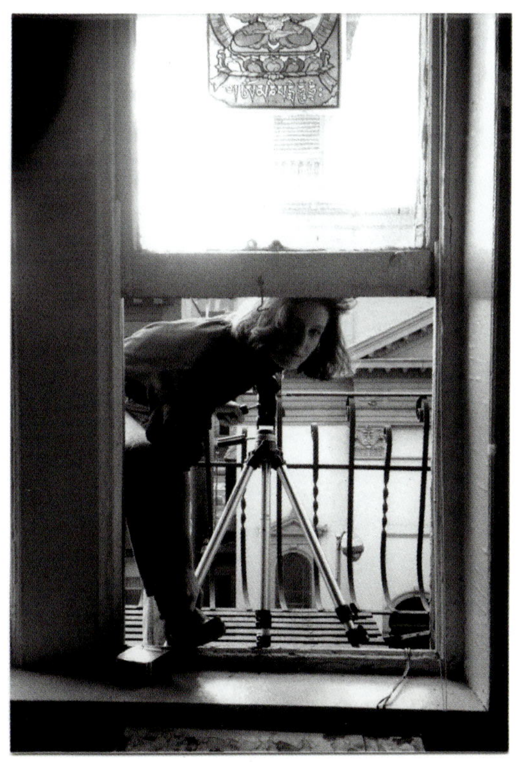

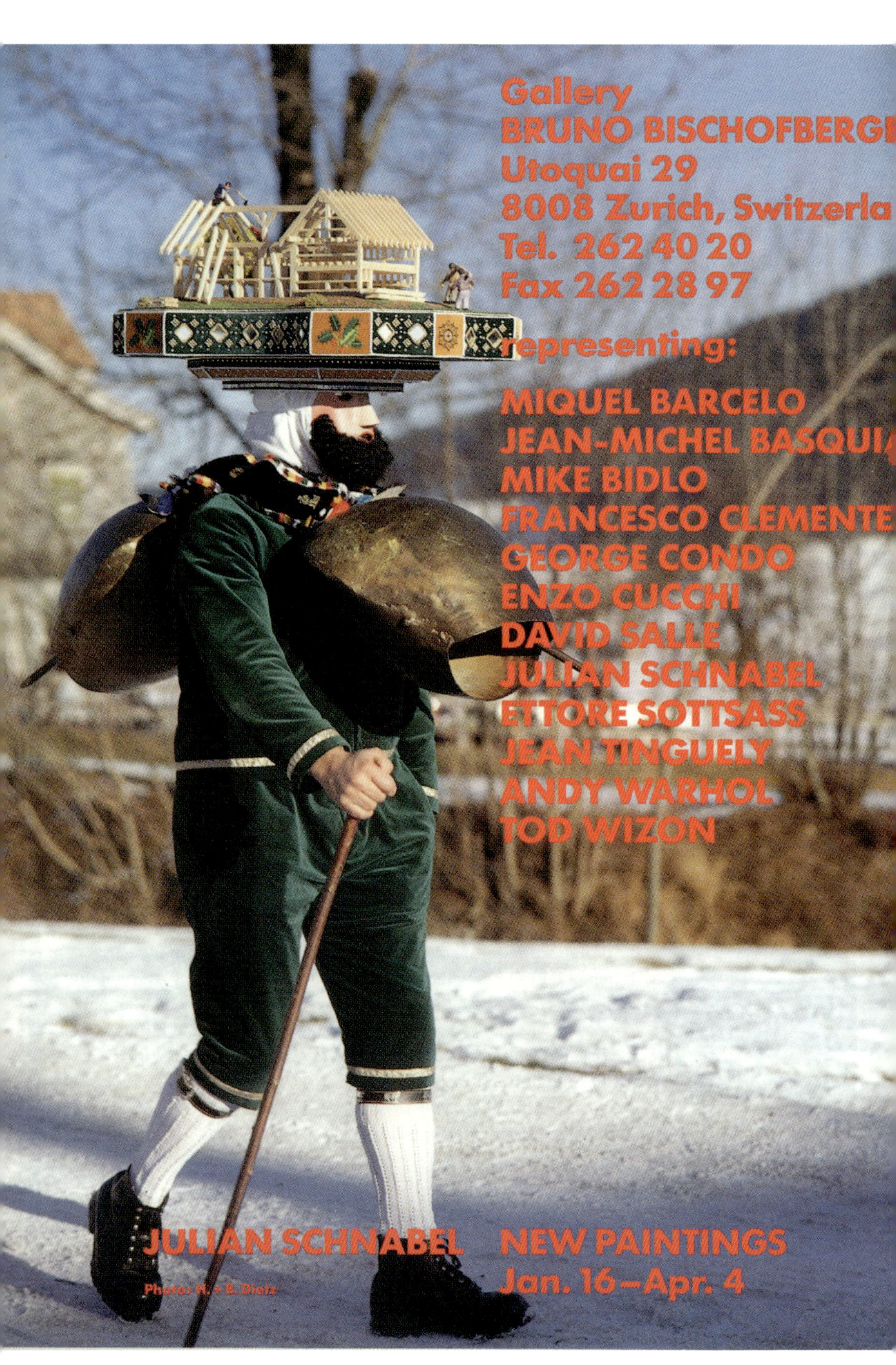

Gallery
BRUNO BISCHOFBERGER
Utoquai 29
8008 Zurich, Switzerla
Tel. 262 40 20
Fax 262 28 97

representing:

MIQUEL BARCELO
JEAN-MICHEL BASQUIAT
MIKE BIDLO
FRANCESCO CLEMENTE
GEORGE CONDO
ENZO CUCCHI
DAVID SALLE
JULIAN SCHNABEL
ETTORE SOTTSASS
JEAN TINGUELY
ANDY WARHOL
TOD WIZON

JULIAN SCHNABEL   NEW PAINTINGS
Jan. 16 – Apr. 4

Photo: H. + B. Dietz

St. M   Feb 92

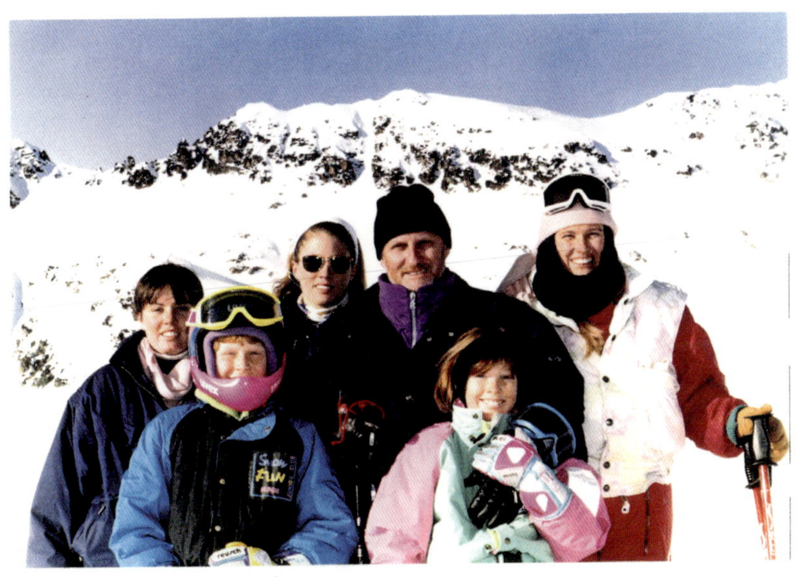

Dear Jeanette and James

thank-you so much for the Dennis
Hopper photograph - Did you know
Julian wants Dennis to play Bruno in
the Jean-Michel movie ......!!!
will be in NY in May - have not worked
on the stone project except for in
my brain and its crystalizing slowly

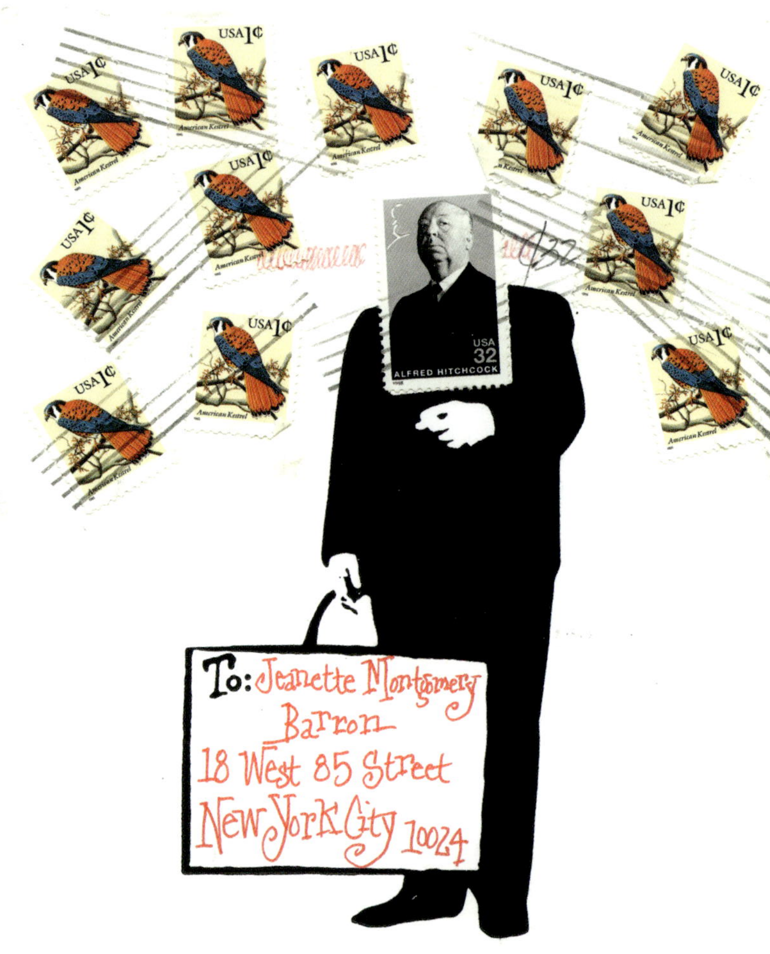
USA 1¢
American Kestrel
ALFRED HITCHCOCK
USA 32
To: Jeanette Montgomery
Barron
18 West 85 Street
New York City 10024

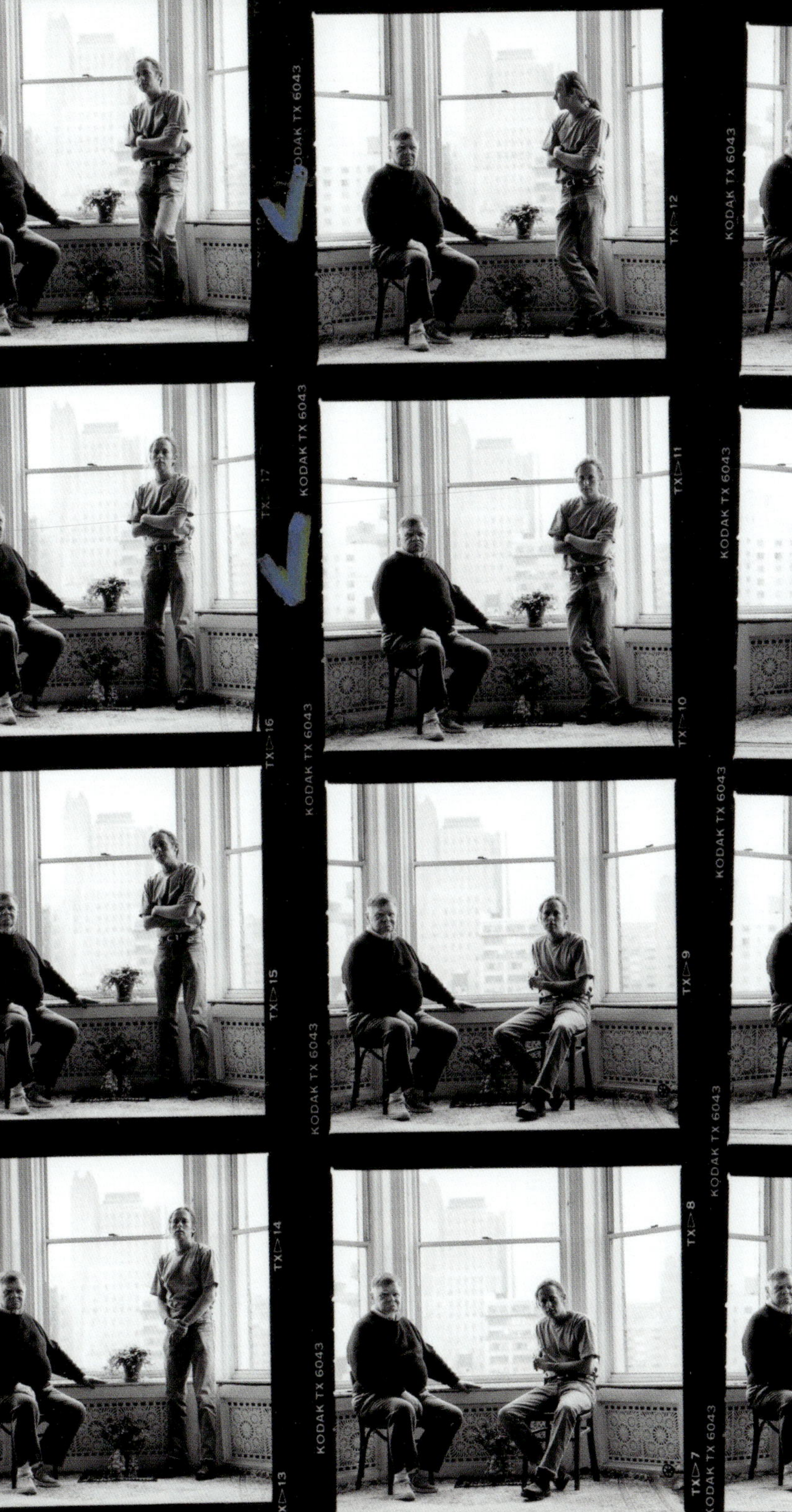

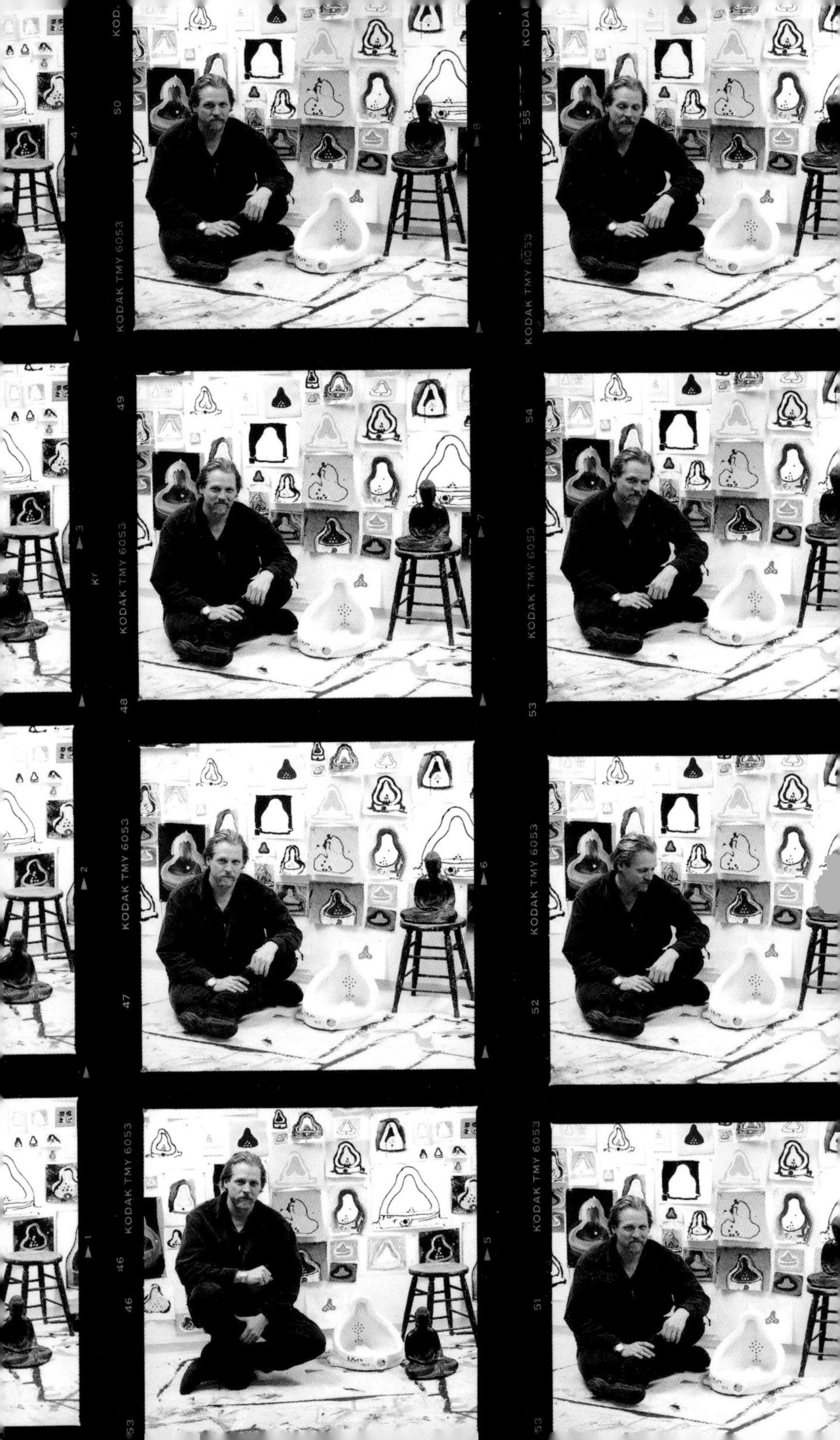

BEWARE!
JEANETTE MONTGOMERY
BARRON HAS A PHOTOGRAPH2
MEMORY...
LIKE MARCEL PROUST
SHE LITERALLY FOCUSES
ON HER SOCIETY AND
SURROUNDINGS WITH
BEWITCHING, BEGUILING
AND BEMUSING CLARITY

MIKE BIDLO

And now I finally understand
What I did in the 1980's

John Ahearn: pp. 78-79
Thomas Ammann: pp. 15-16, 42
Viva Auder: p. 40
Donald Baechler: p. 51
James Barron: p. 56
Jean-Michel Basquiat: pp. 64, 66, 69
Heiner Bastian: pp. 26-27
Mike Bidlo: p. 160
Kathryn Bigelow: p. 5
Bruno and YoYo Bischofberger and family: p. 157
Ross Bleckner: p. 105
Boy George: pp. 46-47
James Brown: p. 111
Matthias Brunner: p. 15, 42
William Burroughs: p. 89
Sandro Chia: pp. 26-27
Francesco Clemente: pp. 10, 12-13, 124-125 (studio)
Quentin Crisp: pp. 46-47
Enzo Cucchi: pp. 96-97
Willem Dafoe: pp. 8-9
Walter Dahn: p. 38
Moira Dryer: p. 137
Eric Fischl: pp. 32-33
Raymond Foye: p. 159
Leon Golub: p. 86
Peter Halley: p. 103
Keith Haring: pp. 46-47, 72-73
Gaby Hoffman: pp. 40, 42
Fatima Igramhan: p. 38
Bianca Jagger: pp. 36, 46-47
Alex Katz: p. 92
Barbara Kruger: p. 107
Jan Krugier: p. 56
Annette Lemieux: pp. 130, 134
Marilyn (Peter Robinson): pp. 46-47

David McDermott and Peter McGough: p. 145
Monty Montgomery: p. 6
Jeannette Montgomery Barron: pp. 4, 7, 11 (by Francesco Clemente), 15, 31, 41-42, 54, 90-91 (by David Seidner), 129 (by Edit deAk), 155 (by Allen Ginsberg)
Wolfgang Müller: p. 38
Luigi Ontani: pp. 59-60
Rene Ricard: p. 59
David Salle: p. 74
Salomé: p. 39
Samia Saouma: p. 10
Kenny Scharf: p. 85
Julian Schnabel: p. 52
James Schuyler: p. 159
David Shapiro: p. 83
Cindy Sherman: pp. 62-63
Mike and Doug Starn (The Starn Twins): pp. 108-109
Philip Taaffe: p. 112
Rigoberto Torres: pp. 78-79
Andy Warhol: pp. 46-47, 64, 66
David Weiss and Peter Fischli and son: pp. 148-149

Opere dalla collezione
Works from the collection

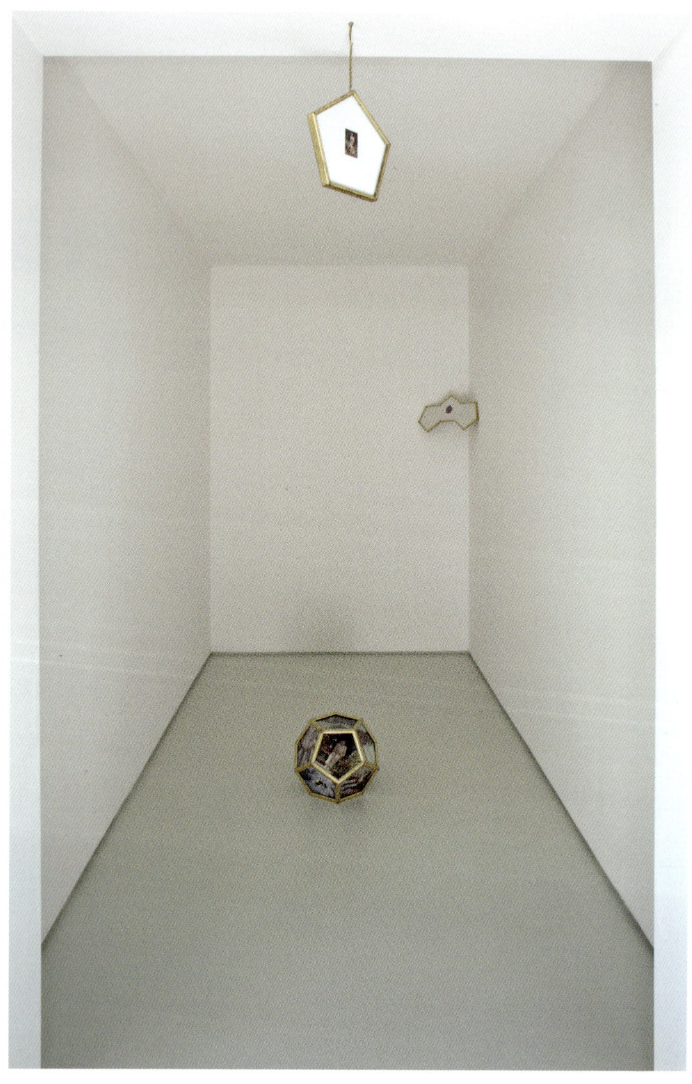

Luigi Ontani
Pentagonia
1979

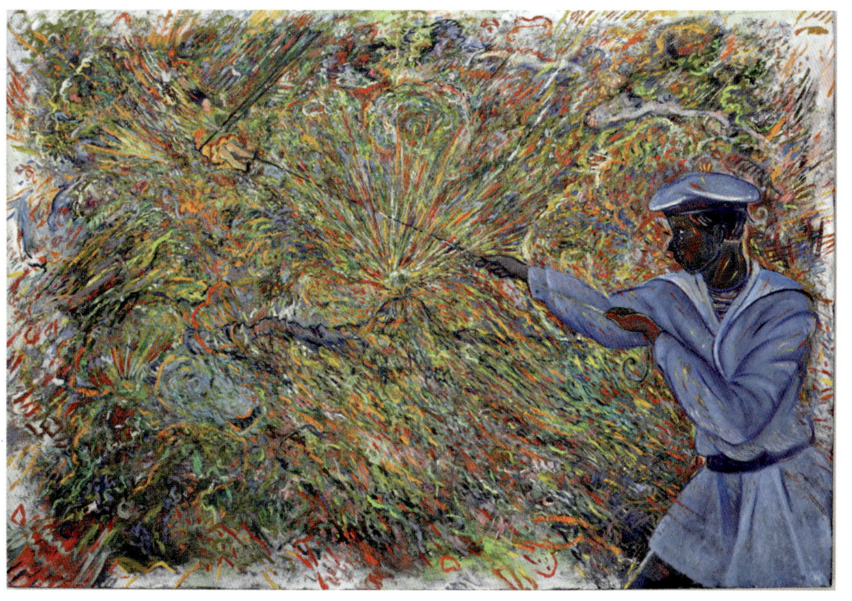

Sandro Chia
La cucina di Dioniso
1980

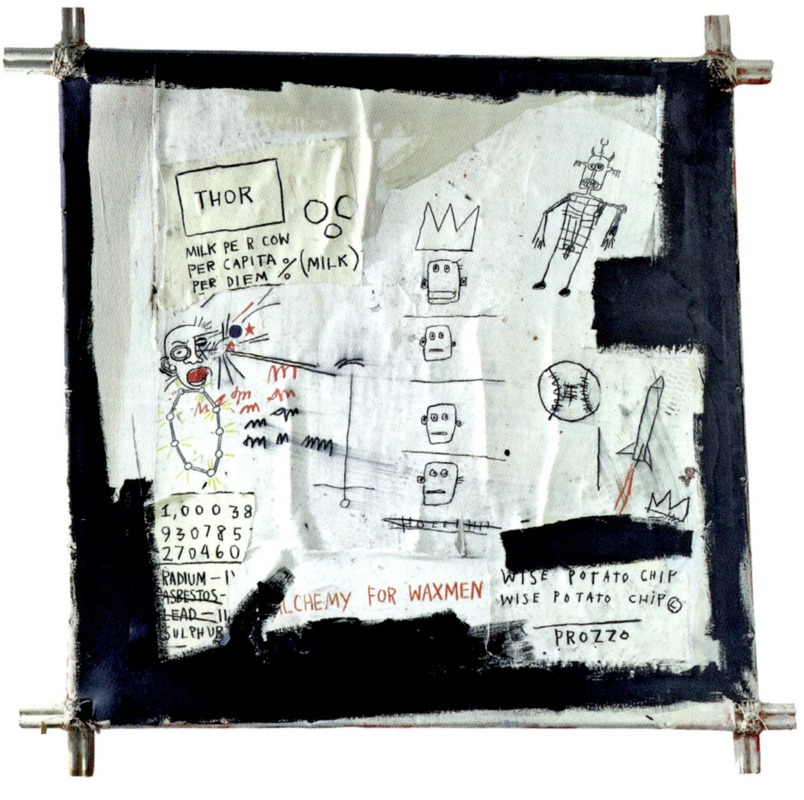

Jean-Michel Basquiat
Alchemy for Waxmen
1982

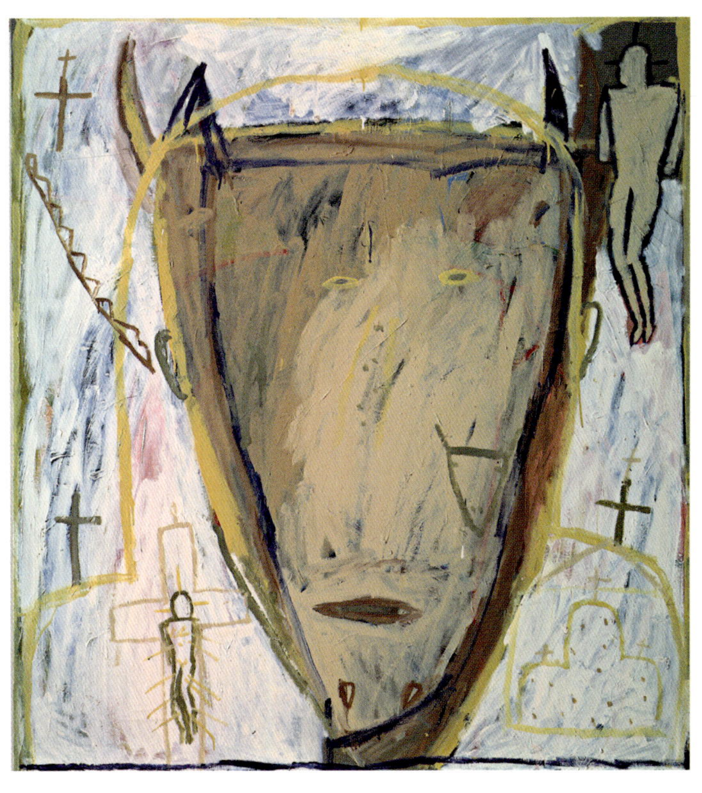

James Brown
Self-Portrait
1982

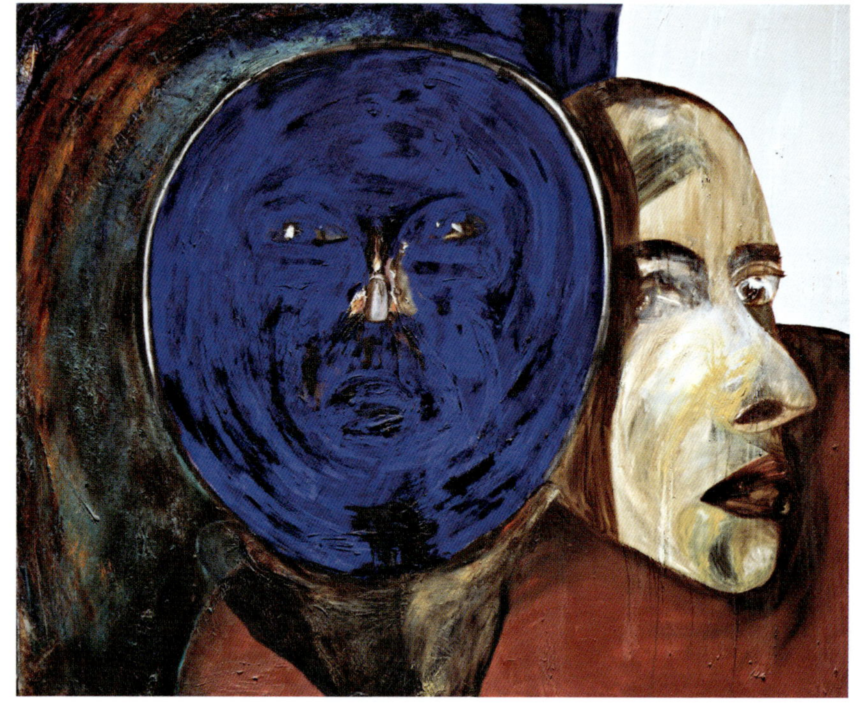

Francesco Clemente
Untitled
1983

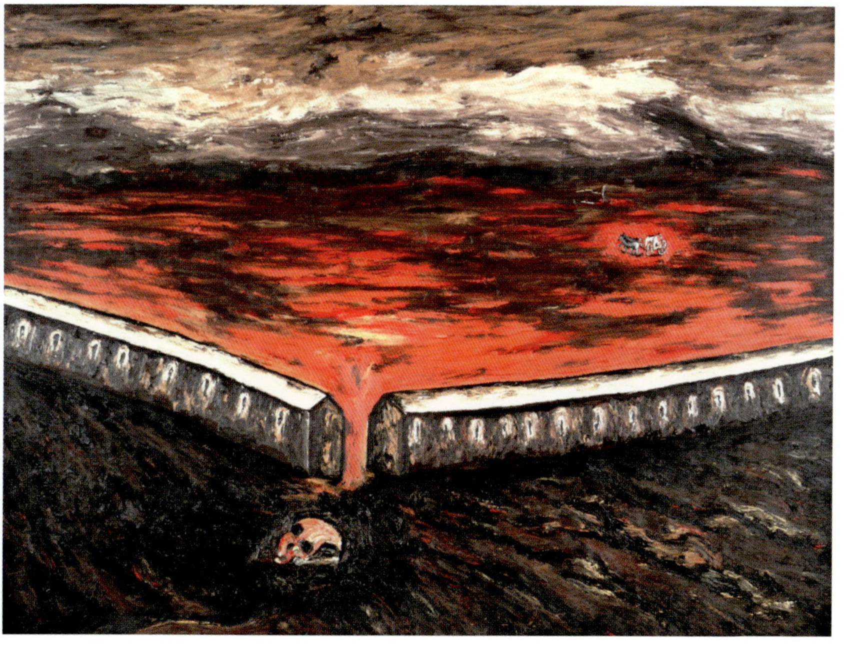

Enzo Cucchi
Le case vanno in discesa
(The Houses are going downhill)
1983

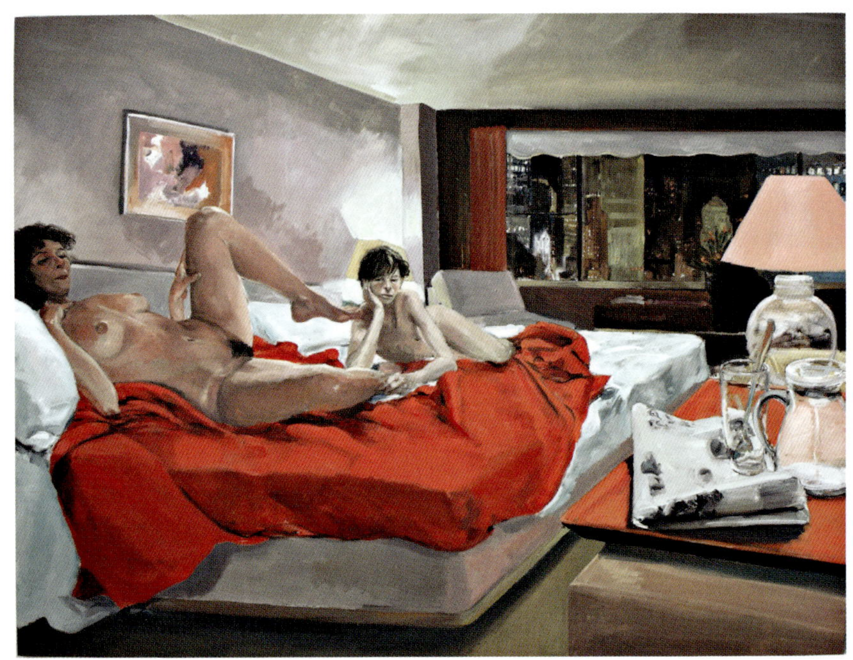

Eric Fischl
Birthday Boy
1983

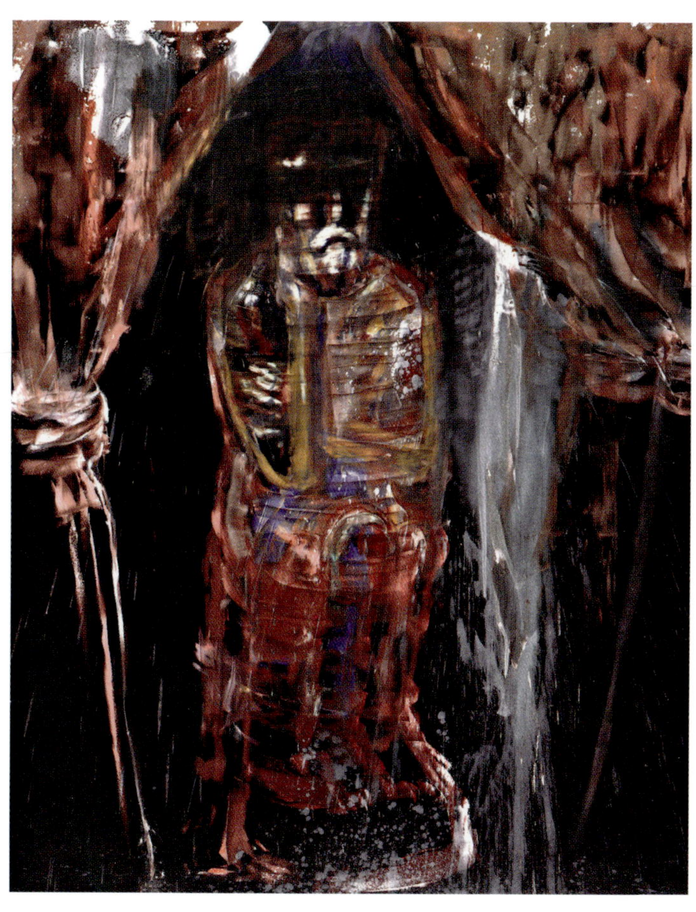

Julian Schnabel
Man of Sorrow (The King)
1983

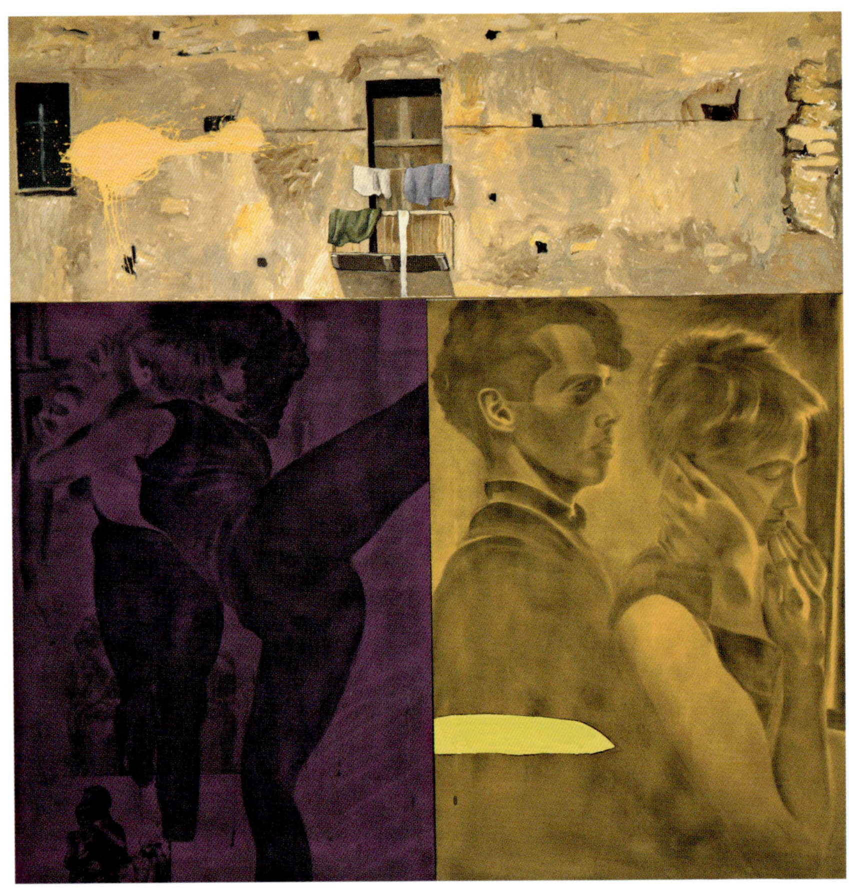

David Salle
The Farewell Painting
1985

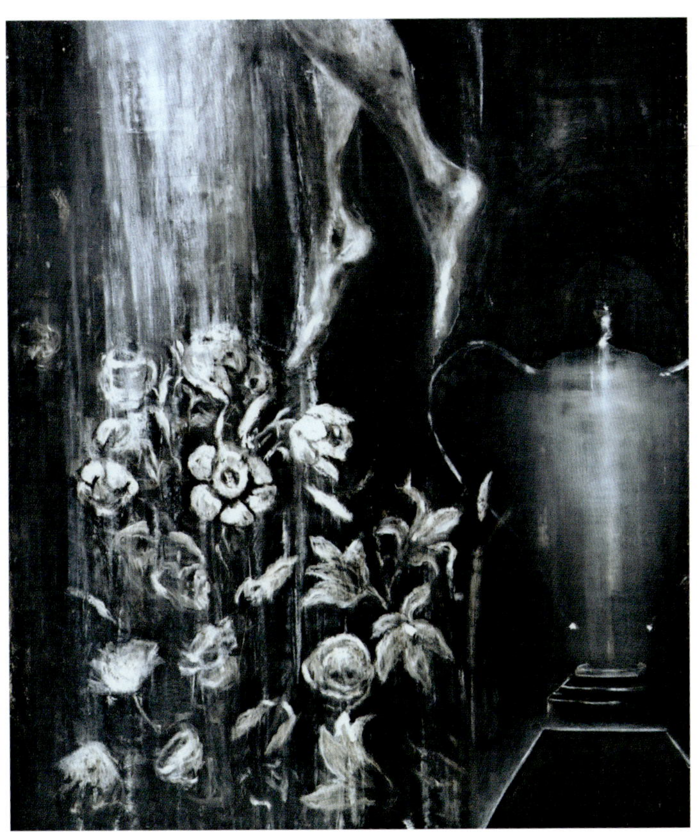

Ross Bleckner
One Day Fever
1986

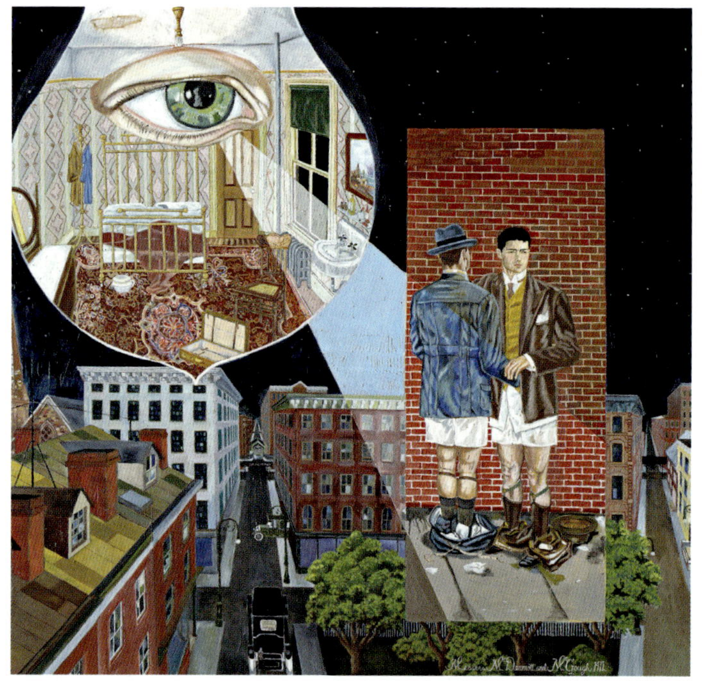

McDermott & McGough
The Night Light
1987

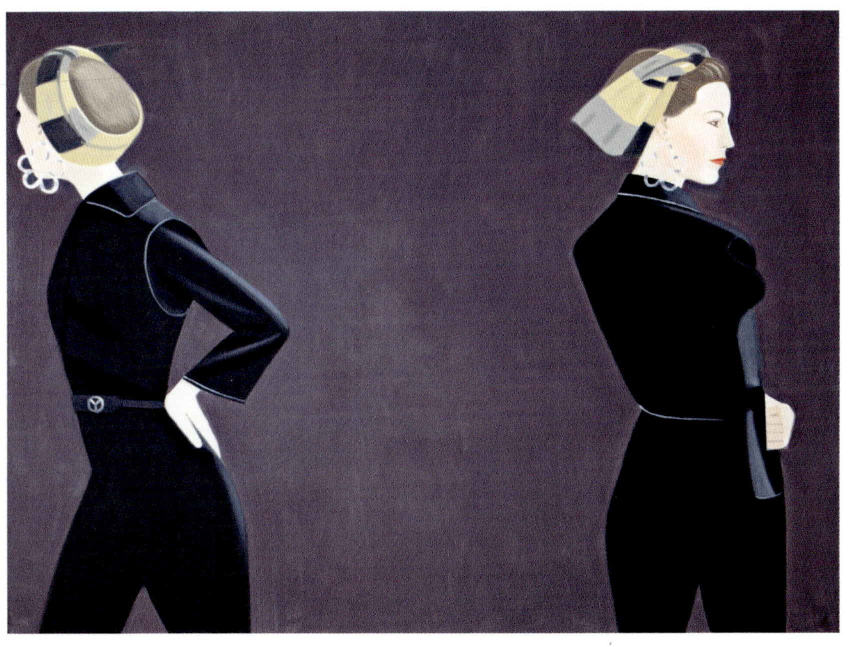

Alex Katz
Ursula
1988

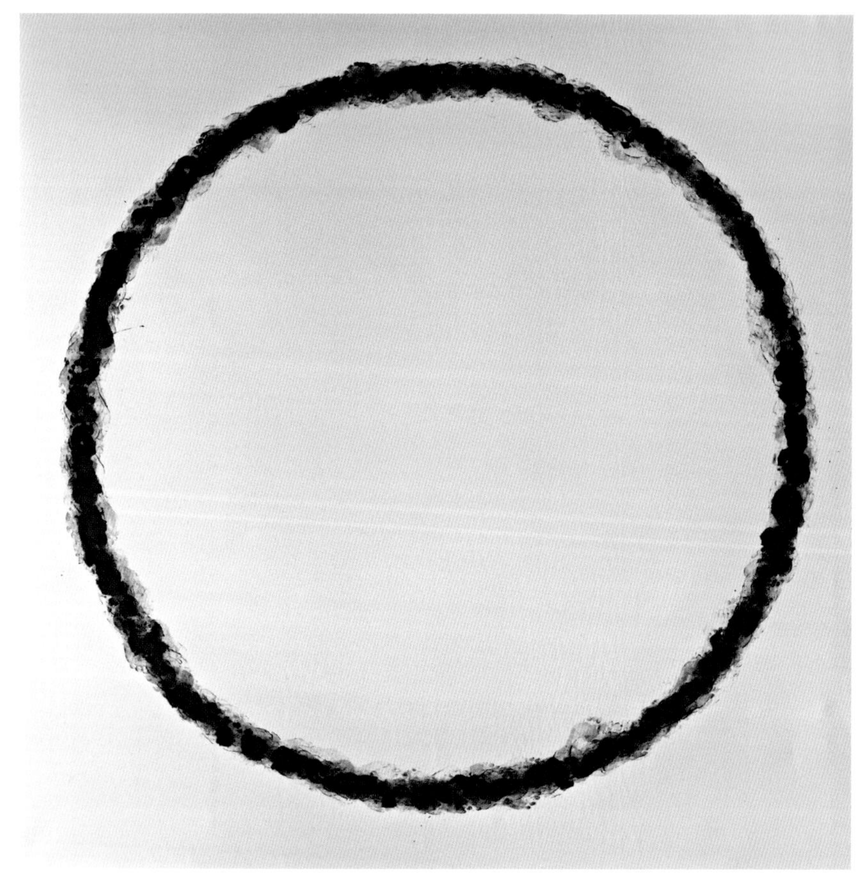

Annette Lemieux
Untitled (Pacing)
1988

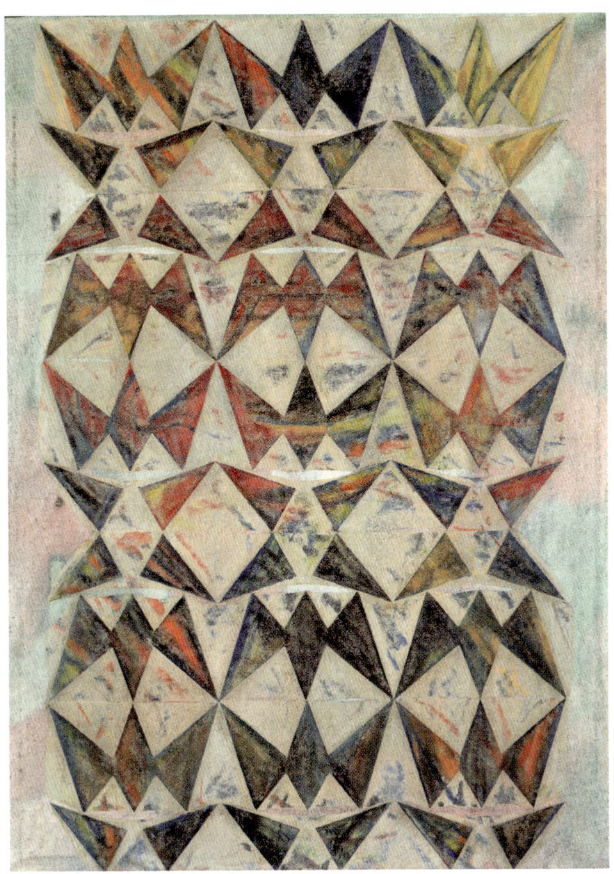

Philip Taaffe
Harlequin
1988

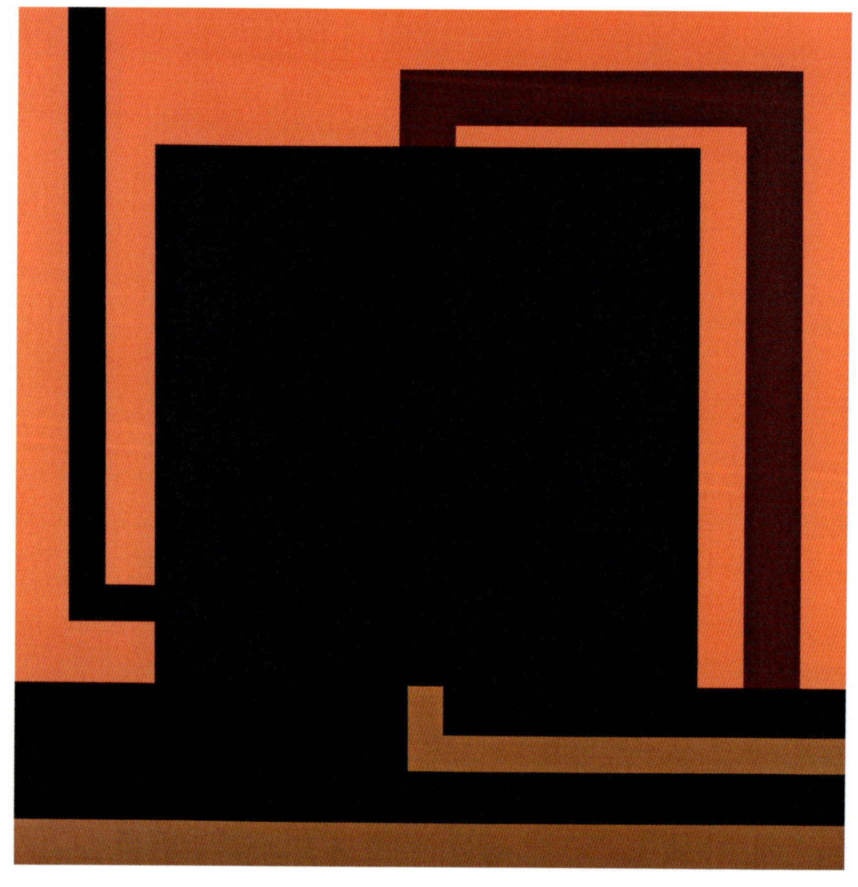

Peter Halley
The Western Sector
1989-1990

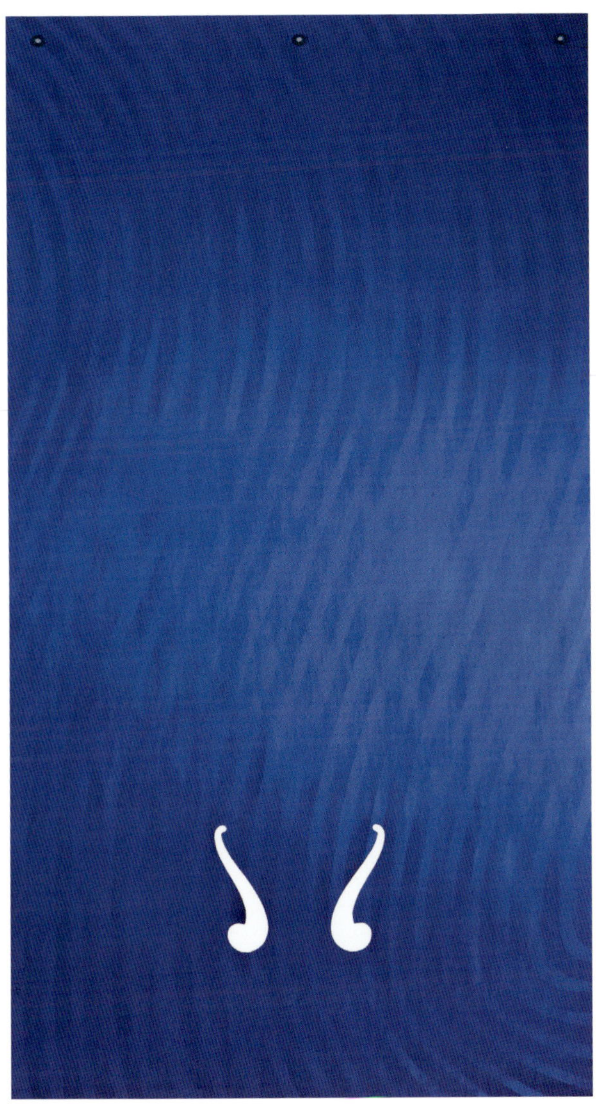

Moira Dryer
Wild One
1990

Donald Baechler
Thinking without Words
2003

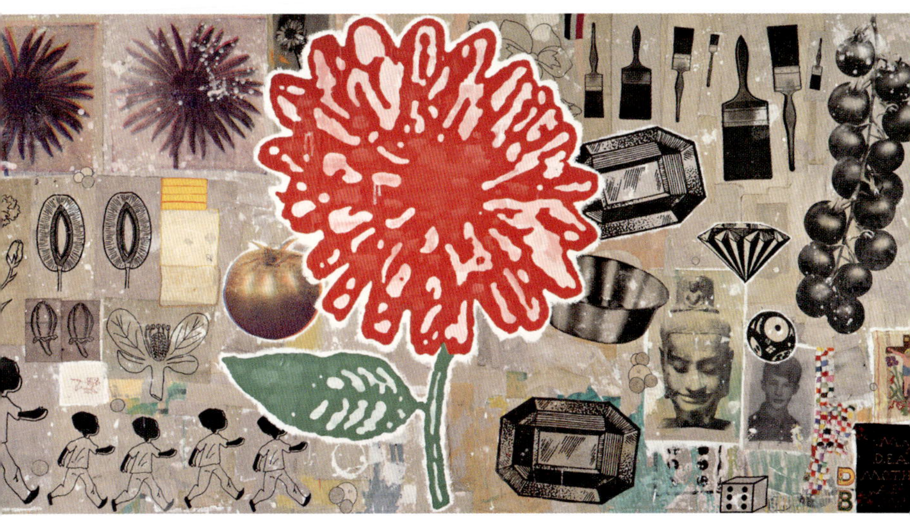

collezionemaramotti

Jeannette Montgomery Barron

MY YEARS
IN THE 1980s
NEW YORK ART SCENE

*Si ringraziano tutte le persone che
hanno collaborato e autorizzato la
pubblicazione dei materiali inseriti
nel volume / Thanks to the people
who helped and authorized the publication
of the materials included in the volume*

Progetto grafico / Book design
Rocco Poiago

Stampato da / Printed by
Grafitalia, Reggio Emilia

Editore / Publisher
Silvana Editoriale, Cinisello Balsamo (Milano)

MaxMara

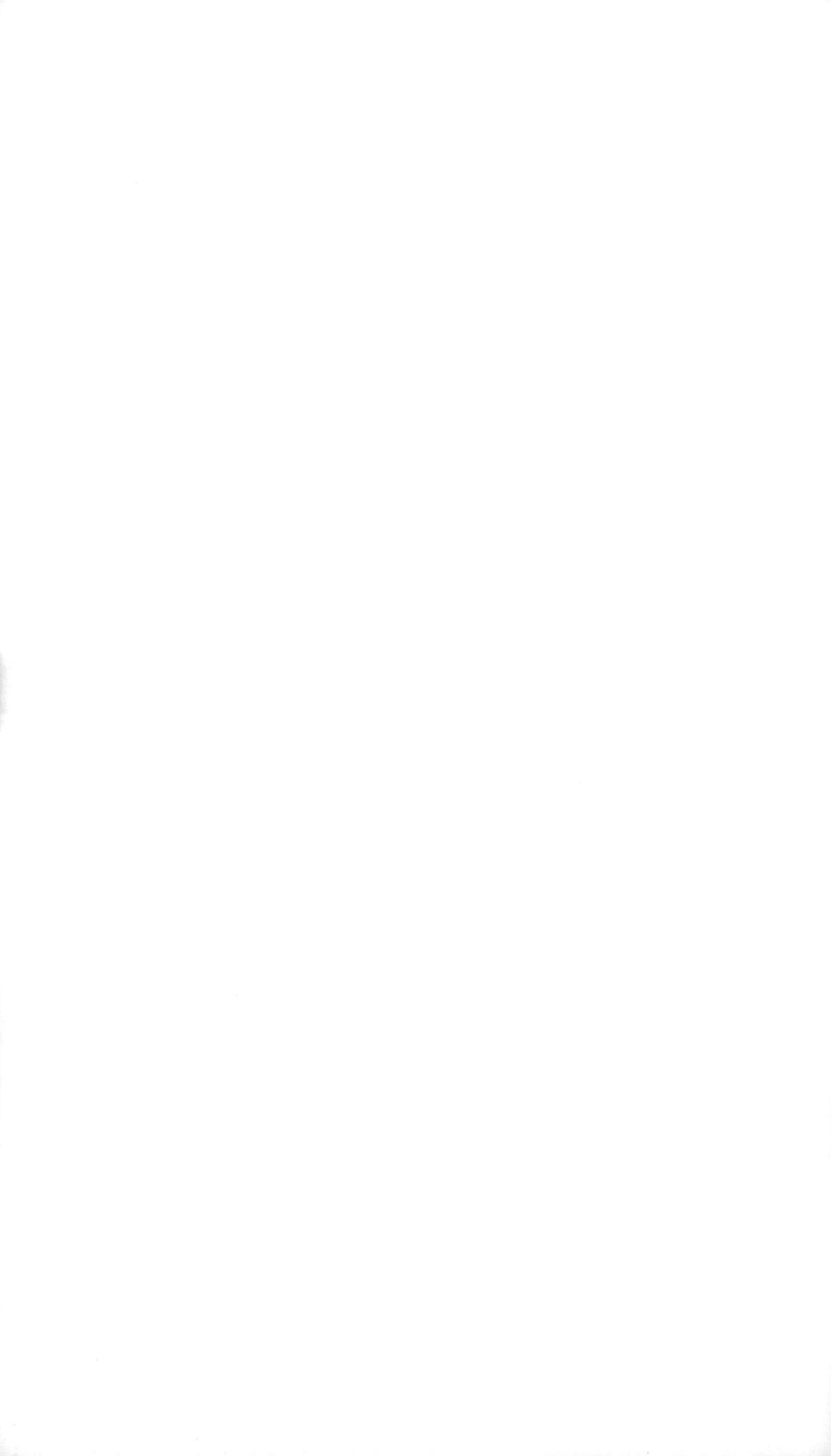

© 2014
Collezione Maramotti, Reggio Emilia;
Silvana Editoriale, Cinisello Balsamo, Milano
per l'edizione / for the edition

Jeannette Montgomery Barron
per le proprie fotografie / for her photographs

p. 11, p. 172
© Francesco Clemente

pp. 18-19
This image was commissioned
by and first published in BOMB
Magazine, from BOMB 4/Fall
1982. © Bomb Magazine, New Art
Publications, and its Contributors.
All rights reserved. BOMB can be
read at www.bombmagazine.org

pp. 22-23
© Anthony Haden-Guest
New York Magazine,
19 Apr. 1982 (excerpt)

p. 50, pp. 150-151, p. 185
© Donald Baechler

p. 53
© Artforum, February 1984,
image from "The Patients and the
Doctors," by Julian Schnabel
Ph. C. Jacqueline Beaurang

pp. 76-77
© Giancarlo Politi Editore,
Flash Art International n° 123,
Summer 1985

p. 82
© David Shapiro

p. 93
© Photograph by Jeanne Strongin

p. 99
© Achille Bonito Oliva

p. 101
© Artforum, September 1986,
"Enzo Cucchi," by Ida Panicelli,
excerpt

p. 104
© The Village Voice, 7 Jan. 1986
© Photograph by Peter Bellamy
© Photograph by Ben Buchanan
© Photograph by Nan Goldin
© Photograph by Danuta
Otfinowski
© Photograph by Nevin I. Shalin

p. 113
© Mark Morrisroe

pp. 126-127
© Interview, Mar. 1988

p. 158
© Robert Homma

p. 168
© Luigi Ontani

p. 169
© Sandro Chia,
by SIAE 2014

p. 170
© The Estate of Jean-Michel
Basquiat, by SIAE 2014

p. 171
© James Brown

p. 173
© Enzo Cucchi

p. 174
© Eric Fischl

p. 175
© Julian Schnabel

p. 176
© David Salle, by SIAE 2014

p. 177
© Ross Bleckner

p. 178
© McDermott & McGough

p. 179
© Alex Katz, by SIAE 2014

p. 180
© Annette Lemieux

p. 181
© Philip Taaffe

p. 182
© Peter Halley

p. 183
© Matthew Dryer

Other sources:

pp. 24-25
Attanasio di Felice, "Painting with a Past," in Portfolio Magazine, Mar./Apr. 1982

p. 75
Peter Schjeldahl, "The Real Salle," in Art in America, Sep. 1984

p. 87
Joshua Decter, "Leon Golub," in Arts Magazine, Mar. 1986

p. 102
Jeanne Siegel, "Geometry Desurfacing," in Arts Magazine, Mar. 1986

pp. 114-115
Jeff Perrone, "Fashion is the Real Thing in Abstraction," in Arts Magazine, Summer 1987

pp. 118-121
William Grimes, "How to Talk Art," in Avenue, Feb. 1988

p. 132
Annette Lemieux in conversation with Brainard Carey, "The Art World Demystified," in Yale Radio WYBC, December 2013 (excerpt)

p. 142
Eleanor Heartney, "Combined Operations," in Art in America, Jun. 1989

Diritti di riproduzione e traduzione
riservati per tutti i Paesi
All reproduction and translation
rights reserved for all countries
© 2014 Silvana Editoriale S.p.A., Cinisello Balsamo, Milano;
Collezione Maramotti, Reggio Emilia

A norma della legge sul diritto d'autore e del codice civile, è vietata la
riproduzione, totale o parziale, di questo volume in qualsiasi forma, originale
o derivata, e con qualsiasi mezzo a stampa, elettronico, digitale, meccanico
per mezzo di fotocopie, microfilm, film o altro, senza il permesso scritto
dell'editore.
Under copyright and civil law this volume cannot be reproduced, wholly or
in part, in any form, original or derived, or by any means: print, electronic,
digital, mechanical, including photocopy, microfilm, film or any other
medium, without permission in writing from the publisher.

Silvana Editoriale e Collezione Maramotti rimangono a disposizione di altri
eventuali aventi diritto che non è stato possibile identificare o contattare /
Silvana Editoriale and Collezione Maramotti are available to any one else
who may have a claim and whom we have not been able to identify or
contact

Il presente volume è stampato in 1000 copie / Printed in 1000 copies

Finito di stampare nel mese di aprile 2014
Printed April 2014

ISBN 9788836628698

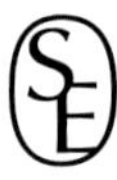

Silvana Editoriale
www.silvanaeditoriale.it

Direzione editoriale / Direction
Dario Cimorelli

Art Director
Giacomo Merli

*Coordinamento organizzativo /
Production Coordinator*
Michela Bramati

Segreteria di redazione / Editorial Assistant
Emma Altomare

Ufficio iconografico / Photo Editor
Alessandra Olivari, Silvia Sala

Ufficio stampa / Press Office
Lidia Masolini, press@silvanaeditoriale.it